MEN, MASCULINITIES AND TEACHING IN EARLY CHILDHOOD EDUCATION

This stimulating book sets out to critically explore the notion of men, masculinities and teaching in early childhood education. It addresses the global pattern of gender, teaching and care where men are in the minority and explores the notion that the greater involvement of men within teaching and associated professions has the potential to transform gender relations for future generations.

International contributors raise critical questions about the construction of masculinities, the continuing reluctance of men to engage in this type of work and the influence of political and public debates on the issue. Through this engaging discussion readers are asked to question whether this is something that we should care about, with key topics including:

- the roles of men in education and care
- teachers' beliefs, norms and values of gender equality
- the construction of male identities
- gendered ideals, and children's interpretations of gender.

Men, Masculinities and Teaching in Early Childhood Education brings together a refreshing and critical set of perspectives linked to an increasingly important educational debate and will be a valuable text for practitioners, professionals, policy-makers and parents/carers.

Simon Brownhill is a Senior Teaching Associate at the University of Cambridge, UK.

Jo Warin is a Senior Lecturer at Lancaster University, UK.

Inga Wernersson is Professor of Educational Research at University West, Sweden.

MEN, MASCULINITIES AND TEACHING IN EARLY CHILDHOOD EDUCATION

International perspectives on gender and care

Edited by Simon Brownhill, Jo Warin and Inga Wernersson

Routledge
Taylor & Francis Group

LONDON AND NEW YORK

First published 2016
by Routledge
2 Park Square, Milton Park, Abingdon, Oxon OX14 4RN

and by Routledge
711 Third Avenue, New York, NY 10017

Routledge is an imprint of the Taylor & Francis Group, an informa business

British Library Cataloguing in Publication Data
A catalogue record for this book is available from the British Library

Library of Congress Cataloging in Publication Data
Men, masculinities and teaching in early childhood education: international perspectives on gender and care / edited by Simon Brownhill, Jo Warin and Inga Wernersson.
pages cm
Includes bibliographical references and index.
1. Male teachers–Cross-cultural studies. 2. Men in education–Cross-cultural studies.
3. Sex differences in education–Cross-cultural studies. 4. Early childhood education–
Cross-cultural studies. I. Brownhill, Simon, editor of compilation. II. Warin, Jo, editor of compilation. III. Wernersson, Inga, 1948- editor of compilation.
LC212.9.M47 2015
370.15'1–dc23
2015004293

ISBN: 978-1-138-79771-0 (hbk)
ISBN: 978-1-138-79772-7 (pbk)
ISBN: 978-1-315-75693-6 (ebk)

Typeset in Bembo
by Cenveo Publisher Services

To our families and friends

CONTENTS

THE CONTRIBUTORS

Vina Adriany is a Lecturer and Researcher in the Department of Early Childhood Education, Faculty of Educational Sciences at the Indonesia University of Education. She obtained her PhD from the Department of Educational Research, Lancaster University, UK. She is a member of the Centre for Women's Studies at the Indonesia University of Education. Her research interests include gender issues in early childhood education, multicultural issues and applying poststructuralist perspectives to early childhood education.

Simon Brownhill is a Senior Teaching Associate in the Faculty of Education at the University of Cambridge. He contributes substantially as a lead trainer to much of the UoC-led training delivered as part of the Centre of Excellence (CoE) in-service teacher training programme in Kazakhstan. His research interests include supporting adult learners, children's story writing, international perspectives of reflective practice and the male role model in the early years (the focus of his doctoral thesis). He is the editor and contributing author of the textbook *Empowering the Children's and Young People's Workforce: Practice-based Knowledge, Skills and Understanding* (Routledge, 2014).

Sally Campbell Galman is an Associate Professor in the Teacher Education and Curriculum Studies Department of the College of Education at the University of Massachusetts – Amherst, USA. Her areas of research interest fall into three broad categories: the anthropology of childhood and the study of childhood and gender; gendered experience, including but not limited to girl culture, carework and mothering; and the working lives of female primary school teachers and the way they make sense of carework landscapes. Along with Laura Alicia Valdiviezo, Sally is Editor-in-Chief of *Anthropology and Education Quarterly*. Sally is author of *Wise and Foolish Virgins: White Women at Work in the Feminized World of Primary School Teaching* (Lexington Press, 2012).

Karin Grahn is a Senior Lecturer in the Faculty of Education in the University of Gothenburg, Sweden. She is currently lecturing on the Sports Coaching programme as well as on the Teacher Education programme for Physical Education. Her research interests include child and youth sports, a gender perspective on coaching and educational practices, gender construction, sustainable coaching practices, coach–athlete relationships, coaching education and gender analyses of textbooks (the focus of her PhD thesis). Gender features prominently in her current research as well as in her thesis.

Ingrid Granbom is a Lecturer at University West, Sweden. She was previously a teacher in early childhood education with nearly two decades of early years experience (1–8). Her research interests include teacher education and lifelong learning, international perspectives of reflective practice, gender, intergenerational learning, pedagogical documentation and issues concerning quality in early childhood. Her doctoral thesis – '"We Have Become Almost Too Good": Teachers' Social Representations of Pre-school as a Pedagogical Practice' (2011) – aims to describe and analyse teachers' constructions of meaning and common-sense knowledge concerning pre-school as a pedagogical practice.

Anette Hellman is a Senior Lecturer in the Faculty of Education, Communication and Learning at the University of Gothenburg, Sweden. Her research interests include norm and normality constructions in children's everyday lives, intersections of age and gender in educational settings, and masculinity and care in pre-school. She was the guest editor and contributing author of *Negotiations of Gender in Early Childhood Settings* a Special Edition of the *International Journal of Early Childhood* – 46 (3) – published in 2014.

Maria Hjalmarsson is an Associate Professor in Educational Work at Karlstad University, Sweden. She is a former leisure-time teacher and achieved her PhD in 2009 with a thesis on the gender order of the teaching profession. Maria's research focuses on the tasks and work of teachers. Recent publications deal with the aspects of governance and voluntariness for children in leisure-time centres, as well as how male primary school teachers view other people's expectations of them as teachers and how they relate to them/these expectations. Maria is currently working on an ongoing project exploring the reform of career employment for particularly advanced teachers aimed at supporting the career of the individual teacher as well as contributing to increased goal achievement and local school development in general.

Kiyomi Kuramochi is a Professor in the Faculty of Education at Tokyo Gakugei University in Japan. She has a doctorate in Humanities. Her research interests include early childhood education and care in Japan and China, peer culture in pre-schools, peer relationships and pre-parenting education in junior high schools. She is a member of the Science Council of Japan. She is the joint editor of *Teaching and Learning to Foster a Zest for Living* (Kyoiku-Jitumu, 2013).

Annica Löfdahl is Professor in Educational Work at the Faculty of Arts and Humanities at Karlstad University (KAU), Sweden. She has a professional background as a pre-school teacher. Her academic teaching is mainly in postgraduate programmes as a supervisor and a scientific leader. Annica's main research interests concern children in school and the everyday life of pre-school as well as teachers' professionalism. She is the author of *Play in Peer Culture*, a book chapter published in *The Sage Handbook of Play and Learning in Early Childhood* (2014).

Christine Mallozzi is an Assistant Professor of Literacy Education in the Curriculum and Instruction Department at the University of Kentucky, USA. She was awarded the Carol J. Fisher Award for Excellence in Research from the University of Georgia. Her research interests include gender and teacher education, middle grades reading education, feminist theories and discourse analysis. Her work involves studies of women teachers' bodies and gender issues among teachers. She is the co-editor and contributing author of the book *Literacies, Learning, and the Body: Bringing Research and Theory into Pedagogical Practice* (Routledge, 2015).

Chie Nakazawa is an Associate Professor in the Faculty of Education at Tokyo Gakugei University in Japan. Her research interests include lifelong learning from a gender perspective, gender and sexuality education in and out of schools, and lifelong and community learning/education in Sweden and Japan. She is one of the authors of the Survey Analysis on Sexuality of Youth in Japan (Shogakukan, 2001, 2007 and 2013).

Jo Warin is a Senior Lecturer in the Department of Educational Research at Lancaster University and Co-Director of the Centre for Social Justice and Wellbeing in Education. She teaches on the online Doctoral Programme in Education and Social Justice and supervises many PhD students. She began her professional career as a teacher of English, Drama and Theatre-in-Education (TIE) before gaining her PhD. Jo's research concerns identities and especially how constructions of identity can both support and constrain processes of learning and change. Her book, *Stories of Self: Tracking Children's Identity and Wellbeing Through the School Years* (Trentham Books, 2010), together with three related peer-reviewed journal articles, presents a particularly innovative research approach through participatory work with a group of young people through 14 years of schooling (from ages 3 to 17).

Inga Wernersson is a Professor of Educational Research at University West, Sweden. She was a Professor of Education at the University of Gothenburg from 1998 until 2012. Her doctoral dissertation, completed in the late 1970s, reported the very first study on gender (sex roles) in Swedish classrooms. In her current role she is Chair of the Council for Postgraduate Studies in Education with specialisation in Work Integrated Learning. Her research interests focus on structural and individual consequences of gender orders and identities related to education. She has also been engaged in further training for teachers for the promotion of gender equality.

FOREWORD

Mike Younger

To focus on the gender agenda in education and schooling in the countries of the so-called 'developed world' over the last forty years is to experience a feeling of déjà vu, a sense that we have been here before and are watching an ever-turning wheel, as the pendulum has swung from a concern with promoting equal opportunities for girls, through a preoccupation with under-achieving boys, to a renewed determination to ensuring justice, equality and fulfilment for girls and women.

As time has passed, so an evolving consensus has emerged in many parts of the academic community. Despite the moral panic of the last decade of the twentieth century and the first decade of the twenty-first, and the pre-occupation with 'failing boys' as the new disadvantaged among school students, there is a growing awareness of the complexity and the multi-faceted nature of the debate about boys' and girls' engagement, motivation and achievement. There is a growing resistance to the 'poor boys' discourse and to 'male repair' agendas, to interpretations which see boys as being disadvantaged in their schooling by feminist approaches and policies, to recuperative masculinity approaches which seek to confirm commonality and identity among men.

Thus there has emerged a reaction against short-term essentialist policies related to boy-friendly pedagogies, a riposte against those who advocate teaching strategies which apparently favour boys and 'guy-ify' schools and teaching, a contesting of the validity and appropriateness of affirmative action for boys programmes. Instead, we have an increasing recognition of the diversity and variety of gender constructions and a re-emerging emphasis on inclusivity and diversity; we have attempts to take a more nuanced discussion of gender into schools sites and to develop school-based intervention strategies within a gender-relational context.

As the debate has gained in sophistication and discernment, so the recognition has grown of the persistent under-achievement of some white working-class girls, of the need within schooling to challenge traditional gender stereotypes, to give girls space to develop a strong sense of themselves and their value, and to give them the confidence to make their own choices, free of any sense that the script has been written for them. The interplay of these factors led to an emerging re-engagement of the gender discourse with the needs of girls.

This was intensified by the experiences which many girls and women encountered in some parts of the media and from some men within society, with the development of social media enabling a disturbing level of misogynistic abuse, creating a sewer for anonymous prejudice and hate.

It is perhaps inevitable that such a contentious issue as the gender issue – buffeted by media, politicians and policy-makers – should lack continuity and focus, and that the search for some equilibrium in policy and practice should be elusive. So it is that themes and strategies have become fashionable, ignored, derided even as time has passed; advocates have been lauded for a time, disparaged later, re-discovered as novel later still.

Yet here we have another volume on men and masculinities which shows precisely why we need balance in the debate. Here Simon Brownhill, Jo Warin and Inga Wernersson have brought together a wide range of authors, each active researchers in early childhood education, to offer a range of perspectives which keep fundamental issues at the heart of the debate. In so doing, they capture issues which are not transitory or short-lived, but of enduring importance to society, individuals and policy-makers. So it is with early childhood education, and with the role of men within it. Warin and Wernersson set the tone of this volume in their outstanding introduction, and in justifying why this book has been written they capture the unique and distinctive contribution of the authors: a concern with 'real-world' research with discussions drawn from a set of original empirical studies which capture the essence of quality educational research; an international flavour, admittedly mostly from countries of the North but unusually featuring research from Indonesia and Japan; and an altogether timely focus on the gender balance of the early childhood education profession in the light of global recession.

Questioning and debate are central to this volume: not only the focus on unanswered questions which arise from these empirical research questions (and are highlighted succinctly at the end of each chapter), but fundamental questions about the nature of masculinity and masculinities, and about the transformational possibilities and the differences which more male involvement would make to the world of ECE and wider society. So we encounter searching questions about men's continuing reluctance to engage in early childhood education, the influence of the media, fears about 'dangerous men' and the connection with homophobia. Equally, authors adopt a critical approach to the male role model argument, and offer new perspectives to suggest that the greater involvement of men in ECE has the potential to transform gender relations for future generations.

The scope of each chapter, and the issues the authors raise, is summarised succinctly in Warin and Wernersson's introductory chapter. At the core of these contributions is a fundamental argument revolving around the potential for gender transformation in society: the notion that we wish (and indeed need) to live in a world where emphasis on gender differentiation is less prominent, where men and women are not disadvantaged by circumscribed and regulated visions of what is appropriate and inappropriate for their behaviours as gendered individuals, where opportunities are equal, open and transparent regardless of gender. The immense value of this text is epitomised in the different ways in which the authors have brought together empirical research from different contexts and reflected on theoretical dimensions to offer reflections on current provision, policy and practice which show how such gender transformation might be possible.

Mike Younger
University of Cambridge
May 2015

ACKNOWLEDGEMENTS

It is with the most heartfelt thanks that the following people are recognised:

- All of those at Routledge and those associated with the publishers who have worked with us in their various capacities on our collaborative book – thank you all *very* much for your wonderful support and encouragement.
- All of the anonymous reviewers who offered us constructive feedback on the initial proposal – we hope that you feel we have done justice to all the time and effort you put into helping us to make our collaborative book the very best it could be.
- Eva Gannerud and Ann-Marie Houghton for their efforts in contributing to the initial proposal.
- Our families and our friends for their continued love and support during the writing of our respective chapters.
- Mike Younger for writing 'a really affirmative and beautifully written foreword' (JW).
- And most importantly, all of the contributors to this book – thank you for your commitment to this stimulating book. We hope you are as proud of your contribution as we are.

Thank you all *very* much indeed.

SPB, JW and IW

LIST OF ABBREVIATIONS

The following abbreviations are used throughout this book:

ACCRT	American Center for Childhood Research and Training
ARNEC	Asia-Pacific Regional Network Early Childhood
BCCT	Beyond Center and Circle Times
Brå	Swedish National Council for Crime Prevention
CPD	Continuing professional development
CWDC	Children's Workforce Development Council
DAP	Developmentally Appropriate Practices
DfE	Department for Education
DOE	Department of Education
ECE	Early Childhood Education
EYFS	Early Years Foundation Stage (0–5$^+$)
GEA	Gender and Education Association
HoCEC	House of Commons Education Committee
IT	Information Technology
ITT	Initial Teacher Training
JSPS	Japan Society for the Promotion of Science
KAU	Karlstad University
KS1	Key Stage One (5–7 years)
KS2	Key Stage Two (7–11 years)
MECSST	Ministry of Education, Culture, Sports, Science and Technology
MHLW	Ministry of Health, Labour and Welfare
NGO	Non-governmental organisation
NPR	National Public Radio
Ofsted	Office for Standards in Education, Children's Services and Skills
ONS	Office for National Statistics
OSCE	Organisation for Security and Cooperation in Europe
PE	Physical Education

PGCE	Post Graduate Certificate in Education
RF	Swedish Sports Confederation (English translation)
TIE	Theatre-in-Education
TTPs	Teacher Training Programmes
UNESCO	United Nations Educational, Scientific and Cultural Organisation

INTRODUCTION

Jo Warin and Inga Wernersson

Why this book has been written

The male early childhood education (ECE) professional workforce represents less than 3 per cent in almost all nations across the globe (Brody 2014). This edited collection sets out to provide a much needed critical exploration of the themes and issues which have grown up in many countries as a response to this well established and persistent phenomenon. A broad range of arguments has been rehearsed in relevant policy and academic bodies of literature, as well as in the media for explaining this pattern. These rationales are matched by an equally varied range of strategies for change. The contributing authors of this book aim to address the concepts, ideas and thinking which inform policy and practice in this area, and which influence provision for children and young people by men who work and train in the early childhood education sector. We use the term 'early childhood education' (ECE) to contextualise the work that contributes to this collection since it is a generic concept that refers to formal and informal educational programmes and learning strategies that are aimed at children from the ages of 0 to 8 years. The vast majority of the chapters here focus on the pre-school or kindergarten age range.

The book has three features which we believe make it distinctive. Firstly, the contributions are based on 'real-world' research with discussions drawn from a set of original empirical studies. Secondly, the book is international in that it draws together a mix of research undertaken across a range of different nations including Indonesia, Japan, the USA, England and Sweden. The contributors also draw on international research that goes well beyond their immediate national contexts, for example Norway, where there is the highest representation of male pre-school teachers (10 per cent). This book is also international in that it discusses a pattern that had been described by Drudy *et al.* (2005) as a global phenomenon. Thirdly, this collection is timely. As we watch the world stage following the global recession, men's and women's employment patterns remain in the limelight with strong competition for jobs in many countries. Some suggest that this will increase the likelihood of men choosing ECE professional work; others point out that, on the contrary, austerity and economic hardship drive men and women back into traditional gender roles (McRobbie 2007, 2009;

Warin 2014) and that increased market competition, influenced by neoliberalism, exploits and perpetuates gender differences. We are also aware that at the present time there is much policy noise in many countries about this phenomenon with some concerted recruitment strategies and initiatives in operation in order to change the gender balance of the ECE profession, indicating the timeliness of this discussion.

The debate about 'missing men' is a controversial and often a very emotional one; it is influenced by the media with sensational and newsworthy stories that threaten to obscure research-informed pathways towards clarification. Local, national and international expressions of concern are fuelled by moral panic and media scare stories with regard to the absence of men in children's and young people's lives. For example, in the summer of 2011, youth riots that took place in the UK were attributed to 'children without fathers' in a highly publicised speech by the Prime Minister David Cameron (Eaton 2011). In April 2014 a large number of suspected cases of abuse were committed in a pre-school in Högsby Municipality of Kalmar County in Sweden, causing a media stir and inducing a fear of male paedophiles that would impact on the likelihood of men's uptake of pre-school teaching. Heated debates persist about the value of having more men in early childhood educational settings and the contribution they can make to the achievements and well-being of boys and girls. These inform concerted local authority/government campaigns and institutional recruitment drives in many countries, urging more men to work with children and young people, yet at the same time casting doubt on men who do. We aim to examine the arguments surrounding the prescription for 'more men in education', critically analysing the tensions and dilemmas that relate to the 'beneficial' presence of men in educational/care contexts, the challenges to masculinities, sexuality and the father figure role.

This book locates itself within the heart of an international time of change and turbulence in education policy. In many Western countries we are seeing widening gaps in achievement between identifiable groups of pupils. While school league tables have drawn public attention to 'gender gaps' there are other less visible influences on school success such as social class and ethnicity which interact with gender. These attainment gaps are the result of competitive 'performance' orientated school policies that are aimed, often implicitly, at creating winners and losers. At the same time, policy-making at a local, national and international level is currently engaged in the active recruitment and employment of men in an attempt to raise standards, offer 'father figures' where these are perceived to be lacking and improve the behaviour of children and young people. This book critically examines these assumptions, offering a refreshing international examination of the realities of being a man who enters and works in the education and care sector.

We believe it is important to counterbalance some of the more extreme versions that this debate has taken by presenting theoretical reflections that are firmly rooted in empirical research. A central aim of this book is to showcase recent empirical research in order to provide a strong evidence base for this important debate while engaging the reader in accessible illustrative material. All the contributors in this book are active researchers who have been engaged in recent years in cross-national comparative conversations on gender, care and teaching. It is always illuminating to see how debates are played out with different emphases and nuances in different countries. For example, there is a striking contrast between the UK's policy rhetoric about a need for male role models (assumed to provide patterns of manliness) compared with policy discourse in Sweden about ECE staff as gender-neutral professionals.

By reading through the range of contributions presented here we hope that readers will be able to apply a reflexive self-scrutiny and recognise the taken-for-granted aspects of cultural and national practices/policies that operate in their own ECE professional cultures, training arena, and research contexts.

The cluster of editors and authors who have contributed to this book have not been randomly selected but in fact have emerged as a coherent network of international researchers with shared interests in research-led discussion on the position of men in ECE. The group has developed within the broader framework of the Gender and Education Association (GEA) through several symposia at its annual and biannual conferences, as well as through Swedish Research Council funded meetings in Sweden, England, Japan and Indonesia. From this group collaborative research papers have been produced, including a Special Issue of *Gender and Education* on the topic of 'Gender, Teaching and Care' (edited by Warin and Gannerud, 2014). A point that we make in the latter publication concerns the problematic dominance of the English language within our collective work. At times this has implicated a complex and sometimes hilarious pooling of language skills. Recently, for example, Adriany, Hellman and Warin engaged in a focus group with some Indonesian male pre-school teachers, drawing particularly on Hellman's and Adriany's language skills and translation abilities.

The three editors collectively point out in their conclusion that this enterprise cannot be characterised as a systematic comparative study; instead it has arisen from a shared wish to engage in dialogue with gender researchers in other countries. International collaborative comparative research in gender and education can prompt us to see ourselves, researchers and educationalists from the outside, helping us to see anew some of the taken-for-granted aspects of our practices and policies relating to gender, education and care. Of course we do not always share the same views about the presence and absence of men in ECE settings within this network with the result that this collection is a set of varied perspectives on this debate, some of which will resonate with readers' views and some of which will challenge them. Our experiences of writing, researching and thinking in this area are informed by the rather different national cultures we inhabit and we gratefully recognise how much we have learnt from each other. However, there is something that we share in common and that is a commitment to the critical argument about the greater involvement of men within ECE teaching that seemingly has the potential to transform gender relations for future generations.

Questions. And more questions

Questions form a key element of this book. When the editors and authors began to discuss this enterprise they acknowledged the value of asking difficult and powerful questions by referring back to the pedagogic strategies of the celebrated drama teacher Dorothy Heathcote (Wagner 1999) who sees one of the goals of education processes as the gradual improvement and refinement of developing better questions. We see the value of this book in these terms as we do not feel that our combined research efforts have produced a set of easy answers. Instead, we hope that the following accounts of our research work and thinking, and the way this has informed our theoretical understanding of some of the more difficult questions, will enable all of us who are interested in this area to ask ever better questions. To that end, an innovative feature is that each chapter will end with a brief concluding section identifying 'Unanswered Questions'. We hope these may guide individual readers in their reflection on this research area and also perhaps be helpful for groups of readers to address together.

We pose two sets of questions here in this Introduction which the reader may like to use to guide their reading of the following chapters. The first is about the nature of masculinity and masculinities and a wish to analyse what keeps men away from the teaching and care of young children. The second concerns the transformational possibilities and the differences more men would make to the world of ECE and the wider society. In the conclusion to this book the three editors pose the blunt question: *Are men so badly needed that it is worth all this fuss?* The chapters that follow investigate the first question by addressing masculinities through an examination of the global 'feminised' pattern of gender, teaching and care where men are in a minority, especially in work with younger pupils. Authors raise critical questions about men's continuing reluctance to engage in this type of work, personal and institutional constructions of masculinities, the influence of public debates, fears about 'dangerous men' and the connection with homophobia. In response to the second question we consider whether it matters that men are less engaged than women in the professional work associated with bringing up the next generation. *Is this something we should care about or not?* The chapters adopt a critical approach to the weary and wrong-headed prescription that we need more men to be male role models. We bring a new set of perspectives to this debate based on the argument that the greater involvement of men within teaching and associated caring professions has the potential to transform gender relations for future generations. Having stated the bald figures at the start of this Introduction of the low percentage of men in ECE across the globe, we need to set out this picture in a little more detail.

What is the current pattern of men working in ECE?

General claims about the global pattern are made by Drudy *et al.* (2005; Drudy 2008) and more recently by Brody (2014) who tells us that the general pattern is for less than 3 per cent worldwide. Brody also tells us that the proportion of male workers is low even in countries such as Norway which has had some very deliberate strategies for increasing male workers, but where only 10 per cent of staff is male. McCormack and Brownhill (2014) identify England, Australia, Canada, the United States and New Zealand as countries where this phenomenon has become a policy concern. Ingersoll and Merril (2010) report from the USA that the proportion of female to male teachers has increased across the compulsory school age range with a recent specific increase at secondary school level and a continuation of the female majority pattern at elementary level. The US Bureau of Labor Statistics (2012–13) study (cited in Uba and Cleinman 2013) suggest 2.3 per cent of the pre-kindergarten and kindergarten teachers are males.

European patterns are particularly interesting because of a specific policy concern in some European countries with recruitment of men and strategies and action patterns designed to promote the increase of male practitioners (see Chapter 1 by Wernersson, this volume). Van Laere *et al.* (2014) give an update on the European pattern and claim that: (1) *no* European country has reached the benchmark set by the European Commission Childcare Network in 1995 to achieve 20 per cent male early childhood workers by 2006; and (2) that in more than half of the EU member states there are *fewer* than 1 per cent of male practitioners in

ECE (authors' emphasis). They also point out, like Brody (2014), that the figures have remained low even in countries where there have been specific actions to increase male recruitment such as in Norway and Denmark. A fairly recent report in Germany (Cremers and Krabel 2012) from the Federal Ministry for Family Affairs for Senior Citizens, Women and Youth puts the number of men working in ECE at 2.4 per cent, thus confirming the general trend.

Discussion has also begun in recent times in Asia. For example, UNESCO's (2007) report for Asia-Pacific argues that a lack of male teachers in ECE has denied boys' access to positive role models, an argument that we problematise below. The Asia-Pacific Regional Network Early Childhood (ARNEC) has just introduced a new programme on its website to include more males in ECE in Singapore (Ho 2014). In Malaysia the lack of male teachers in ECE has been recognised as one of the country's critical problems (Majzub, n.d.) while research conducted by Suyatno (2004) in Semarang Indonesia is concerned with the disproportionate numbers of male and female teachers.

Why should we be concerned about 'missing men' in ECE?

Many people might want to argue that we are not 'missing' men in ECE because this is an area where women can easily gain employment and excel. *Why then should we threaten this significant area of professional employment for women?* Others may argue that there are some far more important concerns to address regarding gender, education and care, for example the need to ensure that girls across the globe are educated. However, we believe that there is a deeper argument that goes right to the heart of the potential for gender transformation in society. *Do we want to live in a world where there is much less emphasis on gender differentiation, where men and women are not disadvantaged by limited and restricted views of what is appropriate and inappropriate for their behaviours as gendered individuals?* The underlying aim of the editors and authors of this book is that we do indeed wish to live in such a society.

However, any trip to a children's toy shop shows us how very far we are from realising this ideal. The segregation of the consumer goods into girls' toys (colour-coded pink) and boys' toys (colour-coded blue for young boys; black for older boys) creates a very concrete and tangible symbol of how slow we have been to fulfil the potential for gender transformation. Indeed, many commentators have suggested that we are witnessing a re-gendering of society. An example of this can be seen in the way that, in many countries, there has been a visible public comparison of boys' academic achievement compared with girls. This has been enabled because of the marketisation of schools and the ways that schools assemble exam performance data into league tables for consumers (parents/carers) to choose between settings and schools. It has been easy to divide school populations along gendered lines to create such comparisons. It is interesting to note that it is altogether more challenging to look at the slippery concept of social class in relation to pupil performance in schools but very easy to utilise the social categories of boys and girls to make such comparisons. Consequently, a very strong and visible public discourse has sprung up about boys' academic achievement compared with girls. This debate has perpetuated assumptions about gender differences and nicely illustrates the concept of re-gendering. This term is used by Martino *et al.* (2009) who point out that we are currently witnessing a backlash against gender flexibility: one may refer to it as a re-gendering rather than a de-gendering. McRobbie (2007, 2009) also demonstrates that a current retrenchment of patriarchy has occurred, as does

Charlotte Benjamin, aged seven years old, who recently wrote the following letter, as reported by Molloy (2014):

> *Dear Lego company,*
>
> *My name is Charlotte. I am 7 years old and I love lego but I don't like that there are more lego boy people and barely any lego girls. Today I went to a store and saw legos in 2 sections. The pink girls and the blue boys. All the girls did was sit at home, go to bed and shop, and they had no jobs but the boys went on adventures, worked, saved people, and did jobs, even swam with sharks. I want you to make more lego girl people and let them go on adventures and have fun. OK!?!.*
>
> *Thanks you,*
> *From Charlotte*

It now seems more important than ever before to disrupt the gender binary. We need to challenge an assumption that masculinity is necessarily aligned with men and femininity with women. We need to 'trouble' gender (Butler 1990), disrupting the gender divisions that 'still deeply bifurcate the structure of modern society' (Lorber 2000) since it is the 'ubiquitous division of people into two unequally valued categories that undergirds continually reappearing instances of gender inequality' (ibid.). In order to realise this extremely ambitious ideal of de-gendering society a necessary small brick in this wall is to attract more men into the teaching and care of young children. So, at the deepest level, it is a way of undoing gender and de-gendering society.

How will the book chapters address the questions we have raised?

The book is organised into three sections: Section One *Policy, Legislation and Perspectives*; Section 2 *Young Children: Gender, Learning and Care*; and Section Three *Gendered Professional Identities and Practice*. We begin Section One with a chapter from Wernersson which acts as a scene-setter since it portrays Sweden's long history of gender awareness and policy directed at gender inequalities, set in the context of wider Nordic policy in this area. Wernersson shows that the gender order is resistant to change and that men have remained as a small minority – 2–3 per cent of the ECE workforce in Sweden – despite these policy efforts. She also frames the main arguments that have been used in this debate, drawing on a theoretical model from Archer (2003) of analytical dualism to examine both societal and individual influences on the call for more men in ECE. This framework, presented as a matrix in her chapter, portrays the intersection of two dimensions of gender differentiation: femininity and masculinity as 'specialisations', and the power/status hierarchy of the gender order. This provides a tool for the book as a whole since the arguments presented in the other chapters can be analysed to examine which of the quadrants they fit into.

Chapter 2 by Brownhill also adopts an emphasis on policy. This time the context is England and the specific policy emphasis that is discussed here is the requirement for men to act as 'male role models', a discourse that has been very dominant in England, especially with regard to a long-standing policy preoccupation with 'boys' underachievement', an emphasis that has been strongly criticised by many gender researchers (see Francis 2008). Adopting a critical approach to this policy emphasis, Brownhill discusses the influence of arguments about father absence from families and the problematic assumption that men can provide 'strong male role models'. Drawing on data from 81 research participants collected via questionnaires and interviews, Brownhill draws out men's experiences of *tension* within their discussions of masculinity and argues for a regrouping and rethinking of this policy.

Löfdahl and Hjalmarrson's ethnographic study in Chapter 3 examines policy at the micro-level of one pre-school classroom in Sweden. They analyse a specific intervention by pre-school staff who were attempting to implement a 'gender-conscious' approach in relation to the resources of the pre-school environment. The staff tried to alter the 'dolls corner' (home corner equivalent) by distributing the toys and resources throughout the pre-school space to make them more readily available to both boys and girls and to prevent the entrenchment of single sex groups clustered around gender-traditional toys. Drawing on Corsaro's theory (2005) about children's interpretive reproduction of the culture around them, the authors show the failure of this strategy and a continuation of gender-stereotypical play. They conclude that the children themselves need to be included in decisions to create change in gender patterns.

The research discussed in Chapter 4 by Mallozzi and Campbell Galman was taken from a larger data set about women's positioning of men as co-workers within the 'feminised' world of ECE. They emphasise the US context of the research where they claim that gender roles in the family are reproduced in ECE and are strongly differentiated. Drawing on interview data with two male and female ECE workers, their portrayal of the influence of US culture brings out militaristic and gun-toting stereotypes where men are seen to bring a disciplinarian function to the classroom. They argue that a male teacher in this context performs a hegemonic form of masculinity that is embraced with vigour as both men and women seek to demarcate gender difference 'in the starkest terms possible'.

In Section Two on *Young Children: Gender, Learning and Care* we are introduced to Hellman's ethnographic study in Chapter 5 which takes place in a Swedish pre-school context. The focus is on meal times in pre-school where findings emphasise embodied aspects of gender in a context that is focused on the care aspects of ECE professional roles. Hellman asks how the power relations between teachers and children perpetuate gendered ideals about boys' bodies and how the teachers reflect on this. She suggests that teachers are less gender conscious in the informal learning environment of meal times and that their unreflective practice breeds gender stereotypes.

Drawing on data from an Indonesian pre-school, Adriany in Chapter 6 argues that if teachers are to challenge young children's gender-stereotypical behaviours they may have to compromise the 'child-centred' ideology which is so highly valued in the Indonesian pre-school context. Her data shows the teachers expressing a view that they must follow the lead of the child and not interfere with nature in the child's development. This means they do not feel able or willing to challenge gender and this deeply held belief leaves them surprisingly powerless.

In Chapter 7 by Granbom we see how pre-school staff in Sweden interpret the curriculum with regard to gender equality by drawing on data collected from 45 participants in seven focus groups. The emphasis in this chapter is on teachers' social representations of gender differences that are constructed in one of these groups, exposing quite strong assumptions about boys' and girls' different toy preferences. She finds that the teachers' construction of gender differences is linked to their value for the children's individuality. She suggests that the staff articulate an idea of 'compensatory education' for children, with each gender group encouraged to develop aspects of their personality that traditionally belong to the opposite sex. This strategy implies an active division of children into single-sex groups as a means to an end. She concludes that the men and women working within ECE need to be well-informed about gender-related issues.

Chapter 8 by Warin, which opens the final section of the book *Gendered Professional Identities and Practice*, is based on recent interviews with pre-school teachers in Sweden and older interview data gathered in a children's centre in the UK. She sought to establish whether men working in this environment become hyper-masculine or whether they were willing and able to counteract traditional gender patterns. Her interest in the construction of masculine identities is based on Butler's (1990) and Goffman's (1971) theories about the performance of self. Data on personal appearances illustrates the men's gender sensitive negotiation of their performances. They revealed a gender consciousness and awareness in the ways they responded to the interviewer and also in their knowledge of the Swedish pre-school curriculum which they claimed to 'actively' work with. Warin argues for training teachers to become 'gender sensitive'.

An ethnographic study in two kindergartens and four nurseries in Tokyo, Japan, is the focus of Chapter 9 by Hellman, Nakazawa and Kuramochi. Based on observational data and focus groups, the study stresses an ideal of the pre-school teacher that cuts across gender and emphasises professionalism. However, the authors also show that gender norms were very much in evidence, especially in discussions about physical activities and physical tenderness. They also draw attention to teachers' deeply embodied use of verbal and non-verbal language, showing how even the teachers' tone, quality and use of language is gender differentiated within Japanese cultural norms. They conclude that pre-school professionalism is simultaneously regarded as 'gender neutral' yet incorporates some visible gender norms.

Chapter 10 by Grahn, the final chapter of the book, takes us into the interesting area of a rather more informal learning context. The chapter aims to reflect upon the male centredness of sports and how gendered ideals influence the teaching and coaching of sports with children and young people inside and outside of schools. The study discussed is based on interviews with Swedish sports coaches (swimming) and the analysis of the texts and pictures in 43 sports coaching textbooks. While the focus is on youth sports Grahn discusses the relevance of her findings to other age groups including impressionable young children. She shows that coaching is portrayed as gendered, performance-oriented for boys and more caring and socially oriented for girls, and claims that adult male ways of playing sports emphasise heterosexuality, competitiveness, strength, aggression and power, excluding other values such as equality, cooperation and caring. She concludes that when coaches, leaders, parents and teachers gain knowledge of the gendered ideals and stereotypes promoted through sports they can actively work against them.

Overall, the authors of this multinational text offer a book which is designed to question current provision, policy and practice. With its exploratory discussion, international perspectives and critiques of policy-making and professional practice we believe that this book will purposefully facilitate an engaging and dynamic examination of men, masculinities, teaching and care. We hope that you, the reader, agree.

NOTE!

'At the time of writing all of the web [links] offered in [the References for each chapter in this] book were active. As information on the web is regularly changed, updated or removed, it is anticipated that some links may not work for the reader. The author[s] apologise ... for this, but it is hoped that readers will recognise that this is out of the authors['] control.'

(Brownhill 2013: 28)

References

Archer, M. (2003) *Structure, Agency and the Internal Conversation*. Cambridge: Cambridge University Press.

Brody, D. (2014) *Men Who Teach Young Children: An International Perspective*. London: Trentham Books.

Brownhill, S. (2013) *Getting Children Writing. Story Ideas for Children Aged 3–11*. London: Sage.

Butler, J. (1990) *Gender Trouble*. New York: Routledge.

Corsaro, W. (2005) *The Sociology of Childhood*. Thousand Oaks, CA: Pine Forge Press.

Cremers, M. and Krabel, J. (2012) *Men in Kitas. A Study on the Situation of Men in Early Childhood Education, Federal Ministry for Family Affairs for Senior Citizens, Women and Youth*. Berlin: Catholic University of Applied Social Science.

Drudy, S. (2008) 'Gender balance/gender bias: the teaching profession and the impact of feminisation', *Gender and Education*, 20 (4): 309–23.

Drudy, S., Martin, M., Woods, M. and O' Flynn, J. (2005) *Men in the Classroom: Gender Imbalance in Teaching*. London and New York: RoutledgeFalmer.

Eaton, G. (2011) 'Cameron searches for the "root cause" of the riots', *New Statesman*, 10 August. [Online.] Available at: http://www.newstatesman.com/blogs/the-staggers/2011/08/cameron-society-riots-broken (accessed 12 December 2014).

Francis, B. (2008) 'Teaching manfully? Exploring gendered subjectivities and power via analysis of men teachers' gender performance', *Gender and Education*, 20 (2): 109–22.

Goffman, E. (1971) *The Presentation of Self in Everyday Life*. London: Penguin Books.

Ho, E. (2014) *Men in Early Childhood Education in Singapore*. [Online.] Available at: http://www.arnec.net/cos/o.x?c=/ntuc/pagetree&func=view&rid=1036916 (accessed 3 July 2014).

Ingersoll, R. and Merrill, L. (2010) 'Who's teaching our children?', *Educational Leadership*, 67 (8): 14–20.

Lorber, J. (2000) 'Using gender to undo gender. A feminist degendering movement', *Feminist Theory*, 1 (1): 79–95.

McCormack, O. and Brownhill, S. (2014) '"Moving away from the caring": exploring the views of in-service and pre-service male teachers about the concept of the male teacher as a role model at an early childhood and post-primary level', *International Journal of Academic Research in Education and Review*, 2 (4): 82–96.

McRobbie, A. (2007) 'Top girls? Young women and the post-feminist sexual contract', *Cultural Studies*, 21 (4): 718–37.

McRobbie, A. (2009) *The Aftermath of Feminism: Gender, Culture and Social Change*. London: Sage.

Majzub, R. M. (n.d.) *Critical Issues in Pre-school Education in Malaysia: Recent Advances in Educational Technologies*. [Online.] Available at: http://www.wseas.us/e-library/conferences/2013/CambridgeUSA/EET/EET-26.pdf (accessed 2 January 2015).

Marková, I. (2000) 'Amédée or how to get rid of it: social representations from a dialogical perspective', *Culture and Psychology*, 6 (4): 419–60.

Martino, W., Kehler, M. and Weaver-Hightower, M. (2009) *The Problem with Boys' Education: Beyond the Backlash*. London: Routledge.

Molloy, M. (2014) 'Girl, 7, praised for letter to Lego about gender stereotyping in toys', *Metro*, 1 February. [Online.] Available at: http://metro.co.uk/2014/02/01/charlotte-benjamin-girl-sends-letter-to-lego-about-gender-stereotypes-in-toys-4286634/ (accessed 12 December 2014).

Suyatno (2004) *Analisis Kesenjangan Gender pada Aspek Kebijakan, Kurikulum dan Sumberdaya Manusia pada Pendidikan Taman Kanak-kanak (TK): Studi di Kota Semarang-Jawa Tengah (Analysis on Gender Discrepancies in Kindergarten's Policies, Curriculums and Human Resources: A Study in Semarang-Central Java)*. Semarang: Universitas Dipenogoro.

Uba, G. and Cleinman, S. (2013) *Men in Early Care and Education: A Handbook for Affirmative Action*. [Online.] Available at: http://caeyc.org/main/caeyc/proposals-2014/pdfs/Uba,%20Gregory_Sat-3.pdf (accessed 2 January 2015).

UNESCO (2007) *Strong Foundation for Gender Equality in Early Childhood Care and Education*. Bangkok: UNESCO Asia and Pacific Regional Bureau for Education.

Van Laere, K., Vandenbroeck, M., Roets, G. and Peeters, J. (2014) 'Challenging the feminisation of the workforce: rethinking the mind–body dualism in Early Childhood Education and Care', *Gender and Education*, 26 (3): 232–46.

Wagner, B. J. (1999) *Dorothy Heathcote: Drama as a Learning Medium*. Portland, ME: Calendar Islands Publishers.

Warin, J. (2014) 'The status of care: linking "educare" and gender', *Journal of Gender Studies*, 23 (1): 93–106.

Warin, J. and Gannerud, E. (2014) 'Gender, teaching and care: a comparative conversation', *Gender and Education*, 26 (3): 193–9.

PART I

Policy, legislation and perspectives

1

MORE MEN? SWEDISH ARGUMENTS OVER FOUR DECADES ABOUT 'MISSING MEN' IN ECE AND CARE

Inga Wernersson

Introduction

Patterns of gender behaviour are simultaneously shifting yet also consistent. The gendered division of labour has been transformed: women are now found in many branches formerly labelled as 'male' but men have not crossed the line to 'women's work' to the same extent. A prominent example of this is the professional teaching and care of young children. Globally few men across the world work as pre-school teachers or childcarers in kindergartens, pre-schools and other similar institutions. This absence of men in ECE and care is the norm for Sweden despite affirmative actions that took place at the start of the 1970s. In this opening chapter a story will be told about male absence in childcare with an emphasis on the arguments used to support the need for, and the dangers of, men working with young children. The aim of this chapter is to unfold some aspects of how the complexity of the gender order presents itself in the relationship between care, men and masculinity.

Analytical dualism

There has been a long struggle for women to establish the rights and realities of finding gainful work in traditionally male areas, but it still appears to have been easier for women than for men to step over social and mental gender borders regarding occupations. To understand this imbalance a multitude of factors should be taken into account. A general theoretical model is helpful to keep track of the tangle of elements involved. How society arranges the care and socialisation of children is related to technical and economic, as well as social, psychological and emotional, aspects of human life. Within a framework of critical realism, Archer (2003) has developed a model of human and social development that takes into account objectives, material circumstances and social structures, as well as collective and individual constructions, interpretations and imaginations of the world. Her methodology, referred to as *analytical dualism*, is useful to separate structural and individual influences without losing their interconnectedness. The individual internalises and is formed by social structures, but is also an agent and an actor in the reproduction and transformation of such structures. It is important, Archer argues, to recognise the temporality in these processes (the individual and structures operate on different timescales) to avoid upwards, downwards and central conflation. Downwards conflation reduces the individual to a product of social discourse (e.g. poststructuralism). Upwards conflation reduces society to individual attitudes, acts and decisions (e.g. methodological individualism). Central conflation is exemplified by structuration theory (Giddens 1979) where the influence of both structure and individual are recognised but viewed as indivisible which makes it impossible to separate one kind of influence from the other. The mutual and complex influence over time between the individual subject, social relations and multiple layers of social structures should thus be kept in mind in trying to understand, in this case, the lack of male professional carers in a changing gender order.

The complex context – general structures

Transformations of significant structures in society enable fresh ideas about possible occupations for individual men and women. The labour market, the general gender-power order and the educational system are fundamental in this case and will be discussed in turn below.

The labour market

When it was introduced on the Swedish scene in the 1960s, the issue of male pre-school teachers and carers for young children was related to the structure for the production of goods and services, i.e. the economy and the structural gender-power order, as well as to sexualities and gender identities. The increasing demand for labour in the postwar era and women's demand for economic independence were significant political issues as a core aspect of a new and fair gender order. In order for mothers to join the paid labour force it was necessary to provide daycare of high quality for young children. In Sweden the Social Democrat government took measures to implement this insight by developing a policy of gender equality and by creating a system of highly subsidised public daycare for all children (Palme 2011).

The diminishing need for labour in certain areas, for example farming and industrial production, and the increasing demand for services and for jobs in the 'knowledge' sector have resulted in a reduction of traditional male jobs over several decades. As early as the 1970s it was concluded that men would need to change their occupational preferences and look to the health and care sectors, for example, to find jobs (SOU 1978: 15). This was one type of indication that daycare/pre-school should develop into workplaces that are also 'normal' for men. All these labour market factors were present in Sweden in the 1960s and 1970s when public daycare started to expand and when the discussion about male professionals in childcare began.

The gender-power order

The structural changes in the labour market described above embrace an *intended* change in the gendered division of labour. In Sweden, as well as in the other Nordic countries, a large majority of women (82 per cent in Sweden[1]) are in the labour force and 'home-making' has become less common as a career. A political policy of gender equality has accompanied this development, implying that it is not *only* labour power demand that has geared the expansion of public childcare. In Sweden daycare is sometimes identified as the single most important factor in the development towards gender equality (Tallberg Broman, 2009). However, if it is *only* women who undertake this public care of children it may be doubtful if, or in what sense, this is a sign of a genuinely fair and equal gender order.

It is important to explore this discussion at a global level via another angle, examining men's participation in actions to develop a fairer and equal gender order in which childcare is an important aspect. The Organisation for Security and Cooperation in Europe (OSCE)[2] has described it as 'essential for achieving sustainable security and upholding human rights' (OSCE 2012). The close responsibility for children is viewed in this context as a means of loosening up masculine structures represented by violence and power struggles. A transformation of the kind of connection between men and children is thus identified, not just as a concern limited to quality and equality in childcare, but also as a key to a different kind of masculinity and another form of the gender order with an impact for peaceful development at a global level.

The educational systems

A gradual change over four decades has turned the Swedish 'daycare centre' into an integral part of the educational system, resulting also in a change of name to 'pre-school'. The same trend is present in most comparable countries (Eurydice 2014). Today there is a stress on these institutions to prepare children as early as possible for school, and 'knowledge' rather than 'care' is stressed as the prime function. The focus is now on reading, writing, mathematics and science and, since 1998, the Swedish pre-school has had its own national-level curriculum (Swedish National Agency for Education 2010). This trend to prolong formal education, starting with younger children, is strongly supported by, for example, the European Union (EU) as summarised in a report from Eurydice (2009):

- Historical changes in education systems … which were constructed from the top (university level) but have gradually spread downwards to embrace younger age groups.
- The extension of education to the masses or the democratisation of education inspired by the convergence of two ideas: the first one emanating from the humanist tradition whereby all individuals have the right to education; and the second, rooted in economic theory, which views children as a reserve of talent which must yield a profit.
- Changes in our view of childhood and, due to the development of child psychology, an increasing understanding of the importance of the first years of life.

(p. 131)

In conclusion, different dimensions of social structure, partly integrated and partly separate, have been changing over a long period of time in ways that point in the same direction: public childcare institutions are necessary and men ought to work there. These transformations of structures constitute (part of) the context in which individual men make their choices and in which other individuals (men and women) react to these choices.

Hard facts: the number of children in Nordic daycare/pre-schools and the men working there

The structural changes described above have resulted in an increasing participation of children in daycare/pre-school all over the Western world. Figures from the Nordic countries and the average for the EU 28 (Eurydice 2014) are illustrative (see Table 1.1).

It is apparent that a larger percentage of children under the age of four are in formal care in the Nordic countries (except Finland[3]) compared to the average for the EU. The percentage differences for children under the age of three are closely related to the details in parental leave regulations. The numbers for pre-school attendance, i.e. preparing for regular school, of children from four years old are similar in all of Europe.

Even if, as I have tried to show above, *structural* changes indicate that a fair number of men would be working in pre-schools, this is not the case. Norway and Sweden are examples of countries where the number of men working in pre-school/daycare has been highlighted in relation to gender equality and quality of care. However, this is not the case everywhere (although it is difficult to get accurate and up-to-date figures on the ratio of men and women working in care for young children). Even in the Nordic countries there are fewer men working in pre-school/daycare than is popularly held to be the case. In 2013 the percentage of men working in pre-school/daycare in Norway was 9 per cent (Statistics Norway 2014); in Iceland it was 7 per cent (Statistics Iceland 2014) and in Sweden it was 4 per cent (Statistics Sweden 2014b). The figure for Denmark in 2007 was 8 per cent and for Finland it was less than 2 per cent in 2008 (Baagøe Nielsen 2011).[4]

In Sweden the issue of male careworkers, in terms of a national policy and structural changes, was highlighted several decades before it became prominent in Europe and other comparable countries. However, this early start does not seem to have resulted in any advantages. Norway, the country that is celebrated for being the most successful in the endeavour to recruit men to work with children, started the process much later (in the 1990s). In the following section I will discuss the arguments used, both at present and in the past, in order to trace why it is so hard for men to choose to work with young children.

TABLE 1.1 Participation rates in formal care and pre-school for children under school age (2011) in the Nordic countries and average for the EU 28

Country	Enrolment in formal care for under 3s and pre-school from 4 to school age (%)	
	Up to 3 years	*4 years to compulsory school age*
Denmark	74	97.7
Finland	26	74.0
Iceland	39	96.5
Norway	42	97.2
Sweden	51	95.3
EU 28 (average)	30	93.0

The institution and the individual: arguments for men in childcare and pre-school

In the light of analytical dualism (see above) structures are understood as partly transformed as a result of changes in people's thinking, needs and actions. In turn, transformed structures and introducing new sets of demands and opportunities have consequences for individual beliefs, actions and imaginations. It is a puzzle as to why individual men do not harness the changes in the structures of gender, labour, childcare and education by becoming pre-school teachers. It is also surprising to see that women tend to stick to a traditional division of childcare labour, although not to the same extent as men. In the following section I will scrutinise the different dimensions in the public discussion about why men are needed, or not as the case may be, in the care and teaching of the young.

Early efforts in Sweden: affirmative action in the 1970s

In Sweden in the 1960s a specific term – *Jämställdhet* – was coined to make the idea of gender equality visible and possible to handle in its own right (Florin and Nilsson 2005). *Jämställdhet* is defined as a state in which '… women and men have equal power to shape society and their own lives. This implies the same opportunities, rights and obligations in all spheres of life' (Statistics Sweden 2014a). This concept was introduced and implemented in working life and in public institutions (e.g. schools and pre-schools) as a principle and a goal. In the curricula of the compulsory school (Sweden: National Board of Education 1969) as well as the secondary school (Sweden: National Board of Education 1971) gender equality was introduced as an object of teaching as well as a spirit that should permeate all kinds of activity. The expansion of public childcare resulted in an increasing demand for well-educated pre-school teachers, and the recruitment of men was one way to meet that demand. From 1971, to promote male recruitment, men could, if they were not competitive, get an extra merit point added to the sum of their marks when applying for pre-school teacher education. This arrangement, a form of positive discrimination, was initially successful and the number of men in pre-school teacher education was nine times higher in 1975 than in 1971 with about 10 per cent of the pre-school teacher students now being male (Wernersson and Lander 1979).

In 1978 one of the teacher unions organising pre-school teachers demanded an evaluation of this affirmative action. One reason for this was the union's assumption that men tended to occupy more than their share of the few superior positions available in pre-schools and had consequently decreased the amount of time they actually spent working with children. The union viewed this situation as problematic since the main reason for accepting the support for men in the first place was for children to have male role models and to experience men as carers. The evaluation showed that the support for men was moderately effective in the first few years but less so later on (Wernersson and Lander 1979). Consequently, this form of affirmative action was removed and this kind of differential treatment is no longer legal in Swedish higher education.

As part of the evaluation, an analysis was made of the arguments used at the time for the promotion of more men in pre-schools. The arguments from the 1970s could be categorised into three main groups with several subcategories as follows:

1. Men were seen to be important as *role models* for children, especially boys, for two reasons. First, there was a psychological argument implying that men were needed to

reinforce 'good' gender identities in boys. The notion of *compensatory masculinity* was important for this argument, implying that boys who grew up without proper male role models tended to become overly violent and aggressive or the opposite – effeminate. Second, there was a sociological argument claiming that pre-schools needed to be a model context where men and women working together showed that gender division was not inevitable in order for gender equality to be implemented in wider society.

2. More men in pre-school would *improve pre-school teaching as an occupation*. First, having more men in this occupation would improve the social status and influence of pre-school teaching as well as provide higher salaries. Secondly, a workplace with both men and women was said to be more satisfying in terms of working conditions. Third, the content and quality of the occupational performance would improve, since both men and women were expected to bring useful, but different experiences.

3. More men in pre-school would change the *social structure at a macro level*. First, it would add to gender equality in general since there should be both men and women in all occupations. Second, it would add to changes in the labour market since men must change their job preferences as a result of a decreasing demand for labour in male-dominated sectors. Third, to work as a pre-school teacher was viewed by some as a political decision as the opportunity to influence new forms of childhood socialisation was recognised as a way to move society to the ideological left.

Since the 1970s there have been many activities (see Ohlsson 2003; Antonsson 2008)[5] aimed at breaking the traditionally gendered educational and occupational choices. 'Girls into science and technology' was the most visible theme in the school context and it was also moderately successful. After the 1970s the parallel, 'Boys into care' and 'Men into teaching', has not been forgotten but moved somewhat into the background.

In 2009 this issue re-emerged due to difficulties in meeting the demand for teachers at all levels in the school system. A report by Högskoleverket (2009) presented arguments that were used to explain why it was important for men to take part in the socialisation, education and care of children. This time the goal was to bring men into teaching in the school system overall, not just in the pre-school area. Somewhat surprisingly the arguments were very much the same as in the 1970s (except for the political argument that teaching children is a way to 'change the world'). It appears as if very little has happened in this area despite actual social and political change and a fair amount of empirical and theoretical research on masculinity specifically and gender in general. In addition to the need for more teachers, the fact that girls tend to outperform boys in most areas of education has put the searchlight on the implications of being male (Björnsson 2005). In current times the issue has re-emerged and it is the Norwegian experience that is viewed as the model.

Norway has recently been recognised as successful in the recruitment of men to childcare jobs. In 2008 the Norwegian government developed a long-term action plan to guide the work for gender equality (Kunnskapsdepartementet [Norway] 2008) where getting more men into kindergarten was one of several goals. The plan identified the traditional differences in choice of occupation and education as one of the most important causes for gender division in society. The main arguments for more males in kindergarten were:

1. To provide boys and girls with female and male role models and to let all children experience both female and male carers.

2. To guarantee a supply of qualified personnel with different kinds of competences in childcare.

A target was set for 2010 to attain 20 per cent men among carers/teachers for young children and there was an emphasis on long-term systematic recruitment efforts. An elaborate and expensive programme[6] was set up incorporating various different measures, e.g. model kindergartens, recruitment guidance and recruitment teams, media visibility, monetary prizes and evaluations. The Norwegian gender equality law gave room for positive discrimination in favour of male applicants in kindergartens.

The paradox of the male carer – a theoretical model

So far I have drawn on Nordic examples but in this section I intend to present a more general outline that could help us to understand why it is so hard to break the tradition that men should not be professionally responsible for children, especially our youngest. This is even more puzzling since within the private sphere of family life the majority of men love their children as fathers, enjoy being with them and are quite capable of caring for them. The arguments for male carers discussed above are taken from the Swedish context but are used in varying forms all over the world (see Carrington *et al.* 2008). I will try to decontextualise the arguments and relate them to underlying assumptions in order to find a more systematic way to reach a deeper understanding of what aspects of structural and individual gender are at work here.

What we are dealing with here is in essence a *political* issue. The question is how one should go about changing an established social pattern in order to make a better one. It is thus a deliberate and goal-directed construction of gender based on ideas of how things *are*, how they *ought to be* and what is *possible*. The contradictions in the arguments show that different ideas are at work simultaneously and also that there is no common understanding of either 'facts' or 'goals'.

As previously discussed, three main categories of arguments have been identified: the role model argument, the argument about the improvement of occupational conditions and the structural gender equality argument. The rationale behind each of these three categories differs in several ways.

First, dimensions of power and ascribed social value within the gender structure make it very different to motivate men to cross gender-borders compared with such a mission directed towards women. Women/girls are supposed to *gain* from, and have been *encouraged* to *dare* to do, what men do. Change for men implies the opposite. It includes a risk of losing rather than gaining something, be it prestige, power or money. Finding acceptable reasons for men to choose traditionally female jobs can thus be difficult. The goals of personal satisfaction and increased freedom to choose education, occupation and lifestyle do not seem to be as strong incentives for change as might be expected. However, an emphasis on men's value as male role models, especially for boys, is one way to signal that men can do something that women cannot do even within this location of feminine competence. This approach makes it possible to claim that it is not a 'step down' for men to work with children, since they add something unique. However, this creates a new problem if the political goal is to promote gender *equality*. Recruitment of men is reached by a certain loss in women's value since it must be implied that women are not doing a good job-raising boys. Consequently, there has been a long-standing strong critique of the 'role model' argument (see Skelton 2011; Martino and Rezai-Rashti 2012). However, recent Swedish studies (Gannerud 1999; Hjalmarsson 2009) show that female teachers tend to apologise for not being 'male role models'. A diluted form of the role-related argument is that men and women have different experiences, for example 'men know how to play football'. However, this argument has become more or less obsolete in a climate where the gendered separation of activities has loosened up. If we take the aforementioned football as an example, there is a likelihood that a Swedish female teacher plays, or has played, football (even though it was a gendered sport in the 1970s).[7] While there are still gendered experiences and attitudes in current times, in most respects these are much less strict today than they were in the 1970s and the sex of a person cannot necessarily predict what kind of experiences s/he will have. To argue that men bring something to the children that women cannot provide is obviously a tempting but highly problematic way to recruit males to pre-school.

In the Swedish context the most common explanation for men's reluctance to choose work in pre-schools is that the pay is too low and the training too long (three years). It is argued, to persuade women that more men are needed in pre-schools, that men can boost the professional strength of this occupation, resulting in better pay and more influence. However, we also see undercurrents of assumed female weaknesses in this argument and an assumption that heroic, self-sacrificing men can save the situation. Another argument in this category, which generalises to job contexts beyond the pre-school, is that a work-place with both men and women is socially superior to a single-sex environment. Unfortunately this may be a weak incentive for recruitment. One would guess that very few people, if any, are likely to choose an occupation mainly to balance the men–women ratio.

The third category of argument (the structural gender equality argument) has the same weakness. To embrace the principle of both men and women in all types of occupations does not imply that one, as an individual, is willing to give it much weight when choosing a career. Unfortunately, this seems to be the only type of argument that does not incorporate traditional gender inequality to promote equality.

I have presented above several different kinds of arguments for more men in childcare/teaching of young children based on political strategies for targeted modification of the traditional order. In the following section I will try to explore in greater depth assumptions about the 'essence' of gender behind these arguments. To simplify and draw these arguments together I employ the two dimensions of horizontal and vertical gender differentiation. The *horizontal* dimension represents femininity and masculinity as 'specialisations' while the *vertical* dimension represents the power/status hierarchy in the gender order. In Figure 1.1 the two dimensions are crossed and the different arguments inscribed in the resulting quadrants.

Figure 1.1 illustrates how very different, even contradictory, assumptions about the world end up supporting the same political conviction that it is a good idea to try to persuade men to work in childcare/pre-school. Since gender equality and respect for the work women do are important values that are difficult to combine with the kind of arguments shown in the two quadrants to the right in Figure 1.1, it is also hard to find tempting arguments for recruitment. For individual men who are convinced that they will experience working with children as rewarding, and who are strong enough to resist suspicions and insinuations, this

	Horizontal differentiation: femininity and masculinity as 'specialisations'	
Assumptions	*Men and women have the same distribution of qualities and abilities*	*Men and women are individually different in terms of qualities and abilities*
Men and women have the same power/status/value	*Argument* An even distribution of men and women doing the same kind of tasks is a model of gender equality for children	*Argument* More men in childcare/pre-school would add male complementary competencies and role models
Men have more power/status/value	*Argument* More men will (as a consequence of traditional power distribution) make the occupational conditions better (but may also reduce the career options for women)	*Argument* Men are superior and will bring important qualities in several dimensions to the profession, occupational conditions and the workplace

Vertical differentiation: gender power/status hierarchy

FIGURE 1.1   Overview of assumptions and arguments for more males in childcare/pre-school

is no problem. It is, however, not surprising if those who are just a little bit interested are frightened away by the complexities and ambiguities. The interplay between individual considerations of risks and benefits related to past and present social structures are clearly recognisable (Archer 2003).

Another complication – suspicions about paedophilia

It never entered into the Swedish discussion in the 1970s that men who wished to work with small children might be doing so for dubious reasons. Suspicions about men's potential paedophilic inclinations were exposed in the 1990s when such a crime was discovered in one particular pre-school (Stolz 2002). Currently, however, many males working in pre-schools in Sweden bear witness to feeling suspected and describe how they are warned not to be alone with the children (Warin 2014). This is a strong barrier, drawing on potential risk and shame, and is likely to be preventing many men from working with children. The actual instance of male sexual abuse towards children in the pre-school is minimal (Sweden: Swedish National Council for Crime Prevention (Brå) 2011) so this fear is not based so much on a real danger but on a media-led moral panic suggesting an undergrowth of ideas and feelings where men are viewed as sexually dangerous and generally unfit to be close to children. The ideal pre-school context where sensible men and women work together to support children to develop into free and independent adults is hence threatened by a picture of males with a twisted sexuality waiting for their chance to molest young children. *How should this threat be interpreted?*

The simplest possibility is that the mere thought of one's child being molested by someone who is trusted by both children and parents/carers is so repulsive for any parent/carer that no further explanation is needed. From another perspective, however, the individual parents' (understandable) panic reactions can be seen in the light of a gender structure that is characterised by male supremacy (see lower right quadrant in Figure 1.1). At the structural level the male paedophile that crosses the gender line is perceived as dangerous and appalling. As such, he serves as a warning for honest men to keep away. The result is that competent and suitable men who are in favour of gender equality support a system they actually want to change by avoiding professional childcare. Such processes help to maintain male power and limit freedom at an individual level for both sexes.

Conclusions

Thus structural changes (in production systems, the labour market, educational system and gender structure) that were expected to shift men into different kinds of traditional 'women's work' have not had much effect when it comes to professional work with young children. As those men who dare to try anyway are quite successful in this kind of work and that most men manage their own children well enough as fathers, all explanations that refer to essential sex differences are inadequate. The aim of this chapter has been to shed some light on 'emergent forces' in the interplay between individual actions and social structures based on a critical realist theoretical approach. It was expected that transformations of labour market demands and expansion of the educational sector would make men change their occupational preferences. However, the idea of a gendered division of labour appears to be strong and closely related to individual identity and/or social power as we see through the arguments used above and the assumptions they are tied to. While the Swedish case is used here as an example, it seems similar to what happens elsewhere. The recent efforts in Norway are viewed as successful, but the goal – 20 per cent men in kindergarten by 2010 – was not reached. There are, no doubt, questions left to be answered, among them those that are offered below.

UNANSWERED QUESTIONS

- Is the weakening of structural markers of difference between men and women in some areas such as career, formal power and lifestyle in fact strengthening the division in other areas? Is it possible that caring for young children as a profession is used to uphold and make visible a gender order that is otherwise diluted and becomes hard to grasp?
- What role does the 'paedophilia threat' play? How far does it function as a symbol of dangerous masculinity, connected to power and supremacy, and how far does it present a rationale for men not to work with children?
- What can be done to make care professions genderless? Should we be much more single-minded and determined to bring the ghost of gender into the light? What strategies can we propose?

Notes

1. As of 2013. Ages 25–64 years. The figure for women born in Sweden or some other Nordic country is 91 per cent. The comparable figure for men is 88 (94) per cent (Statistics Sweden 2014a).
2. The OSCE is an organisation that comprises 57 participating states from North America, Europe and Asia. Its activities cover three dimensions of security: the politico-military, the economic and environmental, and the human.
3. In Finland parents receive an allowance to use by their own choice, for example, one parent or a hired nanny to take care of the child in the home or the child is cared for in a public institution.
4. Denmark and Finland do not publish official statistics on the sex of personnel in daycare/pre-school.
5. Ohlsson (2003) describes one example of systematic efforts to get unemployed men to choose teacher education. Antonsson (2008) describes and evaluates about 400 examples of projects launched by different organisations to break the gender borders in different kinds of occupations during the second half of the twentieth century.
6. With a budget of NOK 15 million (about GBP 1.35 million).
7. Football is the most popular sport in Sweden for both men and women. Of the population (7–70 years of age) 3 per cent of women and 8 per cent of men play football (Riksidrottsförbundet 2014).

References

Antonsson, H. (2008) *Kartläggning av ett halvt sekels jämställdhetssatsningar i Sverige. (Review of Half a Century of Gender Equality Initiatives in Sweden)*, Sweden's Innovation Agency, Vinnova Report VR 2008:07. [Online.] Available at: http://www.vinnova.se/upload/EPiStorePDF/vr-08-07.pdf (accessed 6 January 2015).

Archer, M. (2003) *Structure, Agency and the Internal Conversation*. Cambridge: Cambridge University Press.

Baagøe Nielsen, S. (ed.) (2011) *Nordiske mænd til omsorgsarbejde! – En forskningsbaseret erfaringsopsamling på initiativer til at rekruttere, uddanne og fastholde mænd efter finanskrisen (Nordic Men to Care Work! – A Research Based Review of Experiences from Initiatives to Recruit and Keep Men After the Financial Crises)*. Roskilde Universitet, Institut for Psykologi og Uddannelsesforskning, VELPRO – Center for Velfærd, Profession og Hverdagsliv.

Björnsson, A. (2005) *Kön och skolframgång: tolkningar och perspektiv. (Gender and School Performance: Interpretations and Perspectives)* Myndigheten för skolutveckling. (Agency for School Improvement). [Online.] Available at: https://www.hig.se/download/18.4eec0990121ee2a9a9f80009351/MatsBjornsson.pdf (accessed 2 September 2014).

Carrington, B., Tymms, P. and Merrell, C. (2008) 'Role models, school improvement and the "gender gap" – do men bring out the best in boys and women the best in girls?', *British Educational Research Journal*, 34 (3): 315–27.

Dahlström, E. (ed.) (1962) *Kvinnors liv och arbete. Svenska och norska studier av ett aktuellt samhällsproblem (Women's Life and Work. Swedish and Norwegian Studies of a Current Social Issue)*. Stockholm: Studieförbundet Näringsliv och Samhälle.

Eurydice (2009) *Early Childhood Education and Care in Europe: Tackling Social and Cultural Inequalities*. Education, Audiovisual and Culture Executive Agency (EACEA P9 Eurydice). [Online.] Available at: http://www.eurydice.org (accessed 2 January 2015).

Eurydice (2014) *Key Data on Early Childhood Education and Care in Europe*, Eurydice and Eurostat Report, 2014 edn. Luxembourg: Publications Office of the European Union.

Florin, C. and Nilsson, B. (2005) 'Women's questions on the agenda: the politicization of gender equality in Sweden', in M. Jerneck (ed.), *Different Paths to Modernity: A Nordic and Spanish Perspective*. Lund: Nordic Academic Press, pp. 302–17.

Gannerud, E. (1999) *Genusperspektiv på lärargärning: om kvinnliga klasslärares liv och arbete (Gender Perspective on Teachers Work: On Female Class Teacher's Life and Work)*, Göteborg Studies in Educational Sciences, No. 137. Göteborg: Acta Universitatis Gothoburgensis.

Giddens, A. (1979) *Central Problems in Social Theory: Action, Structure and Contradiction in Social Analysis*. Berkeley, CA: University of California Press.

Granbom, I. and Wernersson, I. (2012) *Män I förskolan – kartläggning och analys av insatser* (*Men in Pre-school – Review and Analysis of Initiatives*). Skolverket (National Board of Education). [Online.] Available at: http://lumaol.files.wordpress.com/2013/01/mc3a4n-i-fc3b6rskolan-kartlc3a4ggning-oh-analys-av-insatser.pdf (accessed 30 September 2014).

Hjalmarsson, M. (2009) 'Förändrade krav i läraryrket?' ('Changing demands in the teaching profession?'), in I. Wernersson (ed.), *Genus i förskola och skola: förändringar i policy, perspektiv och praktik* (*Gender in Pre-school and School: Changes in Policy, Perspectives and Practice*). Göteborg: Acta Universitatis Gothoburgensis.

Högskoleverket (National Board of Higher Education) (2009) *Man ska bli lärare! Den ojämna könsfördel-ningen inom lärarutbildningen – beskrivning och analys* (*Men Should Be Teachers! The Skewed Distribution Within Teacher Education – Description and Analysis*), Rapport 2009:7 R. Stockholm: Högskoleverket.

Jerneck, M. (ed.) (2005) *Different Paths to Modernity: A Nordic and Spanish Perspective*. Lund: Nordic Academic Press.

Kunnskapsdepartementet [Norway] (2008) *Handlingsplan for likestilling i barnehage og grunnopp-læring 2008–2010*. (*Action Plan for Gender Equality in Kindergarten and Elementary Schooling, 2008–2010*). [Online.] Available at: http://www.regjeringen.no/upload/KD/Vedlegg/Likestilling/KD_Handlingsplan%20for%20likestillinweb_09.08.pdf (accessed 2 September 2014).

Martino, W. and Rezai-Rashti, G. (2012) 'Rethinking the influence of male teachers: investigating gendered and raced authority in an elementary school in Toronto', *Review of Education, Pedagogy, and Cultural Studies*, 34 (5): 258–81.

Ohlsson, J. (2003) *Att bryta ett mönster – en processutvärdering av länsarbetsnämndens brytprojekt 'Fler män till lärare'* (*To Break the Pattern – A Process Evaluation of the County Labour Board's Breaking Project 'More Male Teachers'*). Luleå, Sweden: Luleå tekniska universitet (Luleå University of Technology).

Palme, O. (2011) Speech at the Swedish Social Democratic Congress 1972. Reprinted in *Tidskrift för genusvetenskap* (*Journal of Gender Science*), 2–3: 57–65. [Online.] Available at: http://ojs.ub.gu.se/ojs/index.php/tgv/article/view/1006/878 (accessed 2 January 2015).

Riksidrottsförbundet (Swedish Sports Confederation) (2014) *Statistik*. [Online.] Available at: http://www.rf.se/ (accessed 2 September 2014).

Skelton, C. (2011) 'Men teachers and the "feminized" primary school: a review of the literature', *Educational Review*, 64 (1): 1–19.

SOU (1978) *Ny vårdutbildning: betänkande* (*A New Nursing Education: Parliamentary Report*). Stockholm: LiberFörlag/Allmänna förlaget. [Online.] Available at: http://www.weburn.kb.se/metadata/797/SOU_8350797.htm (accessed 2 September 2014).

Statistics Iceland (2014) *Personnel in Pre-primary Institutions by Sex and Occupation 1998–2013*. [Online.] Available at: http://www.statice.is/Statistics/Education/Pre-primary-institutions (accessed 2 January 2015).

Statistics Norway (2014) *Ansatte i barnehager, etter stilling og kjønn* (*Employed in Kindergarten After Position and Sex*). [Online.] Available at: https://www.ssb.no/statistikkbanken/selectvarval/saveselections.asp (accessed 6 January 2015).

Statistics Sweden (2014a) *Women and Men in Sweden. Facts and Figures 2014*. [Online.] Available at: http://www.scb.se/sv_/Hitta-statistik/Publiceringskalender/Visa-detaljeradinformation/?publobjid=22162 (accessed 6 January 2015).

Statistics Sweden (2014b) *Personal i förskolan efter utbildning 2013* (*Personnel in Pre-school After Education*). [Online.] Available at: http://www.scb.se/sv_/Hittastatistik/Temaomraden/Jamstalldhet/Fordjupningar/Utbildning-och-forskning/Forskolan/Personal-i-forskolan-efter-utbildning-2012/ (accessed 6 January 2015).

Stolz, J. (2002) *Pedofildebatten vs. manlig förskolepersonal* (*The Debate on Paedophilia vs. Males Working in Pre-schools*). C-uppsats i kriminologi, Stockholms universitet. [Online.] Available at: http://www.crimi-nology.su.se/polopoly_fs/1.66166.1340743157!/2002c_John_Stoltz.pdf (accessed 2 September 2014).

Sweden: Curriculum for the Pre-school Lpfö 98 Revised 2010 (2010) *Translation into English of the Curriculum for the Pre-school, Lpfö 98*. Available at: http://www.skolverket.se/om-skolverket/publikationer/visa-enskild-publikation?_xurl_=http%3A%2F%2Fwww5.skolverket.se%2Fwtpub%2Fws%2Fskolbok%2Fwpubext%2Ftrycksak%2FRecord%3Fk%3D2704 (accessed 6 January 2015).

Sweden: National Board of Education (1969) *Läroplan för grundskolan (1969)* (*Curriculum for the Compulsory School 1969*). Stockholm: Liber Utbildningsförlaget. [Online.] Available at: http://hdl.handle.net/2077/30902.

Sweden: National Board of Education (1971) *Läroplan för gymnasieskolan: Lgy 70. (1971–1986)* (*Curriculum for the Secondary School 1971–1986*). Stockholm: Liber Utbildningsförlaget. [Online.] Available at: http://www.lararnashistoria.se/node/993 (accessed 6 January 2015).

Sweden: Swedish National Council for Crime Prevention (Brå) (2011) *Child Rapes Reported to the Police. An Update and Comparison of the Years 1995 and 2008. English Summary of Brå Report 2011.* [Online.] Available at: http://www.bra.se/bra/bra-in-english/home/publications/archive/publications/2012-03-13-child-rapes-reported-to-the-police.html (accessed 2 September 2014).

Tallberg Broman, I. (2009) 'Mamma, pappa, förskolebarn. Om förskolan som jämställdhetsprojekt' ('Mum, dad, pre-school child. About pre-school as a project for gender equality'), in I. Wernersson (ed.), *Genus i förskola och skola: förändringar i policy, perspektiv och praktik.* Göteborg: Acta Universitatis Gothoburgensis. [Online.] Available at: https://gupea.ub.gu.se/handle/2077/20411 (accessed 2 September 2014).

Warin, J. (2014) 'The status of care: linking "educare" and gender', *Journal of Gender Studies,* 23 (1): 93–106.

Wernersson, I. (ed.) (2009a) *Genus i förskola och skola: förändringar i policy, perspektiv och praktik* (*Gender in Pre-school and School: Changes in Policy, Perspectives and Practice*). Göteborg: Acta Universitatis Gothoburgensis.

Wernersson, I. (2009b) 'Pedagogerna och jämställdheten' ('Teachers and gender equality'), in I. Wernersson (ed.), *Genus i förskola och skola: förändringar i policy, perspektiv och praktik* (*Gender in Pre-school and School: Changes in Policy, Perspectives and Practice*). Göteborg: Acta Universitatis Gothoburgensis, pp. 23–42. [Online.] Available at: https://gupea.ub.gu.se/handle/2077/20411 (accessed 6 January 2015).

Wernersson, I. and Lander, R. (1979) *Män och kvinnor i barnomsorgen: en analys av könskvotering, yrkesval och arbetstrivsel* (*Men and Women in Childcare: An Analysis of Affirmative Action, Occupational Choice and Work Satisfaction*). Stockholm: Jämställdhetskommittén.

2

MALE ROLE MODELS IN EDUCATION-BASED SETTINGS (0–8)

An English perspective

Simon Brownhill

Introduction

The call for more male practitioners (0–5)/teachers (5–7+) in 0–8 education-based settings in England remains prevalent as boys' underachievement and their disaffection with learning continues to dominate education agendas (PARITY 2013). In an attempt to narrow the 'attainment gap' between boys and girls there is a recognised need, backed by government policy-making (Paton 2013a) and public discourse (Children's Workforce Development Council (CWDC), cited in Ward 2009) for more men to work with young children and act as 'male role models'. This chapter focuses its attention on exploring various *tensions* which surround the persistent male role model argument. It will consider different ways in which the term 'male role model' can be interpreted and whether men who work in the early years (0–8) sector actually *are* role models simply because of their male presence in education-based settings. An examination of professional practices and physical characteristics of the male role model serve as an opportunity to challenge stereotypical thinking which continues to be rooted within the male role model 'ideal'.

Drawing on select findings from doctoral research undertaken by the author, this chapter will explore the complexities of the role model rhetoric by adding further discussion and debate to existing knowledge, understanding and research which has either raised questions or challenged perceptions of the male role model as being 'the answer' to address problematic issues relating to boys' academic motivation, behaviour, engagement and attainment levels.

'Driving' the men agenda

There are numerous arguments which fuel local, national and international campaigns and institutional recruitment drives to not only get more men working in the 0–8 sector but also to retain them. Skelton (2009: 39) refers to these reasons as 'drivers' and efforts to critically explore several of these will be briefly made in this opening section. These include:

- the 'gender gap' and the feminisation of teaching;
- father figures; and
- strong male role models.

The 'gender gap' and the feminisation of teaching

A central argument for the increased calling for and participation of men in education-based settings (0–8) relates to the very 'real and persistent' gender gap noted in the academic attainment of boys in comparison to that of girls (House of Commons Education Committee (HoCEC) 2014: 3). National statistics published by the Department for Education (DfE 2013a, 2013b) clearly show girls outperforming boys in terms of achieving a good level of development at the end of the Early Years Foundation Stage (EYFS) (0–5) and reaching expected levels at the end of Key Stage 1 (KS1) (5–7), a pattern also noted in later Key Stages (KS2–5) (7–18+). While there are a number of factors attributed to this continued variance in performance, one prevalent school of thought asserts that the absence of male practitioners/teachers has resulted in what might be described as an 'epidemic' of boys' anti-learning and anti-school attitudes and behaviours which, in turn, have had a negative impact on their attainment and subsequent test results. Contributing to this epidemic is the feminisation of teaching which is deemed to be as a result of the predominance of female staff in both sectors (0–5 and 5–8+) – current statistics suggest that the UK education and care workforce is made up of 3 per cent males (0–5) and 12 per cent males in the primary sector (5–11) (Paton 2013b). McCormack and Brownhill (2014: 83) report how it is perceived that female practitioners/teachers will 'act ... in stereotypical feminine ways, resulting in their practices, pedagogies, strategies and expectations favouring girls' which subsequently disadvantages boys. This raises an interesting number of *tensions*, particularly as there is no definite research indicating that male professionals have a positive impact on students' academic achievement. Assertions that bringing more men into the 'education fold' with alternative forms of provision, e.g. 'movement, vigour, 'hands-on' [and] natural activity' (Mulholland and Hanson 2003: 214), is challenged by the likes of Francis (2008: 119) who opposes this pedagogical mindset, highlighting what she refers to as the 'absurdity in expecting male teachers to teach ... in predictable or uniform ways on the basis of their maleness'. I personally question the relevance of the gender of the practitioner/teacher as I argue that it is more about the wealth and variety of *pedagogical skills* a professional brings to the classroom to effectively *teach* their pupils rather than it being about whether the practitioner/teacher is 'a man' or 'a woman'.

Father figures

With a steady increase of children in the UK growing up in single-parent families (Office for National Statistics (ONS) 2013), concern has been expressed about the deficient upbringing that these children are likely to be experiencing as opposed to those whose fathers are present. Research by Cushman (2008: 130) found that New Zealand (NZ) head teachers primarily considered male teachers to be necessary for children of single mothers: 'They [children] need a father figure as too many in today's society are fatherless.' Through the employment of more men in settings/schools it is thus argued that those children who come from homes where the father is absent will have access to a substitute/surrogate dad who can relate better to them, support them in their development, model good behaviour and provide them with a required level of stability and consistency which, in turn, will result in a rise in academic attainment. While this is supported by the Office for Standards in Education, Children's Services and Skills (Ofsted), cited in Clark (2008), the *tension* lies in the assumption that children from single parent families are seemingly disadvantaged by being brought up by a lone adult. Christie (1998) argues that some 'present' fathers either have little involvement with their children or actually do not live with them. Cushman (2005: 232) builds on this, highlighting how some children may have a father figure but they may actually be neglectful or abusive; claims that these children are 'better off' are thus strongly refutable. I personally question the father figure argument on the grounds that men who work with children are employed as 'practitioners' or 'teachers', not as 'fathers' – *how is it possible for men to fulfil their professional duties in the setting/classroom while operating as a dad?*

Strong male role models

The demand for more male role models to be in the lives of children, especially boys, is one of the more commonly espoused reasons underpinning the call for more men to work in education-based settings (0–8+). Efforts to justify their presence are varied and a select summary of these is offered below:

- It will help children to have meaningful day-to-day contact with adult males.
- It will help to make settings and schools 'boy friendly' again.
- It will help to address the issue of 'disengaged' learners in the classroom.
- It will help to bring 'strength' in the form of power, authority, discipline and technical competence to the setting/classroom.

The thinking above is advocated by policy-makers, recruitment agencies and employers who all argue that strong, positive role models will greatly advantage the educational needs of boys, particularly those who are disadvantaged and generally disaffected with their schooling. Needless to say, *tensions* surround these claims. Assertions that these role models will help children to have meaningful day-to-day contact with adult males, for example, are challenged when one considers the wealth of males they are likely to encounter in their day-to-day lives, be they older siblings, immediate or extended family members, those in the local community or men in the media. Claims that male role models will help to re-engage learners in the classroom by making settings and schools 'boy friendly' again undoubtedly fuel resentment from female practitioners and teachers who are considered perfectly capable of making settings and schools supportive to the needs of boys (Ashley and Lee 2003); *this is what being a good practitioner/teacher is about – being able to effectively respond to the varied needs of their learners.* It is interesting to note the thinking of Ashley (2001) who argues that what motivates and interests boys is actually what motivates and interests *all* children. This brings the efficacy of pedagogical approaches to address presumed gendered differences into question, particularly as Younger *et al.* (2005), cited in Carrington *et al.* (2008: 117–18), point to the 'dangers of treating boys and girls as monolithic and undifferentiated entities in the classroom with mostly pre-defined and homogenous interests'. The final claim – that male role models will help to bring power, authority, discipline and technical competence to the setting/classroom – emphasises particular characteristics and attributes which subscribe to the notion of hegemonic masculinity (Connell 2005), defined as the dominant way of 'being a man' within a setting or society. While wordage limitations prevent a more detailed exploration of this concept (see Donaldson 1993), it is important to take note of Connell's (2005) use of the term 'masculinities' in recognition of how the presentation of gender is not monolithic and that there are different/alternative versions of masculinity adopted by individuals as a result of their varying ethnicities, class, sexual identities and characteristics. This means that there are multiple ways of 'being a man' which is important if male practitioners/teachers are to encourage boys to value education, which is still largely seen as a female activity. Due to the complex nature of the male role model argument, efforts to critically explore the concept further, both theoretically and empirically, form the basis of the remainder of this chapter.

Exploring the 'male role model'

An investigation into the complexities of the 'male role model' argument was personally undertaken as a piece of doctoral research (Brownhill 2011). One of the aims used to drive the direction of the enquiry was to highlight *tensions* specifically related to the 'male role model' argument. The research sought to examine the thoughts, views, beliefs and feelings of those individuals deemed to be 'role models' by public and professional discourse – men who actively trained/worked in the early years (0–8). All participants in the research – 81 in total – were geographically located in a central county in the Midlands, England. Further details about the research, the collection of data and its subsequent analysis are discussed elsewhere (see Brownhill 2010, 2014, forthcoming). Findings from the primary data raise a number of contentious claims and disparate ideas which exacerbate the ambiguous nature of the 'male role model'. Presentation of these findings, coupled with a critical discourse, is offered below.

Male perspectives of the 'male role model'

A level of confusion initially surrounded the meaning of the word 'male' when discussing the term 'male role model':

> There's a distinction in being a role model and seeing 'male' in that context as just an adjective, so that you're a role model who is male … or you are a male role model in the sense that you are modelling maleness and masculinity …
>
> ('Ben', focus group interview)

Carrington and Skelton (2003) add to this confusion by questioning whether the male teacher, as a role model, is expected to model qualities associated with being a good male *person* or a good male *teacher*. *Tensions* lie in the lack of clarity or consensus with regard to *which* kind of male role model men should be when they are working with young children (0–8), and whether the kind of role model that the practitioner/teacher actually models matches the expectations of those around them, be they head teachers, female colleagues, parents/carers or children themselves. This is likely to be a cause for concern for those men attempting to emulate the male role model status which is readily bestowed on them, especially when they are faced with 'a bewildering, fleeting multiplicity of possible identities' (Hall 1992: 277).

When asked whether they saw themselves as a role model to children in the early years (0–8), 99 per cent (n = 70) of male respondents to the research questionnaire responded in the positive. This challenges the views of Lunenberg *et al.* (2007: 586) who express 'serious doubts about the competence of … educators to serve as role models' even though male respondents substantiated their assertion by claiming that they were a *positive example* (28 per cent, n = 20), that they modelled *positive attitudes and values* (20 per cent, n = 14), or it was because of the amount of time (contact) they actually spent with children (12 per cent, n = 9). Interestingly, in the first two stages of the research undertaken, claims that being a role model was *part of the job* of an educator were made by both male questionnaire respondents and focus group interviewees. There was a clear assumption that being in this *position of authority* (class teacher of 3–8 year olds, questionnaire) automatically equated to the person being a role model. Findings from the final stage of the research (individual semi-structured interviews), however, directly challenged this perception as it emerged that being a role model was considered to be a status which had to be *earned* as opposed to it being an assumed role. This supports the views of Carrington and Skelton (2003: 258) who argue that to be recognised as a role model by their students 'teachers have to win their respect and admiration. This cannot be assumed to take place.' *Tensions* exist due to the fact that policy-making clearly views men entering and working in education (0–8+) as role models to boys whereas my research would suggest that men have to gain this status as opposed to it being seen as 'a given' or a default position. Further *tensions* surround the lack of clarity with regard to explaining exactly *how* male practitioners/ teachers would earn this 'respect and admiration' and how long it would take to earn. If, for example, it took longer than a year then the notion of the practitioner/teacher actually being a role model is challenged considerably, particularly when one considers those professionals who work in Foundation Two (Reception – 4–5) and KS1 (5–7) classes as the full school year only represents just over half of the calendar year.

One of the biggest *tensions* which emerged from my research data focuses on the perceptions of male practitioners/teachers when considering who they thought they were a role model to – boys; girls; boys and girls – and who they believed *saw them* as a role model in the setting/classroom. Findings from the questionnaire suggest that 93 per cent (n = 66) of male respondents saw themselves as role models to both boys and girls, with 86 per cent (n = 62) of male respondents believing that boys and girls saw them as role models. This is in direct contrast with the thinking of Ashley (2002) who believes role models to be people with whom a child has a strong attachment; Ashley claims that children form attachments with their parents and peers but that they do not identify with their teachers or imitate their behaviour. Indeed, findings from Ashley and Lee's (2003: 276) research validate these claims as it was argued that 'boys model themselves primarily on other boys', the direct influence of teachers thus being described as 'limited'. Bricheno and Thornton's (2007: 394) conclusion that children 'd[o] not see their teachers as role models' directly opposes the views of those male questionnaire respondents who perceive themselves to be role models to children. I believe that these men are under some kind of misapprehension; this may be due to what they have read in the media or have heard as part of government campaigns encouraging more men to work in settings and schools. It is thus questionable that if children do not see their practitioners/teachers as role models the perceived value of men in the early years (0–8) is slightly undermined by the lack of children who will actually be trying to emulate them. However, it is worthy of note that even if children do not view teachers as 'role models' for themselves *as children*, teachers do become part of their experience of how adults behave and thus part of the 'material' they use to become adults. In this way it may be argued that any adult (or for that matter any individual of a kind that the child will or may become) may be a role model (good or bad). This is, of course, a matter of what kind of 'timescale' is referred to, be it an academic year or longer.

During the analysis of the individual semi-structured interviews the notion of men engaging in a wealth of physical activity emerged from the data. References to 'physical movement', 'masculine sports' (football) and 'exercise' suggested that men who worked in the early years (0–8) engaged in more physical-based activity than their female counterparts. It is of interest, however, that only two questionnaire respondents identified 'being good at sports' as an important quality/characteristic for a role model to emulate; when given the option, the notion of being 'athletic' was given no recognition of importance at all. One questionnaire respondent (a class teacher of 7–8 year olds) commented that 'I am not very good at sports/athletic – so should I avoid being a primary school teacher?' This highlights a *tension* with regard to perceptions that to be a male practitioner/teacher in the early years (0–8) one has to be 'physically' competent. This perception is emphasised by Cushman (2008: 131) which found that the *second* most cited reason NZ head teachers gave as to why they thought schools needed more male role models was to provide sports leadership. This would suggest that there is *tension* between the expectations of others with regard to the sporting/physical abilities of the male role model and the *actual* capabilities of the role model in being willing or indeed *able* to undertake this role. For those without a 'sporting prowess' there is a danger that men will be 'pigeonholed' ('Will', focus group interview) into undertaking these kinds of activities (a sentiment supported by the author's own personal experiences as a class teacher). This 'pigeonholing' serves as an example of a small number of 'pressures' which were felt by men who worked with young children (0–8) and who took part in my research. By examining the nature of these pressures two distinct categories emerged:

- pressures on the role model's masculinity; and
- pressures of the job.

One of the perceived difficulties of entering or working in the early years (0–8) relates to the negative perceptions of men who actively work in the sector. Others' opinions of being 'effeminate' or 'gay' suggest that working in the early years (0–8) challenges men's sexuality. Concerns of being accused of paedophilic activity mirror the findings of King (2004) who found that male teachers of young children are construed not only as potential paedophiles but also as being homosexual. This highlights a *tension* for men entering or working in the 0–8 sector as their sexual orientation and 'motives' for wanting to work in the sector are brought into question; I argue that these are likely to be two key reasons as to why many men do not work in the early years (0–8). My research also suggests that men fear being 'mocked' as it was acknowledged in the individual semi-structured interviews that fathers and friends of men who worked in the early years (0–8) were considered 'weird' and that it was 'not a proper job' for them to do. Sumison (2000: 94) identifies these perceptions as a 'risk' of working in the sector and these are likely to result in 'emotional distress' for men who choose to work with young children; indeed, it was suggested that men might experience 'feelings of insecurity when in school' ('H', individual semi-structured interview). I thus argue that while the calling for more men is seen as being of benefit for children (0–8) there is a *tension* with regard to whether actually working in the 0–8 sector is emotionally beneficial to those men who choose to enter or work in this educational arena.

An interesting *tension* which emerged from my research centres on the physical character-istics of the male role model. Questionnaire respondents suggested that the role model would wear 'smart clothes'. This supports Thomas' (2014) suggestion that role models are usually *seen as* role models, particularly by pre-teens, because of what they wear. Indeed, during the individual semi-structured interviews the notion of the male role model being 'smartly dressed' and having a 'professional dress code' emphasises the perceived importance of cloth-ing for the male role model. This submission helps to extend the list of 'fixed' or visual attributes identified by children in Hutchings *et al.'s* (2007) research and the listed attributes noted by Bricheno and Thornton (2007) as the clothing of the children's teachers was not an identified feature that they [children] wished to emulate. A lack of clarification, however, relates to what is meant by 'smart' clothing as issues of interpretation exacerbate *tensions* relat-ing to its meaning. For example, this could be interpreted as a male role model wearing a suit, a shirt and tie, designer or fashionable clothing, or clothes which respond to their professional activities, which in the case of supporting children's physical development (PE) would sug-gest a T-shirt and shorts/tracksuit and trainers. A further *tension* relates to who actually defines the clothing as being 'smart' – *is it the male practitioner/teacher or the children that they work with?* Clearly the views of children in terms of what they perceive as being 'smart clothing' is likely to differ significantly to the views of male practitioners/teachers who have to wear them. The idea of the role model being 'smartly dressed' directly challenges the practices of many early years settings (0–5) which typically adopt relaxed dress codes as this helps to reflect the set-ting's ethos and approach to learning and teaching. One may argue whether being smartly dressed is entirely appropriate, particularly for the early years practitioner (0–5), as they spend the majority of their day engaging with 'messy' activities and working with children on the floor. While there is no doubt that practitioners/teachers need to be suitably dressed for work, there is a *tension* with regard to what male role models would have to wear to ensure they have a 'professional appearance'.

Efforts to establish further physical characteristics of the male role model allude to the idea of the role model being 'tall', 'strong' and having a 'big build', as identified during the indi-vidual semi-structured interviews, attributes which Swain (2004: 171) acknowledges as being 'connected with an embodied form of physicality'. This notion of strength, clearly evident in the characteristics identified above, mirrors male role model attributes identified by Hutchings *et al.* (2007) and is supported by comments made by 'Ben' during the focus group interview whose strength and height was called upon by his colleagues when working in school:

Staff would say to me, 'Could you get something heavy down off the top shelf?'

While there are clearly legitimate reasons to ask men for help due to the fact that they are, on average, taller and physically stronger than women, perceptions of the 'strong' male demon-strate a subscription to stereotypical conventions of what it is to be a man in the sense of being physically strong. This presentation of traditional hegemonic masculinity offers some support to the findings of Jones (2006: 72) who found that female teachers in KS1 (5–7) wanted men who worked with younger children to be 'macho'. Indeed, a wealth of identified qualities and characteristics associated with 'leadership' and being 'skilled' from my research (questionnaires) supports the idea of the male role model being someone who emulates masculine traits. *Tensions*, however, lie in the fact that not all male practitioners/teachers are tall or are physically strong – *does this therefore mean that these men are not role models to children?* This is refuted by data from the final stage of my research where it is suggested that the 'physical build of the role model is not of importance', a claim largely supported by the findings of Hutchings *et al.* (2007: 140) who found that 'the teacher's physical attributes were of limited significance'. This brings the relevance and importance of the physical stature and appearance of the male role model into question as I argue that these do not influence whether the male practitioner/teacher is 'seen' as a role model or not – it is more about *who* they are and *what* they emulate as opposed to *how* they look.

Conclusions

This chapter has sought to emphasise the complexities of the simplistic claims of men being 'the answer' to the problems associated with boys in settings/schools (0–8). The male role model argument is one which continues to be promoted in public and professional arenas and this concerns researchers like myself who passionately challenge the varied reasoning advocated for the greater presence of men in the early years sector (0–8). Ludowyke (2001) states that underachievement is not simply the result of one factor (i.e. not having a male practitioner/teacher or a male role model), but is rather a complex interplay of factors including social class, poverty and ethnicity. One could add gender-related stereotypes to this list of factors! With this in mind, I firmly believe that parents/carers, professionals and policy makers should 'regroup and rethink' the whole advocacy of the male role model agenda.

UNANSWERED QUESTIONS

- If being a role model is indeed 'part of the job' of an educator, does that mean that females are strong role models for children?
- Does the gender of the role model have to match the gender of the individual who 'looks up' to the role model, e.g. are males only role models for boys/men?
- What evidence is there of young children (0–5) themselves seeing practitioners/ teachers as role models?
- If more men worked in settings/schools would *girls* be disadvantaged by this?

References

Ashley, M. (2001) *Caring for the Boys: Lessons from Attachment Theory*. Paper presented at the British Educational Research Association Annual Conference, Leeds University, 13–15 September. [Online.] Available at: http://www.leeds.ac.uk/educol/documents/00001857.htm (accessed 26 August 2014).

Ashley, M. (2002) *Role Models, Classroom Leadership and the Gendered Battle for Hearts and Minds*. Paper presented at the Annual Conference of the British Educational Research Association, University of Exeter, England, 12–14 September. [Online.] Available at: http://www.leeds.ac.uk/educol/documents/00002244.htm (accessed 27 August 2014).

Ashley, M. and Lee, J. (2003) *Women Teaching Boys: Caring and Working in the Primary School*. Stoke-on-Trent: Trentham Books.

Bricheno, P. and Thornton, M. (2007) 'Role model, hero or champion? Children's views concerning role models', *Educational Research*, 49 (4): 383–96.

Brownhill, S. (2010) *The 'Brave' Man in the Early Years: The Ambiguities of Being a Role Model*. Paper presented at British Educational Research Association Annual Conference, University of Warwick, 1–4 September. [Online.] Available at: http://www.leeds.ac.uk/educol/documents/193285.pdf (accessed 27 August 2014).

Brownhill, S. (2011) 'The 'Brave' Man in the Early Years (0–8): The Ambiguities of Being a Role Model'. Unpublished doctoral thesis, University of Derby, Derby, UK.

Brownhill, S. (2014) '"Build Me a Male Role Model!" A Critical Exploration of the Perceived Qualities/Characteristics of Men in the Early Years (0–8) in England', *Gender and Education*, 26 (3): 246–61.

Brownhill, S. (forthcoming) *The 'Brave' Man in the Early Years (0–8): The Ambiguities of the Role Model*. Saarbrücken: LAP LAMBERT Academic Publishing.

Carrington, B. and Skelton, C. (2003) 'Re-thinking "role models": equal opportunities in teacher recruitment in England and Wales', *Journal of Education Policy*, 18 (3): 253–65.

Carrington, B., Tymms, P. and Merrell, C. (2008) 'Role models, school improvement and the "gender gap" – do men bring out the best in boys and women the best in girls?', *British Educational Research Journal*, 34 (3): 315–27.

Christie, A. (1998) 'A comparison of arguments for employing: men as childcare workers and social workers in Denmark and the UK (Social Work in Europe)', *Social Work in Europe*, 5 (1): 2–17.

Clark, L. (2008) 'Teachers must act as father figures to white working class boys, says Ofsted', *Daily Mail*, 23 July. [Online.] Available at: http://www.dailymail.co.uk/news/article-1037327/Teachers-act-father-figures-white-working-class-boys-says-Ofsted.html (accessed 26 August 2014).

Connell, R. W. (2005) 'Change among the gatekeepers: men, masculinities, and gender equality in the global arena', *Signs*, 30 (3): 1801–25.

Cushman, P. (2005) 'Let's hear it from the males: issues facing male primary school teachers', *Teaching and Teacher Education*, 21 (3): 227–40.

Cushman, P. (2008) 'So what exactly do you want? What principals mean when they say "male role model"', *Gender and Education*, 20 (2): 123–36.

Department for Education (DfE) (2013a) *Statistical First Release: Early Years Foundation Stage Profile Attainment by Pupil Characteristics, England 2013*, SFR 47/2013, 21 November. [Online.] Available at: https://www.gov.uk/government/uploads/system/uploads/attachment_data/file/259067/SFR47_2013_Text.pdf (accessed 26 August 2014).

Department for Education (DfE) (2013b) *Statistical First Release: Phonics Screening Check and National Curriculum Assessment at Key Stage 1 in England, 2012/13*, SFR 37/2013, 3 October. [Online.] Available at: https://www.gov.uk/government/uploads/system/uploads/attachment_data/file/245813/SFR37-2013_Text.pdf (accessed 26 August 2014).

Donaldson, M. (1993) 'What is hegemonic masculinity?', *Theory and Society, Special Issue: Masculinities*, 22 (5): 643–57. [Online.] Available at: http://ro.uow.edu.au/cgi/viewcontent.cgi?article=1149&context=artspapers (accessed 7 January 2015).

Francis, B. (2008) 'Teaching manfully? Exploring gendered subjectivities and power via analysis of men teachers' gender performance', *Gender and Education*, 20 (2): 109–22.

Hall, S. (1992) 'The question of cultural identity', in S. Hall, D. Held and T. McGrew (eds), *Modernity and Its Futures*. Cambridge: Polity Press and Open University Press.

House of Commons Education Committee (2014) *Underachievement in Education by White Working Class Children*, First Report of Session 2014–15, HC 142. [Online.] Available at: http://www.publications.parliament.uk/pa/cm201415/cmselect/cmeduc/142/142.pdf (accessed 26 August 2014).

Hutchings, M., Carrington, B., Skelton, C., Read, B. and Hall, I. (2007) 'Nice and kind, smart and funny: what children like and want to emulate in their teachers', *Oxford Review of Education*, 34 (2): 135–57.

Jones, D. (2006) 'The "right kind of man": the ambiguities of regendering the key stage one environment', *Sex Education*, 6 (1): 61–76.

King, J. R. (2004) 'The (im)possibility of gay teachers for young children', *Theory into Practice*, 42 (2): 122–7.

Ludowyke, J. (2001) 'Directing change: national enquiry into boys' education', *Professional Voice*, 1 (3): 6–8.

Lunenberg, M., Korthagen, F. and Swennen, A. (2007) 'The teacher educator as the role model', *Teaching and Teacher Education*, 23 (5): 586–601.

McCormack, O. and Brownhill, S. (2014) '"Moving away from the caring": exploring the views of in-service and pre-service male teachers about the concept of the male teacher as a role model at an early childhood and post-primary level', *International Journal of Academic Research in Education and Review*, 2 (4): 82–96. [Online.] Available at: http://www.academicresearchjournals.org/IJARER/PDF%202014/May/McCormack%20and%20Brownhill.pdf (accessed 26 August 2014).

Mulholland, J. and Hanson, P. (2003) 'Men who become primary school teachers: an early portrait', *Asia-Pacific Journal of Teacher Education*, 31 (3): 213–24.

Office for National Statistics (ONS) (2013) 'Families and Households, 2013', *Statistical Bulletin*, 31 October. [Online.] Available at: http://www.ons.gov.uk/ons/dcp171778_332633.pdf (accessed 26 August 2014).

PARITY (2013) *Is Action Overdue on Boys' Academic Underachievement?* Briefing Paper, March. [Online.] Available at: http://www.parity-uk.org/Briefing/BoysEducPaperRev1b.pdf (accessed 28 April 2014).

Paton, G. (2013a) 'Just a fifth of new primary school teachers are men', *The Telegraph*, 26 November. [Online.] Available at: http://www.telegraph.co.uk/education/educationnews/10475740/Just-a-fifth-of-new-primary-school-teachers-are-men.html (accessed 28 April 2014).

Paton, G. (2013b) 'Teaching in primary schools "still seen as a woman's job"', *The Telegraph*, 5 February. [Online.] Available at: http://www.telegraph.co.uk/education/educationnews/9849976/Teaching-in-primary-schools-still-seen-as-a-womans-job.html (accessed 26 August 2014).

Skelton, C. (2009) 'Failing to get men into primary teaching: a feminist critique', *Journal of Education Policy*, 24 (1): 39–54.

Sumison, J. (2000) 'Rewards, risks and tensions: perceptions of males enrolled on an early childhood teacher education programme', *Asia-Pacific Journal of Teacher Education*, 28 (1): 87–100.

Swain, J. (2004) 'The resources and strategies that 10–11-year-old boys use to construct masculinities in the school setting', *British Educational Research Journal*, 30 (1): 167–85.

Thomas, M. (2014) 'The importance of role models', *HealthGuidance*. [Online.] Available at: http://www.healthguidance.org/entry/13288/1/The-Importance-of-Role-Models.html (accessed 29 August 2014).

Ward, H. (2009) 'Extra pay needed to coax more men into early years', *Times Educational Supplement*, 17 March. [Online.] Available at: http://www.tes.co.uk/article.aspx?storycode=6007504 (accessed 28 April 2014).

3

CHILDREN'S INTERPRETIVE REPRODUCTION OF GENDER-CONSCIOUS DIDACTIC AGENDAS IN A SWEDISH PRE-SCHOOL

Annica Löfdahl and Maria Hjalmarsson

Introduction

Many Swedish pre-schools use a gender-conscious pedagogy approach as a strategy to achieve increased gender equality. Drawing on empirical data from an ethnographic study, this chapter discusses what happens when the teachers in a pre-school in Sweden try to implement a gender-conscious pedagogical approach and how the children handle these efforts. Pre-school pedagogy of the twentieth century dealt to a large extent with making children as 'normal' and 'average' as possible, in accordance with accepted curve charts of development and learning. The child was viewed as born with certain characteristics and skills and only the 'right' kind of help in development could restructure and change a child who had been affected by conditions in its home environment in a distressing way. Eidevald and Lenz Taguchi (2011) report on how pre-school teachers were eager to work in a gender-conscious way but lacked the pedagogical tools. Furthermore, they claim that this notion of what was possible for pre-school teachers to accomplish was crucial to the warm reception of gender-conscious pedagogy in the early twenty-first century. They state that children's gender categories became just an additional aspect to change. Towards the end of the 1990s and the beginning of the 2000s the pre-school context in Sweden embraced almost all children aged 1–6 years and the first curriculum (1998) was in its initial implementation phase, emphasising pedagogical working with gender equality. The pre-school teachers, supported by feminist politicians and civil servants on county councils, set to work on the question of gender equality, a task that was not only made possible as a consequence of the notion of gender as a social construction, but also because of the pre-school teachers' willingness to work with the child as an object of change, supported by the curriculum.

The curriculum for the Swedish pre-school (Skolverket [National Agency for Education] 2010) stresses fundamental values such as the equal value of all people, the importance of care and consideration towards others and equality between genders. At the same time, it has been shown that children's social development has a low priority in the Swedish pre-school context, while on a municipal level other skills, for example language development, are of higher priority (Skolverket 2008). This may be understood as a problematic division between focusing on children's social development versus work with pedagogical activities, including academic knowledge. We relate this tendency to research results from some of our previous studies in ECE, showing that academic content is more explicitly connected to teachers' work and may therefore be more easily included in the quality reports teachers produce about their work (strengths and weaknesses), while social development is harder to describe with 'facts' such as test scores (Löfdahl and Pérez Prieto 2009a, 2009b). These tendencies are not specific to the pre-school settings but are also present in Swedish leisure-time centres aimed at younger school children (Saar *et al.* 2012; Hjalmarsson 2013; Hjalmarsson and Löfdahl forthcoming).

Drawing on empirical data from an ethnographic study, this chapter focuses on the tension in the everyday practices of the pre-school between the pre-school teachers' efforts to apply 'gender pedagogy' – for example, distributing the tools and toys used in domestic environments such as a dolls corner – and the children's ways of dealing with the implications of these efforts. We might assume there is a link between the low priority of focusing on children's social development and the tensions that appear in their work with gender pedagogy as this oscillates between offering social skills training and cognitive skills.

Gender conscious pedagogy as a means to achieve gender equality

The concept of gender-conscious pedagogy is a Swedish phenomenon with no equivalent in other countries; it is more common to speak in terms of feminist pedagogy or gender equality work but seldom in the context of pre-school (Eidevald and Lenz Taguchi 2011). Some authors have tried to elaborate the content of gender-conscious pedagogy as a means to achieve increased gender equality. Svaleryd (2007), whose guidelines to the gender-pedagogy approach had a significant effect on Swedish educational settings aimed at younger children in the early twenty-first century, highlights four aspects that are the basis of such work:

1. the need for teachers to be aware of how their own gender norms and values affect their teaching, choice of content and treatment of pupils;
2. the need to make visible and scrutinise the teachers' ideas on femininity and masculinity;
3. the need to make visible and develop the pupils' notions and gender myths with the aim of helping them build their own future on the basis of their own will and personal interests; and
4. the need to work out methods and working materials to be used in regular education to support equal conditions for boys and girls to develop in various ways.

In a similar way, Olofsson (2007) also presented four aspects that are needed for successful work with gender equality in pre-school:

1. Firstly, pre-school teachers should 'add but not deprive', i.e. help boys break negative hierarchies and achieve 'a language of emotions' while girls should be reinforced for courage, strength and toughness (p. 60).
2. Secondly, the children should be met on their specific levels and interests and their own experiences should be the starting point for the pre-school activities. By entering 'the children's world' (p. 60) pre-school teachers can widen this world and show other possibilities.

3. Thirdly, pre-school teachers should focus on the positive and make it even stronger, which in the context of gender equality means that children should not be criticised when they perform according to gender-stereotyped patterns, but be given positive feedback when they dare to cross gender borders.
4. Finally, pre-school teachers should use play as a means of accomplishing pleasurable relations among the children and provide opportunities for the boys to understand the profit of being kind in a playful manner and help the girls understand the positive experience of feeling brave, tough and strong.

The relationship between women and men and girls and boys is important in the constructions of gender. By adopting three 'gender formulas' Hirdman (2001) shows how women are positioned in relation to men. The first formula implies that the man is the norm while women are not counted. The second formula means that the man is the norm while women are viewed and described as inferior or deviant. The third formula holds notions on men and women as essentially different subjects. According to our interpretation, the gender-conscious pedagogy elaborated by Svaleryd and Olofsson (see above) is based on ideas of boys and girls that represent the third formula. As we understand it, these authors view boys and girls as representing distinct characters with different needs, personalities and skills, thus failing to see the differences within 'boys' and 'girls' groupings. In this sense the guidelines to the practical work of gender pedagogy is based on essential and biological views of gender which conceal that a person's sex is not what makes them masculine or feminine.

Aspects of gender and gender equality in Swedish pre-schools

Previous studies that focus on gender and gender equality in various more or less explicit ways appear to confirm a statement in a report from the Swedish Delegation on Equality in Schools (SOU 2010: 66), namely that research has mainly focused on *the child perspective* on gender equality (meaning adults' or society's perspective on the child), i.e. on how children's lives are affected by a lack of gender equality in pre-school (and school) and how teachers should work to improve children's everyday practice in pre-school (and school), and less on *the children's own perspectives*, including how they perceive their situation in pre-school from the perspective of gender equality.

Over the past decade, government pre-school politics have paid particular attention to work on gender quality in Swedish pre-schools. The Curriculum for the Pre-school (Skolverket 2010) stresses that all pre-school teachers should counteract traditional gender patterns and gender roles. Edström (2009) explores if – and in which case *how* – this has had an impact on pre-schools on the municipal level; from studies of four different municipalities she finds that there appear to be significant differences between the municipalities' activities in politics and administration. Furthermore, the municipal quality reports in her study include no to limited information on the municipalities' work on gender quality (these quality reports are accounts from the municipal level on how they manage to live up to the ambitions on work with gender equality). The most striking aspect is not what is written about gender quality in the pre-school context, but rather the lack of such formulations. The descriptions of the quality of gender equality relate foremost to the compulsory school context whereas the work of gender in the pre-school has been neglected.

Several researchers, for example Karlsson (2009) and Odenbring (2010), show how pre-school teachers and children exist in a 'gendered' environment where traditional gender patterns are reproduced and strengthened despite the initiatives in the curriculum and the pre-school teacher's didactic ambitions to avoid stereotyped gender patterns. The Delegation on Equality in Schools concludes in their final consideration that children, materials, the environment, activities and structure get gender-coded and are divided into masculine and feminine aspects. Boys are seen as troublesome, loud-voiced and, above all, impatient. Girls are expected to be quiet and calm, follow the rules, help out a little bit more and take on a greater responsibility for both themselves and their environment (SOU 2006: 75). Pre-school teachers expect different things from boys and girls and strengthen rather than challenge their own stereotyped notions of gender. The children try to negotiate various gender norms and only some of their many actions or positions are categorised as 'girlish' or 'boyish', and certain 'boyish' or 'girlish' practices are viewed as more correct than others. The pre-school teachers work actively to separate boys and girls because they are *viewed* as either boys or girls which conceals the large variation within these gender categories (Eidevald 2009; Hellman 2010; Wedin 2011).

Theoretical framework

This study is framed by Corsaro's (2005) theory of children's peer culture that focuses on how children deal with issues of great importance to their lives and their own development. As a theoretical concept, peer culture can be helpful in describing and understanding what happens when children are together in pre-school. Corsaro's (2005: 110) own definition of peer culture is '… a stable set of activities or routines, artefacts, values and concerns that children produce and share in interaction with each other'. The theory offers an alternative to theoretical individualistic explanations and pays attention to collective actions and social structures. A central aspect in the theory is what Corsaro calls *interpretive reproduction* which means that children learn to interpret and understand their surrounding culture, that is events, norms and values that they encounter through adults' and other children's actions. It means that children 'download', interpret and reproduce the culture that surrounds them, both in the pre-school, at home and in society at large in order to make it intelligible and manageable (Löfdahl 2014a). Children appropriate what adults say and do, not outright, but as reconstructed content in their own activities. In this particular analysis we focus on children's interpretive reproduction according to the specific rules and norms in the pre-school setting that deal with gender and the way the teachers strive to work in accordance with a didactic agenda that avoids gender-stereotyped activities.

The empirical data

The descriptions presented in this chapter derive from an ethnographic study of a group of children at a Swedish pre-school, carried out during a time period of one and a half years. The children involved were 3 to 4 years of age and had just left the infant group to become part of the group of 3 to 5 year-olds. The empirical data consists of field notes, video recordings and informal conversations with the children and pre-school teachers. The research we present in this chapter has been subjected to analysis previously (Löfdahl and Hägglund 2012; Löfdahl 2014b), but in this chapter we aim to broaden the analysis to focus on aspects of gender and gender equality. We are aware that the research may be viewed as reproducing stereotyped notions of boys and girls, and for that reason we emphasise that the empirical data also includes video-recorded sequences that contradict and challenge such notions. Furthermore, the children in this research who are engaged in playing in a home-like environment are all girls, but this fact is not to be understood as indicating that the girls in general always choose such play and the boys never do. The empirical data consists of several situations when girls and boys engage in gender-mixed play. Still, we argue that the selection of this research is suitable for illustrating and discussing possible and non-intended consequences of the gender-conscious pedagogy approach.

Description of the pre-school where the pre-school teachers worked with gender conscious pedagogy

The pre-school teachers at the specific pre-school had chosen to work in accordance with what they named 'gender-conscious pedagogy'. For a long time, they had been interested in how the children should be encouraged to develop an awareness of traditional gender patterns and how they were actively working to 'run counter' to such content in the activities of the pre-school setting. Their intention was to make it easier for the children to make gender-crossing choices and broaden and increase their general repertoire of actions and expressions. With inspiration from the curriculum, the activities carried out were guided by the idea of equal rights for boys and girls to explore and develop interest and skills without limitations set by stereotyped gender roles, expressed for instance as changes in the previous division of certain tools and toys in specific rooms. Aimed at avoiding stereotyped gender role play, the pre-school teachers decided that an area of the pre-school that was formerly denominated the dolls corner (home corner), including a stove, kitchen utensils, prams and traditional housework tools, should no longer be organised in a specific physical location. Toys and other things that previously belonged to the dolls corner were spread out in various places in the pre-school; the stove was put in the otherwise intact corner of building blocks and Lego while the prams were placed in a couple of smaller rooms. We will discuss the pre-school teachers' gender-conscious pedagogy agenda, when put into practice, as part of their didactic agenda in the next section.

Violation of the girls' play corner

After a couple of weeks in the new group at pre-school it seemed as if the younger boys had found a superior position for themselves in relation to the younger girls. Often, the boys pretended they were tough and angry cowboys, to some extent encouraged by the male pre-school teacher who took pictures of them to show at the next parents' meeting, thereby drawing attention to this behaviour. It appeared that the girls were struggling to accomplish a domestic environment where they could engage in the type of play that they enjoyed and were familiar with. In one of the smaller rooms they used a theatre screen backdrop and created a home where they could make a bed for the dolls, hang up curtains, arrange a kitchen where they could cook, take care of their dolls and do the laundry, which they hung up outside the kitchen door. The video recordings show that sometimes the boys seemed a little bit lost in this environment, particularly when they were on their own and without the company of their peers; it appeared that they did not know how to act or if and how they should join the girls' play. Sometimes the boys just watched and sometimes they participated in the role of father or child. But when the boys gathered in a group they seemed to position themselves in a different way in their interaction with the girls. The boys broke into the girls' 'home', messed up their laundry and, provided with a toy tool, hit one of the girls.

The girls had created this environment by themselves but some of the boys had sneaked in, their pockets full of tools (plastic knives, pliers, screwdrivers and hammers), acting like 'toughies', pulling down the girls' laundry, laughing and cheering. The girls protested and resisted, but could not manage to stop the boys, who successfully pulled down the laundry and threw it on the roof of the girls' house. The boys then continued to show their strength and use the toy tools as support. Some of the girls left the room to ask the pre-school teachers for assistance, leaving only 3-year-old Stella (pseudonym) in the play corner with the boys, who began ruining the laundry even more by stamping on it and pretending to hurt Stella by waving the tools in front of her face and making sounds like scissors cutting. Repeatedly Stella said she did not want to be a part of this:

STELLA: Stop it; I don't think it's funny, stop …
> (*The boys continue threatening her, flashing tools at her body and face.*)
STELLA: Stop it!
> (*The boys continue and Stella starts to cry.*)
STELLA: Stop it, stop it!
> (*Stella holds her hand in front of her face to hide. The boys make fun of her by imitating Stella's body language and verbal expressions.*)
STELLA: STOP IT!!

The boys leave the room, laughing and fooling around, saying they are going to throw themselves into the dustbin. They meet the male pre-school teacher, who the other girls went to for help. He tells the boys they are not allowed to behave like that. The girls' play has dissolved and despite the fact that the boys have left the girls' play corner they do not want to continue playing.

Practical implications when gender-pedagogy agenda is put into practice

To return to the Curriculum for the Pre-school and its fundamental values, the example of 'tough boys' and 'the girls' play corner' becomes interesting to elaborate. First, we note that the curriculum guidelines were transformed by the pre-school teachers into more or less explicit rules regarding the children's behaviour, which also included aspects of care in the pre-school teachers' didactic agenda. The teachers' vision was to indirectly loosen up the 'gendering' of the pre-school in a similar way as Wedin (2011) has discussed to be problematic. With the best of intentions, the staff tried to create possibilities for the children to cross gender patterns and broaden their preferences and experiences regarding choices of play and friends. Our interpretation is that the pre-school teachers' actions were meant to be a step towards increased gender equality, which in this sense would mean equal conditions for boys and girls. Simultaneously, we understand that this action was carried out based on notions of boys and girls as homogenous groups, regarding ideas on boys and girls as distinctive characters. As far as we understood, the pre-school teachers did not discuss variations within the categories of boys and girls, which according to Eidevald (2009) implies a risk of concealing the large variation in boys' and girls' positioning of themselves in various situations.

But children are active actors in constructions of their social spaces, and despite the pre-school teachers' gender-conscious pedagogy agenda the children were *doing care* in their own way. The teachers' dissolution of the dolls corner may be interpreted as a type of disparagement and belittlement of the care-orientated play that used to take place there, which stands in contrast to some of the aspects of gender-conscious pedagogy that Olofsson (2007) elaborates, for example children should not be criticised when performing according to gender-stereotyped patterns and pre-school teachers should 'add but not deprive'. The girls' actions may be seen indirectly as a form of resistance to this belittlement. Their response to the pre-school teachers' agenda turned out to be a type of strategy in line with the border work elaborated by Thorne (2005), implying in this specific example that the girls were safeguarding their play and their caring values, while at the same time trying to defend themselves against the boys' violation of their play corner, which rather marked and strengthened the limits between the genders and the dichotomy between boys and girls.

Let us suppose that the pre-school teachers' gender-conscious pedagogy agenda, including the dissolution of the dolls corner, also implied that the caring values associated by tradition with care of the home, children and family got spread out and diluted in a similar way to objects and equipment in the dolls corner. In that sense the gender conscious pedagogy agenda was transformed into a sort of gender neutral agenda, implying that female- and male-coded rooms, toys and other objects should be toned down and neutralised, contributing to an uncertainty in the children about which caring values were welcomed and which were not.

As interpreted by Hägglund and Löfdahl (2010), this brief example holds some aspects of boys' and girls' freedom of action. First, the fact that the dolls corner should not even exist, according to gender-conscious principles, contributes to a situation where the girls have limited opportunity to protest when the boys demolish something they have built by themselves. Second, it may be hard to put words to the boys' actions because the context they violate is not really desirable within a gender-conscious pedagogy. Third, on the one hand the boys are encouraged to act like tough cowboys by the male pre-school teacher who wanted to take photographs, thereby reinforcing their behaviour, while on the other hand they get a reprimand for acting that way in a concrete situation. The children have to relate to pre-school teachers who encourage gender-stereotyped actions, in that sense safeguarding the notions of boys and girls as distinct characters. From the perspective of our new interpretation the children have to relate to the pre-school teachers' gender-conscious pedagogy ambitions as described in the example. It seems as if the children do not actually know whether certain actions are welcomed or not. These may be actions that uphold gender borders or they may be actions that challenge such borders (Thorne 2005). The pre-school teachers seem to indirectly struggle with the tension, as discussed by Wernersson (2009), between focusing on similarities or differences between boys and girls. This will lead to an uncertainty in their response to the boys' tough cowboy play as to whether their behaviour is concerned with gender or not. This uncertainty affects both the boys and the girls when handling situations like the one discussed.

As we understand it, the pre-school teachers aimed at getting the children, both boys and girls, to do the same things and be similar. Drawing from the empirical data we cannot comment on whether the pre-school teachers' actions were successful in the long run, i.e. if the spread of equipment and toys from the dolls corner actually contributed to new children starting to play the way the girls did previously, or if the girls who used to play there widened their preferences regarding play and friends, or, above all, if the children were given the possibility to cross gender categories entirely.

Peer cultures

Some aspects of pre-school culture can be understood from the example as children producing a domestic environment, even if, in accordance with the pre-school teachers' gender-pedagogy agenda, it should not exist. If we let ourselves be guided by the theory on peer cultures in discussing the situation described, the content of caring values stands out as interpretative reproduction of traditional and gender-stereotyped patterns of boys and girls. Children relate to and mould the surrounding culture into situations they are able to recognise and understand, and thereby act in a way they are familiar with. This may be understood as the children interpreting the pre-school teachers' gender-conscious pedagogy agenda in their own way, but also that the children reproduce this agenda, i.e. transform and reshape the didactic content into a more explicit formulated agenda, a specific peer culture that holds in the specific group during a limited time and that is constantly renegotiated when new situations, children and adults enter the pre-school's practice.

Children commonly reproduce forms in the pre-school that objectify care and caring values in a domestic-influenced environment. To the girls in the research, this is a matter of creating a room for their dolls, cooking food for their 'family', and doing the laundry and hanging it out to dry, duties that by tradition are female-coded and are defended by the girls in their resistance to the boys' attack and their request for teacher assistance. Simultaneously, the boys' attack demonstrates caring values as a *contrast* to violence and power which may be interpreted as the division of boys' and girls' actions, strengthening gender stereotypes. This and similar incidents in the children's play create and/or strengthen existing limits between care and non-care and express gender stereotypes as 'caring girls' and 'violent boys'. In that sense, the gender-equality work may contribute instead to the children being *created* as two separate groups with mutually exclusive characters, thereby upholding the differences between boys and girls that the work was aimed to abolish. We argue that the physical location of the play is of central importance; it does not matter that much that the pre-school teachers arrange, spread out or draw together the pre-school material, because the children construct their own meanings connected to the places they use. Maybe it is fair to claim that the dolls corner created by the girls with their own hands contributes even more strongly to making certain identities and positions possible while weakening others. Relations between boys and girls become embedded in material practices when the children mutually and on their own decide how to use the room, as when the girls occupy the room both in a physical manner (provided with things they brought from other places in the pre-school) and in a social manner (by ascribing the room the meaning of a dolls corner) and when the boys in the example violate the meaning of the laundry that has been hung out to dry.

Conclusions

The results show how hard it may be to foresee the practical consequences of implementing an agenda of gender equality. Paradoxically, the pre-school teachers' ambitions and actions meant that the dolls corner, a familiar place to some of the children where they put caring values into practice, was undermined. It would have been interesting to see what would have happened if such familiar places had instead provided a base for creating change. We have shed light upon the distressing aspect of focusing only on differences between boys and girls in the endeavour to achieve gender equality, which may conceal the fact that not all children fit into gender categories. In that sense one may ask to what extent the pre-school teachers' actions were guided by a conscious attitude. Above all, we observe that the organisational changes seem to have been initiated and accomplished by the pre-school teachers themselves, and in that sense the gender-conscious agenda appears to have been implemented as a kind of transfer from active pre-school teachers (sender) to passive children (receiver) or, as the Delegation on Equality in Schools (SOU 2010: 45) puts it: 'This means that gender pedagogy and work on gender equality that does not include the children as active participants and co-creators runs the risk of missing the target.'

UNANSWERED QUESTIONS

- What is needed in order to form a gender conscious pedagogy that takes children's agency into account?
- What challenges are involved in a gender-conscious pedagogy, such as the teachers' own stereotypes on what may be gender stereotype actions? Will this method accept a broad range of children's actions as gender crossing or are there just some predefined actions that fit the concept?
- What challenges will face the future gender-conscious pedagogy in order to avoid defining girls and boys as distinct characters?

References

Corsaro, W. (2005) *The Sociology of Childhood*. Thousand Oaks, CA: Pine Forge Press.

Edström, C. (2009) 'Lite vid sedan om den kommunala dagordningen. En analys av fyra kommuners arbete med jämställdhet i förskolan' ('A little bit beside the municipal agenda. An analysis of four municipals' work with gender equality in pre-school'), in I. Wernersson (ed.), *Genus i förskola och skola. Om förändringar i policy, perspektiv och praktik*, Göteborg Studies in Educational Science, 283. Göteborg: Acta Universitatis Gothoburgensis, pp. 43–59.

Eidevald, C. (2009) *Det finns inga tjejbestämmare – Att förstå kön som position i förskolans vardagsrutiner och lek (There Are No Girl Determinants – To Understand Gender as Position in the Pre-school's Everyday Routines and Play)*. School of Education and Communication, Jönköping University, Dissertation No. 4.

Eidevald, C. and Lenz Taguchi, H. (2011) 'Genuspedagogik och förskolan som jämställdhetspolitisk arena' ('Gender conscious pedagogy and pre-school as an arena of gender equality politics'), in H. Lenz Taguchi, L. Bodén and Ohrlander (eds), *En rosa pedagogik – jämställdhetspedagogiska utmaningar (Pink Pedagogy – Challenges to Pedagogy of Gender Equality)*. Stockholm: Liber, pp. 19–31.

Hägglund, S. and Löfdahl, A. (2010) *Limits of Care: Violating Caring Values*. Paper presented at the OMEP-Congress, 11–13 August, Gothenburg, Sweden.

Hellman, A. (2010) *Kan Batman vara rosa? Förhandlingar om pojkighet och normalitet på en förskola (Is It Possible for Batman to Be Pink? Negotiations on Boyish and Normality in a Pre-school)*, Göteborg Studies in Educational Science, 299. Göteborg Acta Universitatis Gothoburgensis.

Hirdman, Y. (2001) *Om det stabilas föränderliga former* (*Changing Shapes of the Stable*). Malmö: Liber.

Hjalmarsson, M. (2013) 'Governance and voluntariness for children in Swedish leisure-time centres – leisure-time teachers interpreting their tasks and everyday practice', *International Journal for Research on Extended Education*, 1 (1): 86–95.

Hjalmarsson, M. and Löfdahl, A. (forthcoming) 'Confirming and resisting an underdog position – leisure-time teachers dealing with a new practice', *European Early Childhood Education Research Journal*, 23 (4): accepted for publication.

Karlsson, R. (2009) *Demokratiska värden i förskolebarns vardag* (*Democratic Values in the Everyday Life of the Pre-school Child*), Göteborg Studies in Educational Science, 279. Göteborg: Acta Universitatis Gothoburgensis.

Löfdahl, A. (2014a) 'Peer culture and play', L. Brooker, S. Edwards and M. Blaise (eds), *The Sage Handbook of Play and Learning in Early Childhood*. London: Sage.

Löfdahl, A. (2014b) 'Omsorgsvärden i barns lekvärldar' ('Caring values in children's play'), R. Thornberg and E. Johansson (eds), *Värdepedagogik, etik och demokrati i förskola och skola*. Stockholm: Liber.

Löfdahl, A. and Hägglund, S. (2012) 'Diversity in pre-school: defusing and maintaining differences', *Australasian Journal of Early Childhood*, 37 (1): 119–26.

Löfdahl, A. and Pérez Prieto, H. (2009a) 'Between control and resistance: planning and evaluation texts in the Swedish pre-school', *Journal of Education Policy*, 24 (4): 393–408.

Löfdahl, A. and Pérez Prieto, H. (2009b) 'Institutional narratives within the performative pre-school: "If we write that we're no good, that's not good publicity!"', *Early Years*, 29 (3): 261–70.

Odenbring, Y. (2010) *Kramar, kategoriseringar och hjälpfröknar. Könskonstruktioner i interaction I förskola, förskoleklass och skolår ett* (*Hugs, Categorisations and Sub-teachers. Gender Constructions in Interaction in Pre-school, Pre-school Class and the First Grade*), Göteborg Studies in Educational Science, 292. Göteborg: Acta Universitatis Gothoburgensis.

Olofsson, B. (2007) *Modiga prinsessor & ömsinta killar – genusmedveten pedagogik i praktiken* (*Brave Princesses and Tender Princes – Gender Conscious Pedagogy in Practice*). Stockholm: Lärarförbundets förlag.

Saar, T., Löfdahl, A. and Hjalmarsson, M. (2012) 'Kunskapsmöjligheter i svenska fritidshem' ('Learning possibilities in Swedish leisure-time centres', *Nordisk Barnehageforskning*, 5 (3): 1–13.

Skolverket (National Agency for Education) (2008) *Ten Years After the Pre-school Reform. A National Evaluation of the Swedish Pre-school. A Summary of Report 318 2009*. Stockholm: Skolverket.

Skolverket (National Agency for Education) (2010) *The Curriculum for the Pre-school Lpfö 98 Revised 2010*. Stockholm: Skolverket.

SOU (2006) *Jämställd förskola – om betydelsen av jämställdhet och genus i förskolans pedagogiska arbete* (*Gender Equal Pre-school – On the Importance of Gender Equality and Gender in the Pre-school's Pedagogical Work*), Slutbetänkande för Delegationen för jämställdhet i förskolan. Stockholm: Fritzes.

SOU (2010) *Barns perspektiv på jämställdhet i skola. En kunskapsöversikt* (*Children's Perspectives on Equality in School*), DEJA (Delegationen för jämställdhet i skolan). Stockholm: Fritzes.

Svaleryd, K. (2007) *Genuspedagogik* (*Gender Conscious Pedagogy*). Stockholm: Liber.

Thorne, B. (2005) *Gender Play: Girls and Boys in School*, 10th edn. New Brunswick, NJ: Rutgers University Press.

Wedin, E.-K. (2011) *Jämställdhetsarbete i förskola och skola* (*Gender Equality Work in Pre-school and School*). Stockholm: Norstedts Juridik.

Wernersson, I. (2009) 'Pedagogerna och jämställdheten' ('The pedagogues and the gender equality'), in I. Wernersson (ed.), *Genus i förskola och skola. Om förändringar i policy, perspektiv och praktik*, Göteborg Studies in Educational Science, 283. Göteborg: Acta Universitatis Gothoburgensis, pp. 23–42.

4

THE BALLAD OF THE BIG MANLY GUY

Male and female teachers construct the gendered careworker in US early education contexts

Christine Mallozzi and Sally Campbell Galman

Introduction

In the United States (US), where this study took place, the early years teacher cadre is almost entirely female (Zumwalt and Craig 2005; Ingersoll and Merrill 2010: Skelton 2012). While such 'feminisation of teaching' is more complex than just a game of numbers (Griffiths 2006), popular and scholarly American writers alike have accused the mostly female teacher workforce of creating a 'feminised' schooling regime that limits male opportunity (Ringrose 2007; Okopny 2008). One recuperative response in the US and other contexts, and with lacklustre results, has been to 'add men and stir' into early education environments (Drudy *et al.* 2005; Carrington and McPhee 2008; Berg and Lahelma 2010; Lahelma 2011) under the assumption that maleness can correct for the 'natural' faults of females by 'masculinising' an 'inappropriate femininity of culture within schools' (Griffiths 2006: 401). In this way, many men have come to carework careers under flawed premises and strange conditions.

In this chapter we will focus on the US context, examining interview data from two men and two women in early education contexts to explore how male and female careworkers construct and orient themselves in relation to and in concert with masculinities and maleness, and how they do the work of care against a backdrop of facile popular assumptions and recuperative schemes (Martino 2008). Especially attending to women's voices, we affirm that a chapter about how women position men in a 'feminised' terrain is also about how women position themselves and are positioned by others. Our approach, based in social constructionism (Berger and Luckmann 1966), grounded theory techniques (Charmaz 2006), Spradley's (1979) domain analysis and discourse analysis principles (Gee 2011) of a larger data set (see Mallozzi and Galman 2014), seeks to gently interrogate participants' narrative constructions of masculinities within carework.

Guts, guns and glory: the unique conditions of US masculinities

When asked about the role of gender in her pre-service early childhood teacher education classes Jackie (note that all names in this chapter are pseudonyms), a white female, self-identified as a heterosexual, and in her early 20s from a middle-class family, focused exclusively on the one male member of her particular teacher education cohort – Tim – a white male US Marine veteran in his 20s. He represented something gendered and unique: a man preparing to do carework. Her narrative imbued him with special qualities compared to the other female teachers in the sample. The following quote is taken from an interview with Jackie:

> *So, he brings a lot to the group that even a normal guy wouldn't bring ... like I know for his field experience he showed up one day in full uniform and ... he taught the kids how to stand up and how to salute and how to do all that. And, um, so he brings a lot ... like there's this thing going on, like should there be guns in school, you know, should teachers be able to have guns, and obviously he's gonna say, 'Yes, if they're trained correctly and if they know' ... whereas the rest of us are going 'Ah, I'm, if somebody gave me a gun, I don't care how much you train me I don't feel comfortable using a gun with 30 five-year-olds in the room'. But he's of course is all, 'Oh, if I had,' you know, so he brings a lot to, I mean he is like THE ultimate guy with the Marine thing and the background.*

Jackie constructed Tim as a male teacher that goes beyond 'even a normal guy' into the designation of 'THE ultimate guy', based in part on his Marine veteran status. The US Marines have an exaggerated reputation for masculinity which Jackie seemingly 'buys into'. While Tim is no longer an active duty Marine, the status and importance of the Marine identity eclipses his current identity as a careworker in Jackie's eyes, if not in others'. Tim seems to draw on 'THE ultimate guy' image by showing up 'one day in full uniform' and teaching 'the kids how to stand up and how to salute and how to do all that'.

The term hegemonic masculinity, coined by Connell (1987) and reformulated by Connell and Messerschmidt (2005: 832), describes a masculinity that emphasises individualism, aggressiveness, competition, ambition, compulsory heterosexuality, violence and adherence to rigid social hierarchies, 'the pattern of practice (i.e. things done, not just a set of role expectations or an identity) that allowed men's dominance over women to continue ... distinguished from other masculinities, especially subordinated masculinities'. Indeed, it is often at odds with the majority of boys' healthy self-development, and especially with their constructions of themselves as 'good students' – those who might be studious, serious or bookish – and its ongoing popular dominance forces boys and men to make some self-destructive choices between self and ideal (Skelton and Francis 2011). Hegemonic masculinity in US contexts becomes difficult to interrogate as it is propped up by the empty rhetoric of rugged individualism, fervent nationalism and the wild-west fantasies of militarism and perverted manifest destiny (Cesca 2012; Ashwill 2013; Zellman 2014). Nowhere in the US context is the masculine ideal more powerfully showcased than in its gun culture (Burbick 2006). Cesca (2012) writes that gun culture has become synonymous with Americanism, tied to 'our revolutionary founding or the glorification of war' and is symbolic of masculinity and power:

> American guns have become unmistakable displays of virility and strength – of aggression, resolve and heroism. Hell, even the up-and-coming congressional Republicans like Paul Ryan and Eric Cantor have been nicknamed 'The Young Guns'.
>
> *(Cesca 2012)*

The distorted metonymy of the American masculine ideal casts powerful men as weapons rather than people. Furthermore, Americans – and, arguably, the very powerful National Rifle Association and its associated lobbying groups – are so protective of their right to bear arms that even the events in Newtown, Connecticut in December 2012, where 26 five- and six-year-old children and their (female) teachers were slaughtered by a lone gunman, could not foment gun control. Instead, school districts toyed with the suggestion that guns be introduced into elementary and early childhood settings as a protective measure before even minimally restricting gun ownership (Russell 2013). The distorted emphasis on the purported rights of the few over the safety of the many is reflected in the words of one politically right-wing talking principal who told the parent of a child killed in a more recent mass shooting: 'Your dead kids don't trump my constitutional rights' (Visser 2014). Given such responses, the entire argument about guns and rights is arguably less about a constitutional right to bear arms than it is about the conflation of weapons with the masculine ideal.

Jackie's use of the phrase 'there's this thing going on' is not in reference to the specific rhetoric around the Newtown massacre (the interview occurred years before the event) but is more about the idea of guns in classrooms in general. It is reasonable to deduce that 'protecting' children with firearms goes beyond the traditional definition of care and parameters of carework. Following the theme that Tim brings 'something' to carework that she and her female colleagues do not, Tim's capability and willingness to use firearms in the classroom outdoes the fearful women, who Jackie surmises would be immobilised in the same situation and in need of a man like Tim to take charge.

Banking on the idea that 'feminised' schools are in need of 'suitable male role models' (Dermott 2012: 235), the *Troops-to-Teachers* initiative sought to incentivise men returning from military service in one of the many armed conflicts of the early 2000s to re-enter the labour force as teachers, especially in urban, poor environments. *Troops-to-Teachers* and other such programmes offer 'working-class boys routes to high levels of educational achievement but by diverting them towards the "respectable" working-class masculinity of [the] authoritarian, disciplinarian, hyper-masculine armed forces' (Dermott 2012: 237). For middle-class boys, hegemonic masculinity is linked with 'achievement which translates into societal advantage' (p. 237), e.g. task mastery, cultural capital and career success. Dermott's work revealed working-class youths' protest masculinity (i.e. rule-breaking to maintain status though it interferes with skill building and educational success) was corralled through programmes like *Troops-to-Teachers* by redirecting aggression in 'a socially acceptable space in which a "macho/hard" status can still exist' (p. 232). In this way tensions between working-class protest masculinity and social respectability might be rendered more digestible while also masculinising the early care classroom.

The blame game: domestic ideology, hegemonic masculinity and social markers

At an intersection of domestic ideology and hegemonic masculinity, Jackie's middle-class habitus may contribute to her construction of men as the traditional protectors of women and children. US domestic ideology – the system of beliefs and ideas about gendered roles in the private sphere of home that are subsequently mirrored in much of the public professional landscape – emphasises teaching as a highly desirable career for females, but as Jackie illustrated, it does not suggest that women are necessarily the most desirable workers.

Teaching has historically been conflated with marriage, children and family responsibilities, and women's 'natural' nurturance and caring (Acker 1999; Mahalik *et al.* 2005). Women teachers may feel the need to affirm their place in the domestic ideology by inscribing male fellows with exaggerated masculine qualities regardless of the masculine identities claimed by those men. Similarly, men may find themselves exempted from fully claiming the role of 'teacher' because it is typically constructed as a feminine one.

Participant Jay described how female teaching colleagues reconstructed his careworker role by removing him from their own gendered and preferred sphere of influence, emphasising non-pedagogical or non-professional tasks. In this way, women teachers are presented as more agentive than in Jackie's story; they are responsible (we argue, only in part) for forming the role of a male teacher, but through this they are simultaneously blamed for putting men into the overly masculine mould dictated by the domestic ideologies in play, thus limiting the men and by result themselves. Jay, a white male, self-identified as a heterosexual and in his late 20s, comes from a working-class background in the semi-rural north-eastern US. At the time of the interview he was in his second year in the primary level classroom in a large, urban elementary school where the overwhelming majority of his pupils are students of colour and English Language Learners, and whose communities, while culturally rich, are economically poor.

> *Yeah, last year I got all the behaviours also and she* [pointing to the room across the hall] *is just as good with discipline. My co-teacher last year kind of jokingly would say that I am like a drill sergeant … At the beginning of the school year, I was trying to find time to set up my class-room because they were all asking me to carry boxes up the stairs. I was happy this year because there were more guys here so they were being asked to carry all the things up the stairs. And I would say things like, 'Oh, it is because I am a guy right?' I would address it. I did it jokingly but I was getting the point across so they just laughed.*

In addition to his own examples, Jay relayed circumstances of other male teachers assigned to work with discipline problems or to do physical labour. Preceding this focal interview section, Jay was hesitant to explicitly claim his maleness as the singular reason he was assigned 'all the behaviours' – a reference to students on behavioural plans – but he stated that other male teachers do make this claim. Interestingly, he implies the same by emphasising that a nearby female colleague was equally able to discipline children though she was not assigned to do so. The militaristic 'like a drill sergeant' descriptor is shorthand for dominance over others, in this case over students who require discipline, and an invocation of the domestic ideology that emphasises the control potential and physical power of desirable maleness. Jay portrayed himself as passively assigned the role of disciplinarian, claiming that women actively positioned him; however, Jay drew, probably unconsciously, from the racialised privilege of being a white male which resituated him in a powerful position.

Social markers such as race, class and sexuality complicate the face of ideal masculinity present in this narrative. A history of deeply entrenched white supremacist and racist practices has left its mark on US culture, in particular with regard to ongoing racist portrayals of people of colour. One such stereotype – the 'Angry Black Man' (Wingfield 2007) – contributes to negative media portrayals of black masculinity in contemporary and historical contexts. For example, the public image of Civil Rights activist Dr Martin Luther King was a media foil to Malcolm X's image of the Angry Black Man, but it is possible that in contemporary, media-saturated America, King would have been deemed an Angry Black Man as well (Blake 2013). The reverberations of racism and fear are beyond dispute. In the Race Card Project, headed by Norris (n.d.), a National Public Radio (NPR) correspondent, encourages Americans to make six-word observations about race and post them for commentary. One such observation was 'Angry Black men are so scary', made in conjunction with the discussion about the killing of 17-year-old Trayvon Martin, an African American youngster who was gunned down while walking home from buying candy (sweets). The gunman defended his actions using the 'Angry Black Men' trope, saying that he had no choice but to shoot because he assumed Martin, in his hooded sweatshirt, was potentially armed and on the verge of violence. Martin's murder and the gunman's eventual acquittal sparked national conversation about how black men and boys are criminalised as dangerous and untrustworthy in the minds of white Americans.

Both Tim and Jay may exert their power, even disciplinary power, without fear of being cast as 'dangerous'. Jackie even presented Tim's possession of a gun as unproblematic and Jay's colleagues encouraged his vigorous disciplinary regime. The white men's potential anger and punitive power is not viewed as dangerous but rather appropriate and just. Furthermore, it is important to note that Jay's students were mostly non-white and/or non-English speaking. We speculate that Jay's own privileged location may have made him blind to the implicit historical and neo-colonialist weight of his positionality vis-à-vis his participation in hegemony.

Jay did not positively regard the trust his female colleagues placed on him but instead considered it burdensome and proof positive that he is relegated the to 'dirty work' of the father figure, according to the 'wait-until-your-father-gets-home' masculine typing in the domestic ideology in play. Furthermore, Jay asserted the female teachers asking him to 'carry boxes up the stairs' were doing so because he was 'a guy' – in fact the only male teacher – which made him the 'go to guy' for carrying things. The term 'go to guy' echoes a predetermined domestic ideology in which social labour is drawn along gender lines so much so it is normalised; men are expected to use their brawn for the women who are expected to lack physical strength and who must rely on men. Of note, Jay's interpretation, 'Oh, it is because I am a guy right?' rested on a sex-gender role connection devoid of race or class expectation. Had he been a black man, Jay might have argued the women were effectively positioning him as a janitor (caretaker) or maintenance worker, a lower-wage job more likely to be held by a non-white male. Jay seems sensitive to the social implications of being asked to do low-wage work despite a higher status job title, yet despite his working-class background he views the matter as the women's sexual prejudice and ignores any socio-economic implications. Reducing the matter to a male/female issue allows him to blame his colleagues, claim rhetorically popular 'reverse sexism' and avoid uncomfortable grappling with class, something discursively invisible and even taboo in much American culture (Shenker-Osorio 2013).

Anything she can do, he can do better

Folbre (2006) defined 'carework' as the work of caring for dependent others (in this case, young children) that has been historically done by women. Carework is usually cast as 'natural' for females and motivated by 'feminine' feelings of love and care rather than the pursuit of money, status or personal advancement. Folbre wrote that carework typically 'involves close personal or emotional interaction' (p. 186) and is associated with the rhetoric of idealised selflessness wherein women's pursuit of raises or promotions, or women's leaving the profession, are socially unacceptable. Meanwhile, the inverse may be true for men whose tenure in carework is expected to be a period of laudable but temporary service – not unlike a tour in the Peace Corps (Galman 2012).

Educational carework in the US context is further complicated by a history of misogyny and Taylorism through which compulsory schooling was rendered cost efficient and comprehensive by mobilising women as a source of cheap, readily available and easily exploited labour (deMarrais and LeCompte 1998). In part this mobilisation was accomplished by deploying biological-determinist narratives that cast teaching as the duty and bastion of idealised femininity and female care that persist today (Galman 2012); this encourages people to see males in carework as novel, as illustrated by participant Shelby's narrative.

Shelby is a white female, self-identified as a heterosexual and from an upper-middle-class background. She was in her early 20s at the time of the interview and had just completed her student teaching in a rural elementary school in the south-eastern US. When asked about gender in her teaching experiences Shelby commented on a man who was a first grade teacher in the school where she worked as a student teacher:

> *It was really neat to watch him interact with kids 'cause you wouldn't think of some big manly guy being a first grade teacher.* [He acted] *just like any other first grade teacher would and sometimes the kids, I didn't really get to observe his class, I just saw him in the hallway and stuff. But his students really responded to him. I was always so curious to see if he was like as 'nurturing'* [air quotes] *as some of the female teachers were in first grade. But I never got an opportunity to go observe his classroom.*

To Shelby, a 'big manly guy' teaching first grade was unusual for the typical reasons: he was a man doing what was, to her at least, women's work. Shelby admitted that her observations and thus evidence were limited, but she compared the man to 'any other first grade teacher', implying a monolithic view of early years women teachers, nurturing through comforting and genteel kindness, aligning with domestic ideology of the feminine, idealised in cultural tropes of the Victorian Angel-in-the-House and Lady Bountiful (Meiners 2002). Shelby's drawing on this particular archetype, with its history of both subjugation and colonialism, may rest on her experience as a white woman who identifies with some of this imagery, stating she became a teacher partially because it fit with her aims of becoming a wife and mother. It is further important to note that at the primary school level 81.2 per cent of teachers in the US are white and 89.3 per cent of teachers are women (Goldring *et al.* 2013).

However, when asked about gender, Shelby immediately called to mind the presence of men in carework, describing the spectacle of the 'big manly guy' in the early childhood class. This calls to mind the character Detective Kimball in the film *Kindergarten Cop* (Grazer and Reitman 1990) played by the manlier-than-manly Arnold Schwarzenegger. In this film an undercover police officer poses as a kindergarten teacher to protect the innocent and catch the villains; heroics and hilarity ensue. In addition to their brawny size, Shelby's 'big manly guy' and the fictitious Kimball share many characteristics that Dalton (2004) argued are the markings of a Hollywood-constructed 'good' teacher. Both are outsiders – Kimball as a policeman, Shelby's teacher as a man – allowing them to exist outside a typically failing feminised system. Teachers and administrators questioned Kimball's techniques that rely on the principles and routines of military training, akin to Tim's 'stand-and-salute' posture and

Jay's drill sergeant disciplinarian. Kimball is white, so his enactment of the hegemonic ideal is not deemed dangerous or inappropriate, such as a black man might experience. In the end, Kimball is lauded as a superior teacher as he trades in his detective's badge for a permanent teaching position (sans teacher education or certification, we note!) and the reward of romantic, heterosexual love. Meanwhile, Shelby's evaluation that the 'students really responded to him' hint that the cultural consensus on both these big manly guys is that their masculine skill set can easily outpace and improve upon anything the existing throng of women might be attempting.

And then he shows up

The binary thinking of male-masculine/female-feminine dubiously maps onto the binary of action/inaction. Drawing from the Western fine arts milieu, Berger (1972: 47) summed up the cultural expectation that 'men act and women appear'. Action has been constructed as a male province, while like children/objects women are expected to be seen and not heard. Yet even a man's inactive presence in an early education context has been constructed as an action; the act of 'showing up' is valuable and effective compared to women who seemed to have been there all along and are thus part of the problem. One tale of 'showing up' came from participant Robby who, like Jay, had been asked to carry heavy objects and deal with children's behavioural issues. Robby is a white male, self-identified as a heterosexual and in his mid-30s who comes from a middle-class background in a large, urban centre in the northeastern US. At the time of the interview, he was in his final year working at a small state-subsidised pre-school. Robby was celebrated for an almost immediate and dramatic change he prompted in a troubled student that was accomplished by simply showing up:

> Then there were the folks that my first week there, there was a little girl who would sit next to me, and they said, 'This is amazing! All she has done is cry since she's gotten here, but … she has now stopped. Must be that you're a guy.' And I laughed, but they totally meant it.

Like Shelby's 'big manly guy', Robby is an outsider, both by being a new hire and a man. Hired as a teacher and team leader, he was brought into the school to shake up the system, which reinforced his outsider status and the expectation that he act as a pseudo-administrative, higher-status teacher. Yet even before he had the chance to unsettle any teacher's applecart, the mere presence of his maleness was considered to have astounding effects on a distressed young girl, arguably surpassing even Hollywood's over-the-top model of a 'good' teacher, wherein even movie characters follow some arc of change (Dalton 2004). Indeed, the miracle of maleness can unfold simply by sitting next to a child, no pedagogy or interaction needed. Of note, despite Western notions of rugged, manly individualism present in this narrative, Robby did not arrive at this point of 'male teacher as saviour' on his own.

Mid-twentieth-century America was a cornucopia of sexist, ahistorical, 'bad apple' theories that blamed the women themselves for the low status of the 'feminised' nursing, teaching and social work fields, made even lower status by the presence of women (Simpson and Simpson 1969). Despite the pervasive notions of the woman teacher as a dutiful, self-sacrificial saviour (Galman 2012), adopting this persona in schools reified female culpability for wave after wave of educational crises. To wit: they have not thus super-heroically reversed the perceived ills of schooling under any and all circumstances, and so they are to blame. In effect, the women truly have sacrificed themselves to their work. Such blame contributed to deterring many high-achieving women and nearly all men, especially men and women of colour, from pursuing carework careers (Bray 2004;Vilson 2014).

The statistical data bear this out.Teaching was once considered a promising entry career, especially for first-generation college students who are more likely to be black or Hispanic and from low-income families (Chen 2005), yet students of colour who qualify for college are encouraged to aim higher than the meagre salaries and low status that the teaching profession offers (Gordon 2000). First-generation students seem to be receiving this message. Although undergraduate education majors have one of the highest completion rates for first-generation students, business, health sciences/services, social sciences and the vocational/technical fields are all more popular majors for first-generation students than education (Chen 2005).The typical teacher education student remains a middle- to upper-income, white, female from a college-educated family (Zumwalt and Craig 2005). The trends with first-generation college students provide no reason to think this will change soon.

Conclusions

The men in this study, like many men in early care environments, were able to displace a room or even entire schools full of female teachers by simply showing up. Female teachers constitute a monotone chorus against which male teachers might sing arias. Meanwhile, many women doing carework seek to reclaim its landscape as a female-only province defined by biological right, and in the case of educators may resist the professionalisation of teaching because professionalisation emphasises earned qualifications and competencies and downplays natural ability (Folbre 2006).This is arguably not a function of the female teachers' interpretations of masculinity but rather the consciousness of themselves and their abilities within patriarchy. For many female teachers, their perceived ability to care is tied to mothering and anatomy, and constitutes a point of womanly and 'natural' pride for which many have been reinforced throughout history (Cortina and San Roman 2006; Galman 2012). It is easy to see why a female teacher might resist interrogating this idea of being deeply 'good at' caring because outside the universe of carework female competencies are problems to be solved rather than assets to be valued.

Men and their work are made exceptional and their difference – which is to say their maleness – is exaggerated to justify that exceptionality and elevation. Connell and Messerschmidt's (2005) work on hegemonic masculinity aligns well with the desirably masculine: aggressive, ambitious and physical. Others (see Skelton and Francis 2011: 470) argue that multiple forms of desirable masculinity exist such as 'Renaissance Masculinity'; these forms revise the narrow idea of hegemonic masculinity, but among school careworkers the hegemonic form of masculinity continues to be embraced with vigour as men and women seek to demarcate difference in the starkest terms possible.

We argue that because US culture supports and reproduces hegemonic forms of masculinity – casting ideal men as stereotypical breadwinners, powerful, militaristic protectors and strongmen – and as minimally or incompetent nurturers, men are less able to embrace renaissance or other non-hegemonic masculinities. Men can be teachers, and ultimately be promoted into administrative ranks while occupying a range of hegemonic or quasi-hegemonic masculine identities and still be counted among 'the "desirable subjects" of the [childcare] marketplace' (Skelton and Francis 2011: 472). In carework settings the power of such tropes is magnified as careworkers themselves may enact and reproduce the patterns of care within the US nuclear family and its attendant domestic ideologies, which in the US context are remarkably conservative, traditional and persistent (Coontz 2000).

In this way, it becomes acceptable and even desirable for men to occupy only margins of care, even when employed as careworkers in early education contexts. Male teachers in US schools work in the same classrooms with the same professional preparation and the same titles, yet their work is intractably differentiated along gender lines. While female teachers do carework male teachers do higher-status and more masculine work, bleeding well into the boundaries of administrative activity while the humdrum realities of teaching remain the domain of numberless female plebs.

UNANSWERED QUESTIONS

- Female participants in this study marvelled at the unusualness of men in early years education despite the fact that this is a well-established demographic pattern. In what ways does this emphasis on men's uniqueness in these settings serve to other maleness by making it spectacular? How might such a discursive habit serve hegemonic expectations?
- How does the 'feminisation of teaching' thesis work in narrowing men's occupational choices as well as reifying cultural premises of female inadequacy?
- How does US culture lend itself to particularly rigid gendered expectations for male workers, students and others? Are there affordances as well as constraints within this context?

References

Acker, S. (1999) 'Caring as work for women educators', in E. Smyth, S. Acker, P. Bourne and A. Prentice (eds), *Challenging Professions: Historical and Contemporary Perspectives on Women's Professional Work*. Toronto: University of Toronto Press. pp. 277–95.

Ashwill, M. A. (2013) 'When nationalism and militarism become one', *Huffington Post*, 7 August. [Online.] Available at: http://www.huffingtonpost.com/mark-a-ashwill/american-nationalism_b_3564377.html (accessed 3 January 2015).

Berg, P. and Lahelma, E. (2010) 'Gendering processes in the field of physical education', *Gender and Education*, 22 (1): 31–46.

Berger, J. (1972) *Ways of seeing*. London: Penguin Classics.

Berger, P. L. and Luckmann, T. (1966) *The Social Construction of Reality: A Treatise on the Sociology of Knowledge*. New York: Anchor Books.

Blake, J. (2013) 'How MLK became an angry black man', *CNN*, 16 April. [Online.] Available at: http://www.cnn.com/2013/04/16/us/king-birmingham-jail-letter-anniversary/index.html (accessed 3 January 2015).

Bray, P. M. (2004) 'Young women majoring in mathematics and elementary education: a perspective on enacting liberatory pedagogy', *Equity and Excellence in Education*, 37 (1): 44–54.

Burbick, J. (2006) *Gun Show Nation: Gun Culture and American Democracy*. New York: New Press.

Carrington, B. and McPhee, A. (2008) 'Boys' "underachievement" and the feminization of teaching', *Journal of Education for Teaching*, 34 (2): 109–20.

Cesca, B. (2012) 'Breaking the American gun culture once and for all', *Huffington Post*, 21 December. [Online.] Available at: http://www.huffingtonpost.com/bob-cesca/breaking-the-american-gun_b_2348282.html (accessed 3 January 2015).

Charmaz, K. (2006) *Constructing Grounded Theory: A Practical Guide Through Qualitative Analysis*. London: Sage.

Chen, X. (2005) *First-Generation Students in Postsecondary Education: A Look at Their College Transcripts* (NCES 2005-171), US Department of Education, National Center for Education Statistics. Washington, DC: US Government Printing Office.

Connell, R. W. (1987) *Gender and Power*. Palo Alto, CA: Stanford University Press.

Connell, R. W. and Messerschmidt, J. W. (2005) 'Hegemonic masculinity: rethinking the concept', *Gender and Society*, 19 (6): 829–59.

Coontz, S. (2000) *The Way We Never Were: American Families and the Nostalgia Trap*. New York: Basic Books.

Cortina, R. and San Roman, S. (2006) *Women and Teaching: Global Perspectives on the Feminization of Teaching*. New York: Palgrave Macmillan.

Dalton, M. M. (2004) *The Hollywood Curriculum: Teachers in the Movies*, 2nd edn. New York: Peter Lang.

deMarrais, K. B. and LeCompte, M. D. (1998) *The Way Schools Work: A Sociological Analysis of Education*. New York: ABLongman/Addison Wesley.

Dermott, E. (2012) 'Troops to teachers: solving the problem of working-class masculinity in the classroom?', *Critical Social Policy*, 32 (2): 223–41.

Drudy, S., Martin, M., Woods, M. and O' Flynn, J. (2005) *Men and the Classroom: Gender Imbalances in Teaching*. New York: Routledge.

Folbre, N. (2006) 'Measuring care: gender, empowerment, and the care economy', *Journal of Human Development*, 7 (2): 183–99.

Galman, S. C. (2012) *Wise and Foolish Virgins: White Women at Work in the Feminized World of Primary School Teaching*. Lanham, MD: Lexington Press.

Gee, J. P. (2011) *An Introduction to Discourse Analysis: Theory and Method*. London: Routledge.

Goldring, R., Gray, L. and Bitterman, A. (2013) *Characteristics of Public and Private Elementary and Secondary School Teachers in the United States: Results for the 2011–12 Schools and Staffing Survey* (NCES 2013-314), US Department of Education. Washington, DC: National Center for Education Statistics (http://nces.ed.gov/pubsearch).

Gordon, J. (2000) *The Colour of Teaching*. London: RoutledgeFalmer.

Grazer, B. and Reitman, I. (1990) *Kindergarten Cop* [film]. United States: Universal Pictures.

Griffiths, M. (2006) 'The feminisation of teaching and the practice of teaching: threat or opportunity?', *Educational Theory*, 56 (4): 387–405.

Ingersoll, R. and Merrill, L. (2010) 'Who's teaching our children?', *Educational Leadership*, 67 (8): 14–20.

Lahelma, E. (2011) 'Gender awareness in Finnish teacher education: an impossible mission?', *Education Inquiry*, 2 (2): 263–76.

Mahalik, J. R., Morray, E., Coonerty-Femiano, A., Ludlow, L. H., Slattery, S. M. and Smiler, A. (2005) 'Development of the conformity to feminine norms inventory', *Sex Roles*, 52: 317–35.

Mallozzi, C. A. and Galman, S. C. (2014) 'The guys and the rest of us: tales of gendered aptitude and experience in educational carework', *Gender and Education*, 26 (3): 262–79.

Martino, W. J. (2008) 'Male teachers as role models: addressing issues of masculinity, pedagogy and the re-masculinization of schooling', *Curriculum Inquiry*, 38 (2): 189–223.

Meiners, E. (2002) 'Disengaging from the legacy of Lady Bountiful in teacher education classrooms', *Gender and Education*, 14 (1): 85–94.

Norris, M. (n.d.) *The Race Card Project*. [Online.] Available at: http://theracecardproject.com/ (accessed 3 January 2015).

Okopny, C. (2008) 'Why Jimmy isn't failing: the myth of the boy crisis', *Feminist Teacher*, 18 (3): 216–28.

Ringrose, J. (2007) 'Successful girls? Complicating post-feminist, neo-liberal discourses of educational achievement and gender equality', *Gender and Education*, 19 (4): 471–89.

Russell, L. (2013) 'In response to Newtown shootings some states move to put guns in classrooms', *CNN*, 12 June. [Online.] Available at: http://schoolsofthought.blogs.cnn.com/2013/06/12/in-response-to-newtown-shootings-some-states-move-to-put-guns-in-classrooms/ (accessed 3 January 2015).

Shenker-Osorio, A. (2013) 'Why Americans believe they are all middle class', *The Atlantic*, 1 August. [Online.] Available at: http://www.theatlantic.com/politics/archive/2013/08/why-americans-all-believe-they-are-middle-class/278240/ (accessed 3 January 2015).

Simpson, R. L. and Simpson, L. H. (1969) 'Women and bureaucracy in the semi-professions', A. Etzioni (ed.), *The Semi-professions and Their Organization: Teachers, Nurses and Social Workers*. New York: Free Press, pp. 186–97.

Skelton, C. (2012) 'Men teachers and the "feminised" primary school: a review of the literature', *Educational Review*, 64 (1): 1–19.

Skelton, C. and Francis, B. (2011) 'Successful boys and literacy: are "literate boys" challenging or repackaging hegemonic masculinity?', *Curriculum Inquiry*, 41 (4): 456–79.

Spradley, J. (1979) *The Ethnographic Interview*. Fort Worth: Harcourt Brace Jovanovich College Publishers.

Vilson, J. L. (2014) *This Is Not a Test: A New Narrative on Race, Class and Education*. Chicago: Haymarket Books.

Visser, J. (2014) '"Joe the plumber" to California massacre victims' families: "Your dead kids don't trump constitutional rights"', *National Post*, 28 May. [Online.] Available at: http://news.nationalpost.com/2014/05/28/joe-the-plumber-to-california-massacre-victims-families-your-dead-kids-dont-trump-constitutional-rights/ (accessed 3 January 2015).

Wingfield, A. H. (2007) 'The modern mammy and the angry black man: African American professionals' experiences with gendered racism in the workplace', *Race, Gender and Class*, 14 (1/2): 196–212.

Zellman, J. (2014) 'The one question I am asked in every country I visit', *Huffington Post*, 11 April. [Online.] Available at: http://www.huffingtonpost.com/joanna-zelman/the-one-question-i-am-ask_b_5108706.html?utm_hp_ref=tw (accessed 3 January 2015).

Zumwalt, K. and Craig, E. (2005) 'Teachers' characteristics: research on the demographic profile', in M. Cochran-Smith and K. M. Zeichner (eds), *Studying Teacher Education: The Report of the AERA Panel on Research and Teacher Education*. Mahwah, NJ: Lawrence Erlbaum, pp. 111–56.

PART II
Young children
Gender, learning and care

5

BIG AND MUSCULAR BOYS

Teaching of normality in pre-school through food and eating

Anette Hellmann

Introduction

Gender research has shown how gender stereotypes and gender norms are much more likely to emerge within contexts where bodies are the centre of attention (Connell 2000) and in practices where teachers' self-awareness tends to be low (Johansson 2011a; Hellman 2012). This chapter will discuss care and the learning of gender and normality in a specific situation that emphasises the body and that is often coded as 'caring' and 'feminine'. The situation selected for analytic focus is the period of the pre-school day when children are eating their mid-day meal. The analytic starting point for this discussion is the concept of gender and space (Thurén 1996; Connell 2000) and norms (Salih and Butler 2004).

Drawing on empirical data from a larger study about boyishness and normality produced through an ethnographic methodology at a Swedish pre-school (2005–7) (Hellman 2010), this chapter analyses care and learning of gender and normality at meal situations through the concept of educare. Meal situations are particularly interesting in terms of educare and gender because they are coded as 'feminine' (Månsson 2011) and 'caring' situations where 'learning' occurs (Johansson and Pramling-Samuelsson 2001). The results show that both female and male teachers tend to assume an authority over children's bodies and promote a gender stereotypical learning of body ideals. They do this even though the Swedish pre-school curriculum enshrines the key concepts of democracy and children's competency, meaning that pre-schools are obliged to counteract gender stereotypes (Skolverket 2010). It is argued that the promotion of gender equality in pre-school needs to be founded on a concept of care that is understood as both an ethical practice and also a quality that teachers themselves reflect.

The chapter considers the following questions:

1. In what ways do power relations and communication between teachers and pupils in meal situations perpetuate norms about boys' idealised bodies?
2. How, if at all, are teachers' reflective practices linked to notions of care, fostering and learning?

This chapter will discuss the central values in Swedish policy documents and pre-school practice. Using examples from the ethnography, I will discuss how hierarchies of power manifest themselves during the meal situation, first between adults and children and second between 'real men/boys' and everyone else. I note how the caring context of the meal situation conveys norms about strength and the idealised body that are less visible than might be expected in a learning situation; this, I suggest, may be due to the levels or nature of teachers' reflexivity.

Central values in Swedish pre-school policy documents and practice: children's influence, equality and integration of care, fostering and learning

Swedish pre-schools have been ascribed as having an important role in forming children's identity and attitudes. During the last decade values about children's influence have emerged and gained a prominent role in policy documents for pre-schools (Skolverket 2010) as well as in pre-school practice. The most admired child among teachers in Swedish pre-schools is 'the competent child', someone who takes responsibility, negotiates and uses their influence in a constructive way (Emilson 2008). At the same time, teachers also expect 'the competent child' to learn how to follow the rules set up by the teachers (Hellman 2010).

Another important value is about gender equality. The National Curriculum for pre-schools in Sweden specifically stresses the importance of gender equality and the rights of boys and girls to form their identities free from gender stereotypes (Skolverket 2010). At the same time, gender stereotyped norms about 'real boys' and 'real girls' are directed towards children in pre-schools. The relationship of care and education is crucial to a number of relevant gender debates that connect with the focus of this chapter, notably the call for male role models and the feminisation of pre-schools. Underpinning the call for male role models is the influence of sex role theory. The feminine dominance within pre-schools, together with the moral panic about absent fathers, still serves to support the call for male role models of hegemonic masculinities for boys rather than girls (Connell 2000; Whitehead 2002). Care, female teachers, girls and certain spaces labelled as 'feminine' are tied together in this pre-school discourse. Care is linked to the institution, female teachers, the building's architecture as well as the design, and informal situations such as meals that operate as a hidden curriculum. Researchers such as Renolds (2004) and Nordberg *et al.* (2010) have pointed out the importance of 'loosening the ties' between care, girls, girlishness, women and femininity, and create possibilities to analyse care also in relation to boys, boyishness, men and masculinity. Such a reformulation might lead to increased interaction between and greater reflexivity of learning and caring practices that offer a more holistic challenge to unhelpful gender stereotypes that may occur during meal situations.

Pre-schools in Sweden encompass both daycare and kindergarten traditions as educational institutions for young children between the ages of one and six. They provide care and education which are regarded as crucial for children of this age. Learning activities such as circle time are tightly structured and planned (Emilson and Johansson 2013); consequently, education, play and learning are discussed in relation to the National Curriculum. In contrast, teachers unreflectively tend not to make connections with the National Curriculum and care and, consequently, situations linked to care, like meal situations, are generally less planned, reflected upon and evaluated (Hellman 2012). A distinguished quality in Swedish pre-schools is manifested in the pre-school National Curriculum, teacher education and in pre-school practice where the aim has been to 'provide children with good pedagogical activities, where care, nurturing and learning together form a coherent whole' (Skolverket 2010: 4).

Research context

Swedish pre-schools are open from about 06.30 in the morning until 18.00 in the evening with many children eating more than one meal a day in this environment. During the whole day learning, nurturing and care should intersect and form a coherent whole. Male and female teachers trained as pre-school or daycare teachers work together to plan and deliver the pre-school curriculum. This includes activities like eating, dressing, changing of diapers (nappies) and taking a rest after dinner, which are all seen as important situations for both care and learning. In addition to recognising the learning practices associated with traditional caring activities, all learning should be conducted in a caring atmosphere where teachers and children can create meaning by sharing common knowledge (Johansson 2011b).

The research

This chapter analyses select data from an ethnographic study on gender and normality in two Swedish pre-schools (Hellman 2010). The pre-schools were selected because they were organised into age groups that differed in terms of age organisation. The pre-schools were situated in an urban area of mixed social and cultural background. Participants from the pre-schools included seven female teachers, one male teacher and 20 children (twelve boys and eight girls aged between three and six years old).

Most research into masculinity and education tends to study the margins rather than the norm (Thorne 1993; Nordberg *et al.* 2010). This ethnographical study was conducted from a norm critical perspective where deconstructing how hegemonic norms are created becomes important. The ethnography included 2000 hours of participant observations made over a time period of two years and in different contexts within the pre-school, together with data from 30 interviews (individual and in groups) with teachers and children. When observing play and other activities field notes of conversations and non-verbal practices of how teachers and pupils moved between different areas were recorded. All interviews where taped and transcribed for ethnographic analyses of certain 'tracks' of meaning (Sanjek 1990) that were present within interviews and observations. Some of these 'analytic tracks' were based on Thurén's (1996) concepts of strength, hierarchy and space. According to Thurén, gender norms manifest themselves with varying strength in different contexts. One analytic track was therefore to trace when certain gender norms became relevant, for example in combination with age or in caring and routine practices, and when they became less relevant.

In addition to this, when the study was finished, teachers were sent the manuscript so that they had the opportunity to give their comments on the text. The teachers welcomed this approach and reported they felt safe, data production wise, since they knew that they would be given the chance to comment on observations and interviews before the research was published. The process also meant that I gained new data based on their reflections on the draft 'write-up' of the research. A common theme within the teachers' comments related to the process of situated reflection, or rather the lack of reflection, that was captured in the ethnographic observations. Teachers struggled to understand and explain their apparent lack of reflection, especially relating to values which they are expected to follow and promote in the curriculum.

Power relations and norms

The theoretical framework used in this chapter concerning norms about gender (boyishness, girlishness) is understood not as given but as situated in a relational process where negotiation is central. These norms are performed and continually created through language, gesture and gaze. While norms may seem natural, neutral and necessary in social life the meanings or power positions they are given are neither natural nor neutral. The categories and different positional responses are never merely given; rather they are under constant (re)negotiation resulting in naturalised dominant norms. The enactment of norms has 'real' consequences. The impact of norms about gender and masculinity, the use of categories such as boys, girls, children and adults, and the hierarchies between these different categories changes depending upon the context (Thurén 1996; Connell 2000). Within an everyday activity, such as a meal situation, there is a risk that norms and stereotypical expectations develop a hegemonic status that perpetuates rather than problematises gender stereotypical behaviours and beliefs. The hegemonic power of these norms, such as norms about 'big boys', is maintained by the continual repetition of unquestioned interactions in our daily activities, which become invisible and less likely to be reflected on because they are part of our everyday routines.

Gender stereotypes in this chapter refer to categorisations that are typically regarded as more appropriate than others because they reflect certain specific hegemonic practices of boyishness for boys and girlishness for girls.

Research findings

In the following sections I will present how norms about strength and achievement were used in order to motivate and resist. Thereafter, I will discuss promoting idealised bodies for boys and finally a section will be offered about 'to be or not to be big strong boys'.

Using norms about strength and achievement to motivate and resist

The pre-school meal situation was often filled with power struggles, especially concerning the right for adults to make decisions about children's bodies. The expectation is that children have to eat by themselves and the adult's role is to ensure that this happens by motivating, threatening and modelling the expected behaviour so that the children want to eat by themselves. To get children to eat what adults have decided is good for them becomes a rule or eating convention that affects everybody, teachers as well as children. Some of the teachers believed that it was important for children to eat according to pre-school rules or eating conventions. For example, children were expected to taste everything, eat porridge before they had a sandwich at breakfast, or eat the main dish before the fruit at lunchtime. Children's protests against these meal situation rules or eating conventions may have been in response to their sense of violation of their right to eat what they wanted, or because the caring context of a meal situation provided an opportunity to neglect and challenge these eating conventions.

In the following observation from one of the three daily meals (breakfast, lunch and afternoon snacks) in a Swedish pre-school, spinach soup was served for lunch. Some of the children did not want to eat their soup, so the teacher 'Monica' tells them about *Popeye* (a popular comic figure who gets big muscles and great strength by eating spinach) in order to motivate them (note that all names in this interaction are fictitious):

MONICA: Do you know what Popeye likes to eat, something that makes him strong?
GUSTAF (5 *years old*): I know! Spinach!
MONICA: Yeah, that's right Gustaf. Now, if you eat up your spinach I can measure your muscles afterwards and see if they became as big as Popeye's.
GUSTAV: In that case, I'll rather eat pancakes, just like Pippi Longstocking. And I don't think I'll need so much spinach since I've already became strong by wrestling.

In this interaction Monica tries to motivate the children to eat by presenting them with an expected ideal for boys that consists of big muscles and strong bodies. Perceived norms about strength and achievement were often used in the pre-schools to motivate children, especially boys, to eat in a way decided by adults. Children often tried to resist these norms set up by adults, negotiating, or as in Gustaf's case, adopting the rationality of the teacher. Gustaf clearly does not want to taste the spinach soup; instead he wants to eat pancakes and justifies his decision to the teacher by adopting the same strategy of using a fictional character that represents strength. Pippi Longstocking is an independent, competent and strong girl and one of the most admired figures for children in Sweden, who is known to eat pancakes in order to be strong. Gustaf skilfully mirrors the teacher's way of motivating him. Gustaf's resistance is based on using the teacher's rationality of a strong role model; however, in mentioning Pippi Longstocking he makes the case for something he wants to eat, that is pancakes rather than spinach.

Unfortunately Gustaf's comments will not be accepted, even if he follows the logic set up by the teacher. The children can never eat pancakes if they do not eat their spinach soup first – this is a non-negotiable rule or eating convention for children at this pre-school. The teacher's way of using strong hero figures as role models in order to get strong and big bodies is a sort of 'bait' that she uses to get children to eat certain food in what is deemed to be an appropriate 'healthy' order. Gustaf may already know this eating convention based on his previous experience of pre-school meal situations. However, in challenging the teacher, he discovers the flaw in the teacher's rationality. A strong and competent body is an ideal norm and an important way to achieve that for children is to obey the adults who are reminding them of the often unwritten but nonetheless powerful eating conventions that govern meal situations. Gustaf's attempt to negotiate what he ate challenges the rationality in the teacher's argumentation which thus becomes visible. A strong body is an ideal worth achieving at this pre-school and the way to accomplish the ideal was by eating up food chosen/selected by the teachers.

It was common in the study that the children, like Gustaf, protested and tried to negotiate pre-school eating conventions that involved eating their food, tasting everything and eating food in a certain order. I understand the fact that children showed such strong resistance to dominating norms during meal situations as the pressure to follow norms set up by adults was particularly strong in particular situations (Thurén, 1996). Power struggles and teachers' attempts to influence children's behaviour and make decisions over children's bodies were evident at both pre-schools in the wider study about boyishness and normality in pre-school (Hellman 2010).

The different views shared by teachers during interviews and observed in action meant that there was also evidence of negotiation and power struggles between teachers about rules in meal situations. Certain teachers claimed that children ought to eat particular foods or eat foods in a specific order according to the dominant rules at their pre-school. Other teachers believed that these rules were too restrictive and wanted freedom to interpret them. For this second group of teachers the most important thing was that the children gained a positive experience of eating together. The power struggles, whether between teachers or teachers and children, reveal firstly that pre-school teachers are expected, according to the curriculum, to promote democracy and to give children influence. Secondly, it emerged that eating together at pre-school is not only a matter of feeding hunger. Meal situations are also a practice filled with power structures where normality and rules for social relations are established and challenged.

Promoting idealised bodies for boys

As discussed earlier, norms for children in meal situations are linked to following adult rules which are directed towards both girls and boys. In addition to following adult rules that govern meal situations there were achievement norms about eating. Achievement norms linked boys to their future men's bodies, presenting as a goal the desirable position – namely to be a big and strong boy/man. This was illustrated when 'Tommy', the male teacher, was observed talking with the children at his table about eating mustard with the pea soup:

TOMMY (*placing mustard on his plate with his soup*): This is really hot stuff; you have to eat it together with your soup.

TED: What is it?

TOMMY: It's mustard. Try some! It's really something for big, strong and cool guys like me. (*Tommy flexes his biceps and points at each one of the older boys around the table.*)

TED: Yeah, right. (*He shows his biceps as well*) Yeah, this is stuff for strong boys like me and Tommy!

TOMMY: … Ludwig and … Emil.

EMIL AND LUDWIG: Yeah, I was also strong! (*Emil and Ludwig show their muscles and put some mustard in their soup. Kalle, a younger boy, is sitting close to the older boys and he's looking at the mustard without tasting it.*)

KALLE: Maybe I'll like some of that too then … Yeah, I'll have some!

TOMMY: That's my boy! Now when you were so brave, I'll bet your muscles have grown already. Let me see! Wow! Just like your older friends!

When norms about strength, size and achievement were emphasised, the boys were often the centre of attention. Tommy had the intention to make pea soup with mustard an attractive dish for the children and used a specific normative position in order to motivate them. Tommy's comments normalise strength and link it to boys and men, but by implication not to women and girls: 'This food is for strong boys,' says Tommy. He therefore creates a group of those brave enough to try the mustard – 'real strong boys'. Tommy also points at *certain boys* around the table, namely the oldest boys called 'big' who have an existing high status at the pre-school. Of importance here is to recognise the role of one's age as a power structure working together with hegemonic masculinity in order to create 'real boys' at this pre-school. To be counted as 'big/old' (the word 'big' [*stor*] refers in Swedish, especially when used by children, to age as well as size and a muscular body) is a very status-filled position and is here used as a way to create a popular 'we' group. Tommy not only includes himself but refers to the older boys at the table in the group of 'strong boys'. The five-year-old boys then showed that they were worthy to be included by repeating Tommy's actions and showing their muscles.

Masculinity research has studied how masculinity, normality and marginalisation are created in educational contexts (Connell 2000; Skelton 2001; Frosh *et al.* 2002) but more seldom among younger children. As such, a practice relevant for young children in terms of hegemonic masculinity production has not yet become visible. My study (Hellman 2010) confirms that meal situations, more than any other situation at pre-school, produced idealised norms about boys' and men's bodies. The strategies employed by teachers and the interaction occurring between pupils and teachers means those meal situations, more than any other situation at the pre-schools, were marginalising girls, as well as certain boys who did not fulfil the required norms about eating from the position of being viewed as 'big and strong'. Hence, when norms about boyishness are accentuated, actions and bodies are valued in relation to these norms, creating a normative field around 'real big boys'.

Johansson (2011a) discusses how men that uphold idealised and hegemonic norms about masculinity are at risk of either not being labelled as 'masculine' or 'falling down' in status if they do not manage to fulfil the required expectations. Even if individuals that perform body ideals in line with idealised norms achieve a status filled position, it is also important to notice that this is not done without certain risks of 'falling down' in position. Connell (2000) describes how idealised norms about how to behave as a boy always need to be re-established and guarded, even if you are ascribed a high status position like the boys in the earlier observation.

Norms about strength and achievement often influence other children in the meal situation. Sitting next to Tommy and the older boys were some younger boys who were clearly not included when Tommy talked about 'the big boys'. Throughout the observation the young boys watched Tommy and the older boys eating mustard and showing their muscles. The disjunction between themselves and other boys was evident; however, at the same time these presumptive 'big strong boys' were also learning how to behave. It might be the case that Tommy creates an attractive group between the older boys and himself, partly because he wants to motivate Kalle, one of the younger boys, to eat. Younger children and children that received comments from female and male teachers about having bodies that were 'too thin or weak' could only join or belong to the group if they ate the food required. In order to be included in the group they had to achieve certain behaviours, in this case to eat certain food. During this dinner Kalle achieved the requirement and therefore transgressed age categories by succeeding and managing to be part of the group of 'big strong boys'. Boys were expected to fulfil the norm as 'big and strong' and the norm was strongly directed towards them; if girls fulfilled it, they were often seen as an exception of the norm – even if it could be a positive exception.

To be or not to be a big strong boy?

To be strong and labelled as a 'real boy' is a position that has to be constantly maintained through repetitions in everyday practice. In the previous observation this was done through interactions between pupils and a male teacher. In the next observation, the labelling occurs during interactions between pupils and 'Sofia', a female teacher. The three boys who refused to eat what was required supposedly prevented them from becoming a big strong boy. During one meal, 'Anders' refused to taste the pea soup and was disciplined with a reference to the expected performance of a 'real' boy:

SOFIA: Anders, you really need to eat up your soup. You need more vitamins to grow and become big and strong. (*She puts her hands on Anders' biceps.*) You are just too tiny and skinny, dear. Try some soup and afterwards I'll give you a nice fruit for dessert.

KALLE (*leaning over to Sofia and Anders' table*): That's right, Anders. Have some mustard like me. Then you'll become really strong just like all of us big boys here at this table.

ANDERS: I don't want to. I have tried this soup hundreds of times and it still tastes awful. I'd rather have a fruit right now instead.

SOFIA: No, no my dear friend. Eat up your soup and then when all of it is inside your stomach I can take a close look and see if your muscles have become bigger, is that a deal?

The teacher has decided which food counts as healthy and she therefore insists that this is the food Anders needs to eat. Earlier I referred to the invoking of a role model in the form of the character Popeye. Another strategy was to compare children with the dominant and idealised norm; this is what happens when Anders is called 'thin and small' and compared unfavourably with 'the big strong boys'. Anders is denied access to being a 'big strong boy' because he does not follow expectations about eating up, and is therefore not able to demonstrate the norms about strength, size and achievement that are linked to boys in this situation. To have a body labelled as small, thin, weak or young results in marginalisation in terms of 'real' boyishness.

The observations in this chapter correlate with Thurén's (1996) thinking that the strength in which norms about gender are emphasised may shift in relation to space. According to Connell (2000) dominant norms about masculinity are accentuated when boys are disciplined. This is often done with a focus on how boys are supposed to behave as 'real' boys. For example, in meal situations among younger children in a pre-school it was the boys that were encouraged and expected to try food such as mustard or spinach based on its potential to make them strong. Other rationales were not used; for instance, Sofia does not tell Anders that vitamins will keep him healthy and help him to play for the whole day at pre-school. Instead, she tells him that he needs the vitamins so that he will become a big strong boy. Although he has not yet managed to fulfil this status, there is an expectation that he is to be a strong boy, and the option of not to be big and strong is not offered.

As I have discussed in this chapter, meal situations are when hegemonic masculinity is at risk of being produced by children themselves, by female teachers and by male teachers. *But why are these norms accentuated in meal situations?* Taking their starting point in two ordinary pre-schools, Johansson and Pramling-Samuelsson (2001) discuss two different teacher strategies at meal situations. The first is a strategy where the teacher's attention is directed towards how to get the children to eat their food, the emphasis being on rules at the dinner table.

The children do get fed but the situation, according to Johansson and Pramling-Samuelsson (2001), is mainly seen by the teachers as a caring situation and not as a learning situation on which they might reflect. The second strategy is when the teacher's focus is directed towards interacting with the child, answering their questions to enable them to appreciate the benefits of eating the food.

Interviews with pre-school teachers about power struggles at meals revealed how meals are seen as simply 'eating', a practice not connected to learning:

> [*Sofia:*] When I now read about what happened at dinnertime … what can I say; it's awful. But I didn't think. For me, I have always planned and thought through circle time and children's activities very carefully. But I guess I then just thought of meals as eating. My focus was just to try to make him eat up his food. I guess that I also got annoyed by the fact that he was arguing against manners at the dinner table.
>
> *(Field notes, 20 August 2010)*

In discussion with Sofia, she recognised that she did not think as she might have done in another situation. She also describes how she was annoyed that Anders was arguing. Johansson's (2011b) research about pre-school and learning shows how teachers' inter-subjectivity creates different opportunities for learning. Stress and situations that relate to routine and care are identified by Johansson as being at risk of creating spaces where teachers have difficulties interrelating with children and this makes it difficult to create inclusive learning spaces. Hellman (2011, 2012) also describes how stress, discipline, routine and traditional celebrations are spaces where gender stereotypes are reinforced and accentuated. An important reason for this is that teachers tend to have a low degree of self-reflection in caring contexts which are not controlled or monitored in the same way as the learning that happens within the curriculum.

Conclusions

To eat is an everyday practice that promotes gender norms that are at risk of being taken for granted. To question norms such as eating up and eating food in a certain order is to challenge or trivialise what parents, pre-school educators and the wider society may want children, and through them society, to adopt. Food in educational contexts is not only about eating and drinking but is also about the creation of specific subjects. In this chapter I have explained how communication between teachers and pupils during meal situations perpetuate hegemonic masculinities. I also suggest that age and the unequal hierarchies of power between adults and children have a big impact on the way rules in meal situations are constructed and the power and influence that they have over children's bodies.

Thurén (1996) points out how gender norms are demonstrated in practices with different strengths, and that they create a different hierarchy of influence. Meal situations create norms that boys should be big and strong and focus on boys' physical bodies far more than any other pre-school situation. When norms about strength and size were enforced the position of being big and strong was linked to boys and men and not towards girls and women. Also, as a big and strong boy, you were expected to achieve this ideal by eating, which thus became the mechanism through which you gained access to normality. This created pressure for all boys and men in the lunch room to acquire and maintain a position of being big and strong.

If the meal situation had been subject to the same scrutiny as a learning context rather than a caring situation the teachers may have reflected on what learning they wanted the children to achieve and adopted a different strategy. For instance, in the episode involving Anders, Sofia might have identified food which he could eat in the future to acquire the vitamins and benefits he would miss out on by not eating his peas. Just like in sport (Connell 2000), the body and what the body is expected to perform is the centre of attention in meal situations. The body, the most important marker for gender, must (when gender difference is reinforced) be gendered in order to be understandable. However, these processes of hegemonic dominance are often reformulated into something quite natural, even something good for the community (Skelton 2001). I have discussed the teachers' lack of situated reflexive practices in relation to this normalisation. Both female and male teachers produce hegemonic masculinity in meal situations. Rather than presenting femininity as the problem in caring situations like meals, I would like to point out the way teachers situated reflection is related to care and learning.

Meal situations are predominantly linked to care and not to learning. Even if teachers say that they are reflective in other situations, as in circle time, meals are seen as something outside the curriculum. If actions performed here are not seen as part of a teacher's obligation according to the curriculum, normalisation according to dominant masculinity and age are at risk of passing unseen or reformulated into the 'common sense'. It appears that there is a need to pay much more attention to practices of care and how the concept of care is operating in the educare context. While learning is discussed 'on its own' as well as together with care, care is still defined in a more vague way or as a 'combination' with learning in policy documents and in practice. This might be important since it seems that teachers link reflection to learning and care and routine to unreflective practices such as common sense. The principle of educare links learning with caring. Meal situations are clearly a site where not only should teachers encourage their children to eat with care but encourage each other, and acknowledge that there is a need to reflect on care as a context where unreflexive practice can perpetuate problematic gender stereotypes.

UNANSWERED QUESTIONS

- Why does eating become an achievement for children in general and boys in particular? Has it anything to do with norms about individuality in Swedish society and the most status-filled position for children in Sweden, the competent and independent child?
- Why is age such a strong power structure in educational contexts? Why are educational contexts seldom analysed through norms about age, childishness and adultness?
- Why is femininity, rather than teachers' lack of reflection, put forward in the media as 'the problem' for boys in pre-school?

References

Connell, R. W. (2000) *The Men and the Boys*. Cambridge: Polity.

Emilson, A. (2008) *Det önskvärda barnet. Fostran uttryckt i vardagliga kommunikationshandlingar mellan lärare och barn i förskolan*. Doktorsavhandling. Göteborg: Acta Universitatis Gothoburgensis.

Emilson, A. and Johansson, E. (2013) 'Participation and gender in circle time situations in pre-school', *International Journal of Early Years Education*, 21 (1): 56–69.

Frosh, S., Phoenix, A. and Pattman, R. (2002) *Young Masculinities: Understanding Boys in Contemporary Society*. Basingstoke: Palgrave.

Hellman, A. (2010) *Kan Batman vara rosa? Förhandlingar om pojkighet och normalitet på en förskola* (*Have You Ever Seen a Pink Batman? Negotiations of Gender and Normality at a Swedish Pre-school*), Gothenburg Studies in Educational Sciences 299. Akademisk avhandling. Göteborgs Universitet: Acta Universitatis Gothoburgensis.

Hellman, A. (2011) 'Gender learning in pre-school practices', in N. Pramling and I. Pramling (eds), *Educational Encounters: Nordic Studies in Early Childhood Didactics*. New York: Springer.

Hellman, A. (2012) 'Democracy among girls and boys in pre-school: inclusion and common projects', in E. Johansson (ed.), *Democracy, Solidarity and Individualism in Pre-School Practices*, Göteborgs Universitet: Acta Universitatis.

Johansson, T. (2011a) *Maskuliniteter – kritik, tendenser, trender* (*Masculinities – Critical Debates, Tendencies and Trends*). Stockholm: Liber.

Johansson, E. (2011b) *Möten för lärande. Pedagogisk verksamhet för de yngsta barnen i förskolan* (*Intersubjective Interactions in Early Childhood Education*), Skolverket. Stockholm: Fritzes.

Johansson, E. and Pramling-Samuelsson, I. (2001) 'Omsorg – en central aspekt av förskolepedagogiken, exemplet måltiden' ('Care – a central aspect of early childhood education, some examples from mealtimes'), *Pedagogisk Forskning i Sverige*, 6 (2): 81–101.

Månsson, A. (2011) 'Becoming a pre-school child: subjectification in toddlers during their introduction to pre-school, from a gender perspective', *International Journal of Early Childhood*, 43 (1): 7–22.

Nordberg, M., Saar, T. and Hellman, A. (2010) 'Deconstructing the normal boy: heterosexuality and gender constructions in school and pre-school', in L. Martinsson and E. Reimer (eds), *Norm Struggles: Sexualities in Contentions*. Newcastle: Cambridge Scholars Publishing.

Renolds, E. (2004) 'Other boys: negotiating non-hegemonic masculinity in the primary school', *Gender and Education*, 16 (2): 247–67.

Salih, S. and Butler, J. (eds) (2004) *The Judith Butler Reader*. Oxford: Blackwell.

Sanjek, R. (1990) *Field Notes. The Making of Anthropology*. New York: Cornell University Press.

Skelton, C. (2001) *Schooling the Boys: Masculinity and Primary Education*. Buckingham: Open University Press.

Skolverket (2010) *Läroplan för förskolan: Lpfö-98, reviderad 2010* (*Curriculum for Pre-school, Lpfö-98*, revised 2010). Stockholm: Utbildningsdepartementet, Regeringskansliet. Fritzes offentliga publikationer.

Thorne, B. (1993) *Gender Play: Girls and Boys in School*. Buckingham: Open University Press.

Thurén, B.-M. (1996) 'Om styrka, räckvidd och hierarki samt andra genusteoretiska begrepp', *Kvinnovetenskaplig tidskrift*, 3–4: 69–85.

Whitehead, S. M. (2002) *Men and Masculinities: Key Themes and New Directions*. Malden, MA: Polity.

6

GENDER IN PRE-SCHOOL AND CHILD-CENTRED IDEOLOGIES

A story from an Indonesian kindergarten

Vina Adriany

Introduction

For the last ten years, the practices of ECE in Indonesia have been influenced by Developmentally Appropriate Practices (DAP) principles. These new practices have, to some extent, occurred because of the change in the Indonesian political system. Since the downfall of Suharto's regime, Indonesia has been moving towards a more liberal and democratic society. The change in ECE in Indonesia might thus indicate the extent to which education is moving in the same direction (Newberry 2010).

DAP is closely associated with child-centred ideology. A child-centred approach is basically an education approach based on Piaget's (1954) theory, which describes basic stages of human development, generally universally perceived as having the same processes, irrespective of children's social or cultural background. What schools or adults can do, according to this line of thought, is to respect the stage of a child's development. This practice eventually leads to child-centred pedagogy (Burman 2008). Child-centred pedagogy itself is characterised by at least five key ideas (ibid.):

1. In order to be able to learn, children must be socially, emotionally and cognitively ready.
2. Education should respond to children's needs and interests.
3. In order for education to be effective, it needs to be designed in order to fulfil children's needs. Failure to meet those needs is understood to eventually lead to a malfunctioning in an individual's later development.
4. Learning for young children should be joyful and fun.
5. Learning should be based on children's personal experience.

A child-centred ideology has dominated the field of ECE and many practitioners believe that this ideology views young children in a more democratic and humanistic way (MacNaughton 2000; Browne 2004; Burman 2008). Consequently, the child-centred approach has been widely welcomed across the globe, including Indonesia. To some extent, the implementation of child-centred education in Indonesia was introduced by globally corporate enterprises

(Newberry 2010). The American Center for Childhood Research and Training (ACCRT), a research centre that initiated Beyond Center and Circle Times (BCCT) programmes, brought it to Indonesia. Originally introduced by a non-governmental organisation (NGO), the BCCT was, with government endorsement, implemented in most of Indonesia's ECE (Newberry 2010). The key element in BCCT is a child who is self-directed and self-disciplined and whose education is driven by play-based approaches (Newberry 2010). This element of BCCT echoes the basic principles of DAP. Hence, in this context, a new type of child is created in Indonesian society: one who is playful, rational, middle-class and also adapts to global values.

However, playing devil's advocate, one could ask the question: *What is missing in the welcome of the child-centred approach?* To answer this, I would argue that the welcome has overlooked the fact that by emphasising the 'naturalness' of child development the child-centred approach has marginalised particular issues, such as gender and power, in the field of ECE. It is, as Yelland (1998) points out, the field of ECE which in general has often disregarded the issue of gender. Many practitioners in ECE often assume that this issue is not important. This may be due to the way children have been constructed in ECE. Despite the fact that the child-centred ideology promotes children as active individuals, it believes that children's development needs to undergo certain stages. Each developmental stage has its own milestones, and understanding gender issues is not yet considered to be part of the developmental milestones for ECE children (MacNaughton 2000). As a result, despite the fact that it plays an important role in children's lives, gender is not considered to be part of an ECE curriculum in most countries (Davies 1993, 1999, 2003; Warin 1998; MacNaughton 2000; Connolly 2004).

The marginalisation of gender issues from ECE often inhibits individuals from achieving their full potential. Miu (2005) also asserts that existing gender discourses often include an imbalance in power relations that potentially marginalises some groups of children. MacNaughton (2000: 2) also believes that neglecting gender issues in ECE will 'naturalise gendered violence and aggression between boys and girls and between boys and their teachers'. In the long term, ignoring gender in ECE might result in restricted career options for individuals (Miu 2005). In addition to this, Alloway (cited in Martinez 1998) also argues that gender issues have been stifled from ECE, indicating an official silence on gender issues in the larger social context. In Indonesia, for example, the government has started to introduce gender issues into the school curriculum by passing a law that requires all schools to implement a gender-based curriculum. However, the law is only regulated in primary school upwards. Again, this might indicate that gender issues continue to be stifled in ECE.

The research reported on in this chapter was conducted in an ECE institution in Bandung, Indonesia. Studies of gender construction in ECE in Indonesia have been very limited. Again, this might be because gender is not regarded as a fundamental issue in ECE. Furthermore, most of the research on gender in ECE in Indonesia has not directly observed young children. For example, research conducted about pre-school children by Yulindrasari and McGregor (2011) was not conducted in a school setting as their research investigated how gendered parenting was constructed in an Indonesian parenting magazine. One research project that was conducted in a school setting was by Suyatno (2004). His research attempted to demonstrate the extent to which an Indonesian kindergarten's policy and curriculum were gendered, but again this research did not directly observe young children. Therefore, this chapter hopes to provide an international perspective on gender issues in ECE.

In this chapter, I will also aim to further question the child-centred ideology by showing evidence from my research that aims to elaborate how gender ideology is embodied within the child-centred approach. I will attempt to demonstrate how the child-centred ideology consists of gendered elements and how these elements also involve the issue of power relations.

Child-centred ideology

Child-centred ideology is rooted in the early work of Froebel, Dewey and Montessori (Bryant and Clifford 1992; Cuban 1992; Montessori 1995; Dewey 1998; Cossentino 2005). Their work all situates young children as active individuals who follow certain stages of development. This approach was further illuminated by the work of Piaget who argued that the stages of a child's development occur universally, irrespective of the child's social, economic, racial or cultural background (Piaget 1971; Smith et al. 1997). Piaget's theory is often interpreted as implying that a child's developmental stages should be respected by non-interfering adults (Walkerdine 1998). For example, each developmental stage has different milestones and adults should not attempt to go beyond them.

It can be interpreted from these frameworks that young children are situated as active yet passive individuals (Walkerdine 1998; Burman 2008). They are considered active individuals as each child can construct their own knowledge without interference from adults. At the same time, the child-centred approach also sees young children as passive individuals because, in order for them to develop fully, they have to wait until they are emotionally, socially and cognitively ready (Burman 2008). Hence, children's development is also interpreted by some as a period of waiting. It has to be noted, however, that while it was Piaget who argued that young children have a limited intellectual grasp, others have extended his theory to areas such as gender that Piaget himself probably never considered (Short 1994).

The contradiction within the child-centred approach suggests that children's individual interest and freedom determines the successfulness of learning. In order for learning to be effective, education must be designed in accordance with the children's needs. Failure to meet these needs will result in children developing incorrectly (Burman 2008). However, feminist poststructuralist theories began to question many assumptions of the child-centred theory. Many believe that a child-centred ideology only benefits white, middle-class children (Walkerdine 1998; MacNaughton 2000; Burman 2008). This is because early experiments with child-centred theories were conducted with white middle-class children. To use the results of these experiments as a universal norm for all children is thus perceived as problematic. By doing this, child-centred ideology has become a regime of truth which, at its heart, suggests that there is only one way for a child to develop and to go through childhood (MacNaughton 2005; Ryan and Grieshaber 2005; Tzuo 2007; Burman 2008). However, the poststructuralist approach challenges this assumption by arguing that there is no such thing as the child. As Dahlberg et al. (2007: 43) affirm, 'there are many children and many childhoods, each constructed by our understanding of childhood and what children are and should be.' In other words, children and childhood are always produced and reproduced in a particular context.

Another critique of the child-centred approach is that it often overlooks the issue of power relations in the classroom (Davies 1993, 2003; Browne 2004). Predicated on certain assumptions of the child as a free individual, the child-centred theory states that adults or teachers should not interfere in children's activities (MacNaughton 2000; Browne 2004). However, positioning teachers as passive adults will, in fact, perpetuate dominant gender discourses in the classroom when actually teachers could have the power to challenge existing discourses. Research conducted by Browne (2004) also indicates the extent to which teachers are able to use their power in order to bring some gender implication to their daily teaching. A teacher could indeed raise gender issues in their daily teaching.

MacNaughton (2000) has also questioned the extent to which the child-centred ideology is gender neutral. While many practitioners continue to see the ideology as an approach that does not promote particular gender norms and values, MacNaughton believes that it is, in fact, gendered as it maintains and sustains particular gender norms and values that support a binary opposition between males and females in society. Very often in ECE settings, girls show their interest in playing with dolls or selecting pink clothing while boys demonstrate their interest in playing with cars or wearing blue clothing. These are perceived as the children's interests and are restricted by the principle of a child-centred approach; teachers are unwilling to challenge these because to do so may disrespect what children want, an attitude that would be seen to violate the child-centred principle. MacNaughton (2000) and Connolly (2003) have pointed out possible tensions that result from the child-centred ideology, where teachers face the dilemma of whether to challenge children's constructions of traditional binaries or to simply follow and allow whatever the children want to do. MacNaughton (2000: 2) also summarises several discussions about the ideology posed by feminist poststructuralist researchers. In general, she argues that feminist perspective theories believe that 'the innocent and naturalness of childhood is a myth; child-centred pedagogy regulates rather than frees the child; and gender politics flourish in developmentally appropriate programs'. The child-centred ideology has also been criticised for its emphasis on the individual where it perceives the self as an independent being who can achieve self-development, a view which prioritises the flourishing of the individual self in isolation from others. Child-centred theory has also been contested because it tends to subordinate girls. As Connolly (2003: 116) elaborates:

> This model of children's self-directed learning tends to privilege the needs and interest of boys, and conversely, tends to deny and subjugate those of girls. At the heart of this model is the view of the child as a 'little scientist' – naturally inquisitive about their immediate social environment and forever exploring and experimenting with it. This construction of the child as active, assertive and confident reflects the stereotypical traits traditionally associated with males and masculinity.

The process in which child-centred ideology becomes a regime of truth is often established through the process of normalisation. My understanding of normalisation is faithful to the poststructuralist framework that guided my research. I am aware that in ECE the term 'normalisation' often refers to the work of Montessori, in which she regards the concept of normalised children as the ultimate goal of education (Cossentino 2005). The normalised children in Montessori's work possess four characteristics: a love of work, concentration, self-discipline and sociability (Prybylska n.d.). Therefore, a teacher's task in ECE is to correct any deviant behaviour shown by the children. In this research, however, I am using Foucault's (1980) concept of normalisation. Normalisation here refers to the process of comparing the behaviour of a child with that of the developmental norms. For example, a teacher in ECE will judge whether a three-year-old girl has reached her developmental milestones using their professional knowledge. Normalisation functions as a modern disciplinary power that involves the process of 'invoking, requiring, setting, or conforming to a standard-defining normal' (Gore 1998: 237). Here, the normalisation process is used in order to establish the child-centred discourse as the only way to understand children's development in ECE. A process of normalisation is used in order to replace the use of punishment. Thus the children and the teachers are governed, not through the use of repressive discipline but through a process of normalisation (Gore 1993; MacNaughton 2005).

The research

The research adopts an ethnographic approach. In this research, the data were collected using participatory observation, field notes, informal interviews, analysis of school documents and image analysis. However, by the ethnographic nature of the study, the main feature of data collection was observation recorded in field notes. In total, I spent eight months 'in the field', spending more than 600 hours in the research setting. The school that I visited was a kindergarten – *Kopo Kindergarten*. The school adopted a BCCT approach. In my interview with the school's owner it was revealed that the BCCT approach had initially been used by an elite, private school in Jakarta. Here they found that the BCCT model could improve the development of pupils in their school. They then managed to persuade the Indonesian Ministry of Education to franchise the model and implement it in all kindergartens in Indonesia.

A married couple owns the school, which, in terms of staff, consists of a principal, four teachers, a cleaner and 28 pupils ranging over three educational levels: the play group level for children between two and four years of age, kindergarten for children between four and five years of age, and B Level kindergarten for children between five and six years of age. Almost all of the children came from a middle-class background as indicated by their parents' profession. The school, however, implemented a subsidised policy for children from poorer families.

Research findings

The process of normalisation

Gender ideology in the school was maintained through a process of normalisation. In this process, children's behaviour was normalised through a developmental gaze. In the school, normalisation refers to a process of comparing a child's behaviour with the developmental norms. The concept of normalisation can also be understood as a process by which the school constructs an idealised set of behaviours. Part of the teachers' care is to ensure that every child's development should follow certain developmental milestones, and any attempts to deviate from the developmental pathway are seen to disadvantage the child. According to the *Kopo Kindergarten*'s school documents, developmental milestones are divided into seven aspects: positive moral and religious aspects, science, socio-emotional aspects, fine and gross motor skills, cognitive capacity, independence, and language and communication.

The children's development is evaluated through a process of recording, observing, classifying and judging. The evaluation process illustrates the process of evaluation within child-centred discourse, creating norms against which all children are judged (Greene 1999). A child who follows these developmental milestones is considered to be 'normal' and, thus, those who cannot subscribe to these norms are regarded as 'abnormal' or 'the other'. Children who do not conform to the norms are seen as deviant and, consequently, non-conforming children from different cultural and racial backgrounds will be seen as 'different'. Children who show non-conforming gendered behaviour will obviously be excluded from the category of normal children. Gender development is not discussed in the school's documentation and is entirely absent from the school's consideration of socio-emotional development. While it can be assumed that the school appears to establish a gender-neutral policy, the absence of gender development in its documentation can also be perceived as a silencing of gender issues, perhaps because they are considered to be unimportant in ECE (Browne 2004).

The normalisation process in the school had created a binary between normal and abnormal children. This was particularly evident when gender discourses in the school were taken into account. I will explain more about how gender discourse was used as part of the normalisation process in the section below.

'The Princess': the production of femininity and masculinity

At the start of this chapter I showed that many practitioners in ECE believe that ECE is gender-neutral. I, however, contest this belief in light of my findings. Gender discourses in the school were situated within a femininity and masculinity discourse. I am writing this section with an awareness that this may suggest there existed a binary between femininity and masculinity. I did not take this as a given state, but my analysis of the data does suggest a binary opposition between boys and girls that occurred in the school, with the children participating in creating the binary. Both Blaise (2005) and Haywood and Mac an Ghaill (2012) have argued that certain forms of femininity are produced in relation to certain forms of masculinity. Therefore it is important for us to try to understand why such creation takes place. Efforts will be made below to identify why such production occurred and how the construction of femininity and masculinity were exercised, negotiated and contested by the children.

Within the femininity discourses found in the school were those associated with 'the princess'. In my research, the children used 'princess' interchangeably with Barbie. It appears that, for the children, the princess is Barbie and Barbie is the princess. This is probably because of the same characteristics possessed by both the princess and Barbie. The princess and Barbie discourses were a signifier for girlhood that illuminated femininity and was considered a fundamental element of being a girl. The discourse was reiterated every day in the school, particularly during the morning and playtime. The pervasiveness of the princess discourse can be seen in the following field notes (all names are fictional):

> In the dining room, Ita brings her collection of four Barbies. She names all her Barbies Mariposa. Nadya tells me that she has six Barbies at home. She names them Mariposa, Alexa, Rosela, Aneka, Erica and Rapunzel. Ajeng tells me that she too has six Barbies at home. Their names are Arieka, Cinderella, Princess Barbie, Elena, Wonderful Princess and Gendut (Fatty). I ask Ajeng why she names her last Barbie Fatty. She says because this Barbie is from her friend. Nadya says that fat is not a beautiful thing for a Barbie.

I ask Ajeng if this Barbie is really fat. Ajeng says it's not really fat, but, since she doesn't really like it, then she calls it Gendut (Fatty).

(Field notes, 25 November 2011)

The notes above demonstrate the extent to which the princess discourse was taken up by the girls in the school. In the construction of the princess discourse, it was obvious that it had been reiterated on a daily basis and shared collectively by the children, and had become a key point for any girl to become a member of the group.

While the princess discourse worked to establish membership among the girls, it also became a tool to create otherness, particularly among the boys. For example, the girls in the school had the power to situate the boys who played or even just talked about *Barbies* in school as 'other'. These boys were seen as others by the girls. The girls challenged the boys verbally by harassing them and by excluding them from the play (see field notes below). In choice time, I joined three girls in the tree house. Their names, for the purposes of this chapter, are Winda, Ita and Ajeng. Ita and Ajeng bring along their Barbie dolls. Indra is about to climb into the tree house when Ita raises her voice and asks him not to enter the house. Ita says the house is forbidden for boys today. I engage in a conversation with the girls:

VA: Can I play here with you?
AJENG: Yes, of course Bunda.
VA: And can Indra play with us too?
AJENG *(ALMOST SHOUTS)*: No, Bunda! Boys don't play Barbie.
VA: Really?
WINDA: My brother plays Barbie with me sometimes.
VA: I see.
ITA *(SHOUTING)*: No, boys don't play Barbie.
VA: Why?
ITA: I told you, Bunda. Then, they will become like girls.
VA: But, Winda's brother plays with Barbie.
WINDA *(SOFTENS HER VOICE)*: No, he doesn't.
VA: Erm … so what do boys play with?
ITA: A pistol. Not a real pistol, a toy one.
VA: Can girls play pistol, too?
WINDA: Only when it looks like a dolphin.
AJENG: But it's better to play princess stick.

(Field notes, 3 November 2011)

The situation where boys were constructed as 'the other' due to their interest in princess toys is evident if we take the example of Ardi, a four-year-old boy who deliberately showed his attraction to the princess. Very often, Ardi's behaviour was challenged and corrected by the teachers and the other children in the school, as shown in the following notes:

In the circle session, as usual, Bunda Sari asks the children about their feelings. Ardi tells her that he feels so happy because he will go to the shop to buy shoes with princess characters. Bunda Sari looks surprised with the answer. Ardi is one of the most aggressive boys in the class who often kicks and pushes his friends. Kiki, a four-year-old girl, also looks surprised. She says that princess shoes are only for girls, not for boys. Kiki wonders why Ardi does not understand that.

(Field notes, 18 August 2010)

The teachers' and children's responses to Ardi's interest in Barbies and princesses indicated how the school had become a site for normalisation: 'that is, they are places in which the idea of how the "normal" child is constructed' (Paechter 2007: 61). Part of the normalisation process was how boys and girls in the school learned how to become a proper boy or girl. One of the gender rules in this school was obvious: boys did not play Barbie. Barbie has, indeed, become an icon for femininity (Kane 2006). Ardi's interest in Barbie dolls and princesses was, therefore, seen as 'sissy behaviour' that needed to be regulated and normalised. The other children in the school consistently policed Ardi's behaviour when he did not display the correct form of masculinity. The acceptable form of masculinities in the school was related to aggressive behaviour among the boys. The boys would enact any behaviour as long as it was not related to princess stuff. It was evident that in the school femininity and masculinity were constructed in relation to each other.

The teachers at *Kopo Kindergarten* also believed that gender construction was the result of a child's socialisation. This is an essential part of gender discourse within the child-centred approach (Yelland 1998; Kamler, 1999; MacNaughton 2000). Here, a child's gender construction is simply the result of copying their peers or adults. This was evident when the teachers talked about Ardi. Ardi is cared for by his grandmother and an aunt as both his parents work long hours. According to Ardi's grandmother, it was better that Ardi was left with them since his parents often came home very late at night and he only saw them at the weekend. The teachers, Bunda Siti in particular, believed that Ardi's behaviour was the result of being raised by female-only carers. In other words, Ardi's tendency to like princesses and Barbies was the result of a feminisation of parenting; in other words, the parenting practices of his grandmother and auntie were not suitable for Ardi. The teachers had obviously highlighted the role of socialisation in ECE. The teachers also tolerated Ardi's behaviour by explaining that he did not really understand it. The teachers perceived his behaviour as an indication of his level of immaturity.

When the children are asked about their feelings, Winda says she feels happy because she has just been given a new Barbie doll. Ardi says he feels so happy because he wants to buy a new Barbie doll. This answer from Ardi elicits laughter among the other pupils and the teachers. Teacher Sari looks surprised and asks him, 'A Barbie doll for you?' Ria says a Barbie doll is not for boys, it is only for girls. Winda also confirms that it is exclusively only for girls. Kiki wonders why Ardi doesn't know about this. Teacher Sari tells Winda that Ardi does not understand this yet.

(Field notes, 6 October 2010)

The teacher's statement also shows an influence of the child-centred approach, since children are not considered as being able to comprehend the idea of gender consistency (Woolfolk *et al.* 2008). Ardi's behaviour, then, is normalised by the teachers as part of his developmental milestones.

The power of play

The construction of femininity and masculinity in the school is the result of a broader discourse of play. Play is a fundamental concept within the child-centred theory where it is perceived as a right of the child. In *Kopo Kindergarten*, the teachers repeatedly said that the children learn while playing. One of the principles of the child-centred theory asserts that learning should be both joyful and playful. Consequently, any teacher who fails to include play in their teachings will be considered a bad teacher (Connolly 2003). While the concept of playing appears to be harmless, it is within play that gender construction often flows freely. Teachers are unable to challenge gender constructions that take place during playtime, because they might be seen as interfering with children's learning and development. This was evident in my research. In an interview with the school's principal, I found that the teachers in the school were actually reluctant to accept the pervasiveness of the princess play among the girls. They believed that the princess dolls and play taught girls to be consumers, since they had to purchase everything. However, the teachers did not want to challenge this because they were afraid that they might be seen as disrespectful toward the children, an attitude that goes against child-centred principles, as shown in the following interview extract with one of the teachers:

> We just want to facilitate what our pupils want. Like Barbie stuff, we don't initiate that. Princess stuff … (pause). They are so materialistic because we have to provide the clothes, accessories and everything else (laughs).

The concept of play not only prevents the teachers from interfering with the construction of the princess but it also inhibits the teachers from challenging aggressive behaviours among the boys. Even though it was one of the school rules that children should not behave aggressively by kicking, hitting or fighting, the teachers approved these behaviours if they were conducted in a play situation. The boys were often engaged in superhero play that involved aggressive behaviour. By granting children's aggressive behaviour in this form of play, the teachers seemed to glorify play as something useful and ideal for the children. Therefore, as Burman (2008: 265) argues, they ignored 'the coercive, cruel and dangerous aspects of many forms of play'. The pervasiveness of princess and Barbie discourse and the teachers' tolerance towards boys' aggressive behaviour illustrate how the teachers tended to overlook the fact that play always involved gendered power relations (Gagen 2000; Harker 2005).

Conclusions

My findings suggest that the child-centred discourse has inevitably sustained gender regimes in the school. It is evident that school can become an institution that controls both children and teachers. It controls the teachers because they are often unable to exercise their agency as they are continually subjected to regimes of supervision from the school and, therefore, perpetuate existing gender discourses. As I have elaborated in the Introduction, introducing gender issues into ECE could help eradicate sexism and discrimination. Therefore, if the teachers could not challenge the gender discourses in the classroom, these could become barriers in themselves. Thus, in order to avoid this situation, I suggest schools must first give more space for teachers to exercise their agency. If schools promote the child as an active individual who can construct their own meanings, I recommend that teachers also need to be constructed as active individuals. Situating teachers as active individuals will enable them to critically examine the power relations embodied within the child-centred discourse. By developing more critical ways of perceiving child-centred discourse, teachers would be able to negotiate their role in challenging children's gender construction without feeling the guilt of being disloyal to the child-centred discourse. I am not suggesting, as the phrase goes, 'throwing the baby out with the bathwater'; I do acknowledge the positive value within child-centred discourse, but at the same time, I think it is important to recognise the control the child-centred discourse can potentially elicit. My critique of child-centred discourse is derived from the fact that it has become a regime of truth, the only way to understand child development.

However, simply challenging the child-centred approach will not be sufficient if teachers themselves already have gender discourse embodied in their thinking. In my findings, I have presented the story of Ardi whose behaviour was often 'polished' and corrected by the teachers. It does suggest that, even when teachers use their power, they often use it to uphold dominant gender discourse. Thus it is important to first deconstruct teachers' gender ideology, and the first step to doing this could be by emphasising the issue of gender as part of teacher training programmes (TTPs).

The invitation to see child-centred discourse in a more critical way is also a call for reform in TTPs. TTPs should welcome other theories of child development as well as child-centred practices. Edwards *et al.* (2009: 55) have suggested teachers and practitioners in ECE should use what they call a post-developmentalism approach in ECE. By post-developmentalism, they mean 'theoretical movements that have been used to question modernist assumptions of truth, universality and certainty, with respect to children's learning and development in early childhood education and care'. Post-developmentalism enables teachers to question the current practices of ECE that are characterised by child-centred discourse and developmentalism. It allows teachers to use multiple perspectives and theory in understanding children's development.

Post-developmentalism is a multiple approach in nature and encompasses many perspectives and theories. Blaise (2013: 118–24) asserts that post-developmentalism perspectives include poststructuralism, queer theory, post-humanism, girlhood and masculinity studies, postcolonialism and post-Confucianism. Each perspective offers a new way of understanding children's development. However, in order for a school to be able to implement these, schools must first acknowledge the importance of bringing gender issues into ECE. This, in Indonesia and probably anywhere else, is a challenge in itself since not many schools have such awareness. In 2008, the Indonesian government passed Ministry of Education Regulations No. 84 (Year 2008) about Gender Mainstreaming in Education. However, the law only regulates primary schools upwards. Gender issues are still stifled by Indonesia's Ministry of Education policy. The Ministry of Education Regulations No. 58/2009 regarding standards for ECE elaborate as well as regulate the practice of ECE in Indonesia in terms of:

1. Children's developmental milestone standards
2. Educators' and teachers' standards
3. Process and evaluation standards
4. Facilities, management and financing standards.

However, even in points 1 and 2, gender issues are not mentioned in the policy.

Even though gender has often been overlooked in ECE curricula, changes can be initiated by teachers, even though most teachers who are confined by child-centred discourse tend to perceive pre-school children as yet unready to understand issues such as gender (MacNaughton 2000; Browne 2004; Martin 2011). Research by Davies (1993) indicates the extent to which teachers can invite the children to challenge existing gender discourses in the school, while in Korea Yoon (2007) also showed the extent to which teachers could involve children in discussing various types of masculinities and femininities. Another research study conducted by Blaise (2009) also describes the process by which she invited young children to talk about different forms of femininities and sexualities. Her research not only showed that pre-school children were capable of discussing such issues, but also illuminated the teachers' role in introducing different constructions of gender to children.

Teachers need to realise that expanding children's understanding of gender does not mean disrespecting their best interests. As Davies (1987) and Warin (1998) both propose, teachers need to keep a balance between respecting children's need to sustain their gender identity while, at the same time, providing the possibility for them to expand their knowledge of gender construction.

UNANSWERED QUESTIONS

- To what extent can teachers challenge children's gender construction while at the same time remaining respectful of children's interests?
- How can teachers ensure that moving beyond a child-centred approach does not automatically mean becoming a teacher-centred approach? In other words, how can teachers be aware of their own power when dealing with young children?
- How can teachers translate post-developmentalism in teaching pre-school children?

References

Blaise, M. (2005) 'A feminist poststructuralist study of children "doing" gender in an urban kindergarten classroom', *Early Childhood Research Quarterly*, 20 (1): 85–108.

Blaise, M. (2009) '"What a girl wants, what a girl needs": responding to sex, gender, and sexuality in the early childhood classroom', *Journal of Research in Childhood Education*, 23 (4): 450–60.

Blaise, M. (2013) 'Gender discourse and play', in E. Brooker, M. Blaise and S. Edwards (eds), *The Sage Handbook of Play and Learning in Early Childhood*. London: Sage, pp. 115–27.

Browne, N. (2004) *Gender Equity in the Early Years*. Berkshire: Open University Press.

Bryant, D. M. and Clifford, R. M. (1992) '150 years of kindergarten: how far have we come?', *Early Childhood Research Quarterly*, 7 (2): 147–54.

Burman, E. (2008) *Deconstructing Developmental Psychology*. East Sussex: Routledge.

Connolly, P. (2003) 'Gendered and gendering spaces', in C. Skelton and B. Francis (eds), *Boys and Girls in the Primary Classroom*. Berkshire: Open University Press, pp. 113–33

Connolly, P. (2004) *Boys and Schooling in the Early Years*. London: RoutledgeFalmer.

Cossentino, J. (2005) 'Ritualising expertise: a non-Montessorian view of the Montessori Method', *American Journal of Education*, 111 (2): 211–44.

Cuban, L. (1992) 'Why some reforms last: the case of the kindergarten', *American Journal of Education*, 100 (2): 166–94.

Dahlberg, G., Moss, P. and Pence, A. (2007) *Beyond Quality in Early Childhood Education and Care: Language of Evaluation*, 3rd edn. New York: Falmer Press.

Davies, B. (1987) 'The accomplishment of genderedness in pre-school children', in A. Pollard (ed.), *Children and Their Primary School. A New Perspective*. London: Falmer.

Davies, B. (1993) *Shards of Glass: Children Reading and Writing Beyond Gendered Identities*. Cresskill, NJ: Hampton Press.

Davies, B. (1999) 'What is feminist poststructuralist research? Examining texts of childhood', in B. Kamler (ed.), *Constructing Gender and Difference*. Cresskill, NJ: Hampton Press.

Davies, B. (2003) *Frogs and Snails and Feminist Tales*. Cresskill, NJ: Hampton Press.

Dewey, J. (1998) *Experience and Education*, 60th Anniversary Edition. West Lafayette, IN: Kappa Delta Pi.

Edwards, S., Blaise, M. and Hammer, M. (2009) 'Beyond developmentalism? Early childhood teachers' understandings of multiage grouping in early childhood education and care', *Australasian Journal of Early Childhood*, 34 (4): 55–63.

Foucault, M. (1980) *Michael Foucault: Power Knowledge*. Hertfordshire: Harvester Wheatsheaf.

Gagen, E. A. (2000) 'Playing the part: performing gender in America's playground', in S. L. Holloway and G. Valentine (eds), *Children's Geographies: Playing, Living, Learning*. London: Routledge, pp. 213–29.

Gore, J. M. (1993) *The Struggle for Pedagogies: Critical and Feminist Discourse as Regimes of Truth*. New York and London: Routledge.

Gore, J. M. (1998) 'Disciplining bodies: on the continuity of power relations in pedagogy', in T. S. Popkewirz and M. Brennan (eds), *Foucault's Challenge: Discourse, Knowledge, and Power in Education*. New York: Teachers College Press, pp. 231–54.

Greene, S. C. (1999) 'New directions in child development: old themes, new direction', in M. Woodhead, D. Faulkner and K. Littleton (eds), *Making Sense of Social Development*. London: Routledge, pp. 250–68.

Hammersley, M. and Atkinson, P. (2007) *Ethnography: Principles in Practices*, 3rd edn. New York: Routledge.

Harker, C. (2005) Playing and affective time-spaces. *Children's Geographies*, 3(1), 47–62.

Haywood, C. and Mac an Ghaill, M. (2012) '"What's next for masculinity?" Reflexive directions for theory and research on masculinity and education', *Gender and Education*, 24 (6): 577–92.

Indonesian Ministry of Education (2009) *Policy No. 58 Year 2009 About Standards for Early Childhood Education, 58 CFR*.

Kamler, B. (1999). *Constructing Gender and Difference. Critical Research Perspective on Early Childhood*. New Jersey: Hampton Press.

Kane, E. W. (2006) '"No way my boys are going to be like that!" Parents' responses to children's gender nonconformity', *Gender and Society*, 20 (2): 149–76.

MacNaughton, G. (2000) *Rethinking Gender in Early Childhood Education*. Sydney: Allen & Unwin.

MacNaughton, G. (2005) *Doing Foucault in Early Childhood Studies*. Oxford and New York: Routledge.

Martin, B. (2011) *Children at Play: Learning Gender in the Early Years*. London: Trentham Books.

Martinez, L. (1998) 'Gender equity policies and early childhood education', in N. Yelland (ed.), *Gender in Early Childhood*. London: Routledge.

Miu, L. (2005) 'Exploring Teachers' Understanding and Practice of Gender Equity: Case Study of a Kindergarten in Hong Kong'. Dissertation presented as part fulfilment of the requirements of the degree of Master of Education, University of Hong Kong, Hong Kong. [Online.] Available at: http://hdl.handle.net/10722/25711 (accessed 5 January 2015).

Montessori, M. (1995) *The Absorbent Mind*, revised edn. New York: Owl Books.

Newberry, J. (2010) 'The global child and non-governmental governance of the family in post-Suharto Indonesia', *Economy and Society*, 39 (3): 403–26.

Paechter, C. (2007) *Being Boys Being Girls: Learning Masculinities and Femininities*. Berkshire: Open University Press.

Piaget, J. (1954) *The Construction of Reality in the Child*. New York: Basic Books.

Piaget, J. (1971) *Psychology and Epistemology*. Harmondsworth: Penguin.

Prybylska, N. (n.d.). *Normalization of a Child in the Montessori System*. [Online.] Available at: http://pmswebsite.fatcow.com/teacherarticles/Prybylska,Normalization.pdf (accessed 2 February 2013).

Ryan, S. and Grieshaber, S. (2005) 'Shifting from developmental to postmodern practices in early childhood teacher education', *Journal of Teacher Education*, 56 (1): 34–45.

Short, G. (1994) 'Children's grasp of controversial issues', in M. Woodhead, P. Light and R. Carr (eds), *Growing Up in a Changing Society*. London: Open University, pp. 333–50.

Smith, L., Dockrell, J. and Tomlinson, P. (1997) *Piaget, Vygotsky and Beyond*. London: Routledge.

Suyatno, M. (2004) *Analisis Kesenjangan Jender pada Aspek Kebijakan, Kurikulm dan Sumberdaya Manusia pada Pendidikan Taman Kanak-kanak (TK): Studi di Kota Semarang-Jawa Tengah (Analysis of Gender Gap in the Policy, Curriculum and Human Resources of Early Childhood Education: A Study in Semarang-Central Java)*. Pusat Penelitian Gender/PSW Universitas Dipenogoro, Semarang.

Tzuo, P. W. (2007) 'The tension between teacher control and children's freedom in a child-centred classroom: resolving the practical dilemma through a closer look at the related theories', *Early Childhood Education Journal*, 35 (1): 33–9.

Walkerdine, V. (1998) 'Developmental psychology and the child-centred pedagogy: the insertion of Piaget into early education', in J. Henriques, W. Holloway, C. Urwin, C. Venn and V. Walkerdine (eds), *Changing the Subject: Psychology, Social Regulation, and Subjectivity*. London: Routledge, pp. 153–202.

Warin, J. (1998) 'The Role of Gender in the Development of the Young Child's Sense of Self Within the Social Context of Early School Experiences'. Unpublished PhD thesis, Lancaster University, Lancaster.

Woolfolk, A., Hughes, M. and Walkup, V. (2008) *Psychology in Education*. Harlow: Pearson Education.

Yelland, N. (1998) *Gender in Early Childhood*. London: Routledge.

Yoon, J. (2007) 'A Case Study of Korean Girls' Constructions of Girlhood in a Kindergarten Class'. Unpublished PhD thesis, University of Texas at Austin, Texas, USA.

Yulindrasari, H. and McGregor, K. (2011) 'Contemporary discourses of motherhood and fatherhood in *Ayahbunda*, a middle-class Indonesian parenting magazine', *Marriage and Family Review*, 47 (8): 605–24.

7

TEACHERS' BELIEFS, NORMS AND VALUES OF GENDER EQUALITY IN PRE-SCHOOLS

Ingrid Granbom

Introduction

The majority of children in Sweden take part in pre-school activities which suggests that the pre-school environment plays an important role in children's everyday experiences. The Swedish curriculum for pre-schools (Skolverket 98/2010: 4) claims that '[t]he pre-school should counteract traditional gender patterns and gender roles.' However, pre-school teachers' interpretations of the curriculum are based on the beliefs, norms and values of society, concerning, among other things, equality between genders. This chapter explores the complex and dynamic knowledge involved in pre-school teachers' construction of meaning concerning pre-schools as an arena for equality. Pre-schools should actively promote gender equality in their work with children and this chapter reveals some of the difficulties that pre-school teachers face in their quest to complete the directives of the curriculum.

Drawing on data from the author's research (Granbom 2011), this chapter focuses on how shared knowledge of pre-school practice, with a particular focus on gender equality, are articulated and generated by pre-school teachers. I will critically discuss the question of whether male teachers will simplify difficulties faced when pre-schools should counteract traditional gender patterns and gender roles. I will also explore whether conditions for promoting gender equality will change as a result of an increased proportion of men working in pre-schools except, of course, in the trivial sense of numbers.

In order to promote gender equality in pre-schools, I will argue for the importance of emphasising and highlighting fundamental values, ideas and norms in the form of social representations. I also argue that the complexity of gender equality and how to achieve it in the pre-school environment, with or without male teachers, is an important task to discuss for professionals who work in pre-schools. The research reported on in this chapter is based on a small sample of research addressing gender equality in pre-school, describing and analysing male entrance into the pre-school as a way to achieve greater equality. The literature discussed in this chapter, which describes the theory of social representations, is used as a way to analyse and highlight taken-for-granted assumptions about gender and gender equality.

Theoretical framework

The empirical illustrations presented in this chapter are drawn from the author's previous research (Granbom 2011) concerning teachers' talk about pre-school as a pedagogical practice. The aim of this research was to describe and analyse pre-school teachers' constructions of meaning, or more specifically, to investigate pre-school teachers' social representations of pre-school as a pedagogical practice and how these representations are communicated in dialogue between them. In this chapter I will focus on two excerpts from the study which illustrate how pre-school teachers struggle to create an environment based on gender equality. The point of departure in analysing these quotations is that beliefs and values concerning gender equality are reflected in the different ways in which pre-school teachers make materials available. How time and space are organised in order to support an environment in which children get the opportunity to develop their ability and their interests independently of gender affiliation is, according to my starting point, an expression of underlying social representations. The curriculum (Skolverket 98/2010: 4) is clear in the demands on how pre-school teachers should pay attention to work on gender equality in pre-school. It is formulated as follows:

> *The ways in which adults respond to girls and boys, as well as the demands and expectations imposed on children, contribute to their appreciation of gender differences. The pre-school should counteract traditional gender patterns and gender roles. Girls and boys in the pre-school should have the same opportunities to develop and explore their abilities and interests without having limitations imposed by stereotyped gender roles.*

According to the theory of social representations, experiences from interactions with people in everyday life shape our conceptions of the world. This theory is a dialogical theory of knowledge which studies 'phenomena which are at the centre of social life and of the daily reality of individuals, groups and societies' (Marková 2000: 445). The theory is about how people jointly form shared or partly shared representations of the surrounding world. These representations develop into a sort of everyday-knowledge or 'common-sense knowledge' which helps people orientate in social reality. Social representations influence and constitute our lives; in this case the organisation of pre-school included, for example, selected parts of the gender order. Howarth (2006: 74) claims that 'we must emphasise the point that representations not only influence people's daily practices but *constitute* these practices'. The theory of social representations can provide tools and concepts that contribute to a deeper description and understanding of how the work to counteract traditional gender patterns is advanced and the problems this work may confront. A key feature of the theory is its explicit focus on common-sense knowledge (Liu 2004). The notion of relational categories is a concept used in the theory of social representations as a model to highlight the social knowledge and ideas circulating in the discussion. Relational categories are characterised by the pair of concepts that are mutually interdependent. People make distinctions and think in opposites. These contrast categories are characterised in that they are mutually interdependent. They must be understood in relation to each other rather than as opposites in the sense of 'either/or'. They are thus not dichotomies in importance (two mutually exclusive categories). Instead, they should be considered as two equivalent categories based on interdependence (Marková *et al.* 2007).

The research

The research presented is based on data generated from seven focus groups, 45 participants in total. The participants were all working in pre-schools and each group were fellow workers, meaning that they worked as a team even if they did not share the daily practice. It is argued that focus groups can be a useful method in studying social representations as opinions, attitudes and ideas expressed in the group can enthrone and highlight the underlying social representations (Jovchelovitch 2001; Wibeck 2002). Marková *et al.* (2007) characterise focus groups as being a thinking society in miniature. Marková (2003) claims that social representation research aims at identifying, describing and analysing the contents and meanings of common-sense knowledge communicated in life. In this particular case this means common-sense knowledge about gender equality in the pre-school context.

The environment and the promotion of equal opportunities

It appears from my study that gender equality is an up-to-date development area in many Swedish pre-schools today. Teachers in my focus groups expressed that they felt that they had relatively good knowledge of the subject. They emphasised that the physical environment was organised to support both girls' and boys' development and to stimulate their interest. In this chapter I will focus on one of the groups, which I have called *Solen*, and their discussion about how they work in order to counteract traditional gender patterns. The *Solen* focus group consisted of eight participants from the same pre-school but from three different departments; all of the participants were women. The following extract concerns a discussion where the group describes how they observed that boys and girls frequently chose to play separately. This was seen as a problem because there was a wish for the children to play games together, regardless of gender. Note that all names presented below are fictitious.

SONJA: *We touched on the subject at the meeting ... we just felt it a bit ... /like ... you know, it can't be too girlish/... no, we don't want it too sweet and cute ... then it will be just girls who are drawn towards it, there also have to be some material for boys ...*

SOLVEIG: *But when it comes to fancy dress we have a lot of boyish ... /yes we do/ ... like knight costumes and all sorts of things ...*

SARA: *We tried with the Lego as well/mmm/to really consider something that would be appealing to the girls, maybe like horses or something like that, to make them become attracted to it as 'girlie' toys. And we have bought pink and light blue Lego ...*

SONJA: *We have quite a few ... because there was an article in the Primary School Magazine that there were no 'Lego women' ... /yes/ ... I don't know how they expressed it, but there were only men who were Lego people. But I must say that we have plenty of the small women too* [small world resources]*, and I guess they will soon discover that ...*

SIRI: *But then we just expect the boys to like the tough things and that the girls like the softer ones, but that might not always be true ...*

SONJA: *But our thinking must be on the right track as we are working towards an environment where they can make their own choice /mmm/ but then it also has to be ...*

SOLVEIG: *But it can't be that the girls just dare to play with one thing and ...*

SARA: *No, but there has to be ... /no exactly/ ... but quite often we think that ... or thinking ... well, we have to focus more on ... like in the play of building, there always have to be pieces that are appealing to girls so they can interact in the game ... and that would be the same when it comes to the fancy dress clothes, there has to be knight ... yes, knight costumes that are appealing to the boys so they feel included even in that game.*

It is evident in the discussion presented above that the participants highlight the importance of the educational environment to please both girls and boys. I make the interpretation that the participants in this group convey ideas about how children's preferences differ depending on their gender and that there is a risk that the pre-school environment primarily responds to girls' wishes and needs. It reveals that any material offered in the pre-school is purchased on the basis of gender. Pre-school teachers make a distinction between boys' toys and girls' toys and this emphasises the importance for pre-schools providing for both. Some of the boys' toys are, however, 'adjusted' in response to girls' needs and desires through colour choices and accessories that are believed to be attractive for girls. Siri, in the extract above, argues that one should not assume that one's gender determines the choice of activity or toy. After this Sonja argues that the basic idea still is that the children should be able to make their own choices 'in the future', with Solveig emphasising that the focus should not be one-sided in focusing on girls having to change. The quote ends with Sara, who once again emphasises the importance of toys being designed with the aim of attracting children to activities traditionally attributed to the opposite sex, for example that the boys will be attracted to role play when the pre-school environment offers clothes that encourage boys to take on the role of knights in their play. I assert that there is an idea of a dichotomous 'boy-and-girl' view of the world. In my analysis of the above quote, I have found that *children's preferences – girls' and boys' preferences –* is a relational category that is central when participants in the focus group discuss pedagogical practices from a gender perspective. The relational categories are comprehensive and essential to the way people communicate, which means that they are often implicit and taken for granted. The basic assumption is that boys and girls do not have the same needs and interests. In the following excerpt this point is further clarified:

SARA: *But* [there] *will always be a difference, we are not alike and our thoughts are different / but it is women who have ... / Yes we can't make the girls think like boys because they are girls.*
SONJA: *No, we don't want that ...*
SARA: *No, and not the other way around either, we have to ... obviously they are different ... but we have to try to provide toys that are sort of similar ... There have to be just as many alternatives for boys as for girls / ... /*

Sara clearly clarifies the dichotomous division between boys and girls by stressing that there are differences between the sexes and that both girls and boys are to retain their individuality: 'we cannot get the girls to think like boys; they're girls.' I believe that participants give here the expression of a compensatory education where the basic idea is that gender is the determining selection of activities, but the activities that girls and boys engage in should be valued equally. A compensatory education means that each gender must be allowed to develop aspects of their personality that traditionally belong to the opposite sex. This means, according to my interpretation, an educational practice that is based on the child's biological sex.

The previous extracts show the difficulties that pre-school staff face in their efforts to follow the curriculum directives regarding their responsibility to counteract traditional gender patterns. Hellman (2010) shows similar results in her research: that children, as well as adults, categorise some of the positions performed by the children as 'girlish and boyish' and that some of the ways of practising boyishness and girlishness also are seen as more acceptable than others. This is obviously a position that can cause problems because it may involve a limitation of opportunities for children to develop skills and interests without restriction based on gender stereotypes. Kampman (1996) claims that teaching staff expect different behaviours from girls and boys: girls are seen as helpers and the behaviour of boys is seen as in need of restraint. Eidevald (2009) shares this view, claiming that different expectations for boys and girls are made visible. Even when they have similar positions boys and girls are often treated in different ways by teachers. One example of this is when girls are 'acting out' and not following the perceived norm of how girls should behave. Girls are generally considered to be more mature than boys, an assumption that leads to girls' behaviour being regulated earlier and with a greater intensity – they 'can do it better'. This indicates that the task to counteract traditional gender patterns and gender roles is one surrounded by difficulties. In the following section I will discuss possible solutions to these difficulties of working to prevent stereotyped gender roles.

Preventing stereotyped gender roles in pre-school

The extracts presented above show that although the task to counteract traditional gender patterns is an important part of the curriculum there are different interpretations of how this will be/should be implemented. It is assumed that everyone wants equality, but what this actually means in everyday practice and how this equality is to be achieved is a subject for disagreement. *Should girls and boys be treated in the same way or is it more important to give the individual space? Can single-sex groups as a method of organisation contribute to increased equality?* In the previous extract participants expressed the idea that girls and boys should develop abilities that they, on the basis of their gender, are considered to lack. Girls need to be more independent and develop their ability to build and construct, an assumption which leads to the purchasing of pink and light blue Lego in order to support the girls. There are strong assumptions that the colour of the material affects the attractiveness of this for girls. The boys are considered to lack the ability to engage in social games leading to the purchasing of knight costumes in order to attract them to such games. Dividing the children into single-sex groups for part of the day in order to increase equality is an approach that has had some impact in Sweden. The method takes as its starting point that girls and boys are presumed to have different needs that they should develop. Another method used as an effort to counteract traditional gender patterns is that some pre-schools in Sweden are specialised in gender-equal pedagogy, which means that they consciously work with the aim of incorporating gender-equal pedagogy in the educational environment. This is done with an awareness that everything, from interior design, materials, choice of toys and literature to the treatment of children and adults is well thought out from a gender equality perspective. In these pre-schools they claim that strict gender coding of the toys affects a child's ability to choose freely because the expectations in the surroundings affect them. Gender-neutral toys and an awareness of gender-equal pedagogy is thus seen as one way to prevent stereotyped gender roles in pre-schools as it may equalise children's opportunities to develop a wide range of concepts and skills. It is obvious that every toy offered to a child also delivers a message or value about the 'proper way' to see the world and behave in it.

One may ask whether the solution for a more equal pre-school is gender balance in the professional working team. Across the globe ECE serve as an example of a workplace with a staff body being almost entirely made up of females. From a historical perspective there are international perceptions that women are particularly suited to caring for children. One consequence of this view of women is that the pre-school, in its organisation and structure, is traditionally marked by women's work (Tallberg-Broman 1991; Havung 2000). A number of independent researchers have come to similar conclusions regarding motives and strategies in order to change the international shortage of men in ECE (see Cameron 2001; Nordberg 2003; Cushman 2010; Baagøe-Nielsen 2011; Granbom and Wernersson 2012). Research shows that equality has been extensively focused on quantity, based on an assumption that more men in care professions leads to increased equality. In a review of international literature concerning men's work in ECE, Cameron (2001) noted three main arguments which aimed to encourage more men to work with pre-school-aged children. One argument is that men in pre-schools can provide children with opportunities for close relationships, something that is considered important because there is a belief that many children are growing up with an absent father. This is something that Nordberg (2003) describes as an attempt at a revival of the 'two-sex family' with mother and father at the pre-school. Problems relating to the nuclear family's disappearance and absent fathers are assumed to be positively addressed with more men present in pre-schools. The second argument proposed by Cameron is that they can act as role models for the children. This is seen as being of particular importance for boys in pre-schools. Male staff can help to show that nursing and masculinity, for example, are compatible, and the boys have someone to identify with and help them to develop their interests. The importance of more men in pre-schools is motivated also by the men's putative advantages when it comes to act as role models for boys who challenge the idea of set limits; this is also noted in Swedish and Nordic research (see Havung 2000; Nordberg 2005; Hjalmarsson 2009). The third argument for more men in pre-schools, as highlighted by Cameron (2001), is that an increasing proportion of men in pre-schools would lead to equality or balance between the sexes. One argument is that children need a balance of experience from different teachers and that men and women *together* could provide the balance. It would lead to a better balance in the staff team and stereotypical views of men would be challenged. One critique of this point of view, which Cameron has noticed in the literature, is that men are more likely to be employed in senior positions and higher-status jobs.

It is widely accepted that more men in ECE is considered desirable and that the expectations of their contribution differs. *But what does this mean for males in their daily work at the pre-school? What roles do males take in pre-schools?* Nordberg (2003: 77) asks the question of whether these men are more radical than other men, or if they reproduce 'rooted patriarchal gender roles that subordinate women and men who deviate from normative conceptions of masculinity' (personal translation). She found that males in her study created a masculine identity by displacing the historical link to maternal care and by describing male staff as more action-oriented and professional. An important finding in her study, however, was that there is a discrepancy between the talk about men's role in the pre-school and the care orientation and empathy which the male pre-school staff expressed in their practice. Men who spoke about the profession in her study were characterised by a stereotypical portrayal of men (strong, dominant), while their practice increasingly challenged gender stereotypes. Havung (2000) shows in her study that male pre-school teachers in Sweden express traditional opinions on women and men, and that they adapt their roles in the pre-school which is, according to their opinions, gender-marked as feminine. They perceived the situation as satisfactory. Despite this, Havung's results indicate that both men and women displayed tendencies towards demarcation and shutting each other out from certain areas. Sport is an example of an area which was strongly perceived as a male domain while interior decoration was perceived as a feminine area. A similar result is illustrated by Sandberg and Pramling-Samuelsson (2005) in a study about pre-school teachers' attitudes towards children's play. Pre-school teachers described their own childhood play as 'exceptionally gender stereotyped' (p. 299). Male teachers described how they used games with rules, exemplified with different kind of sports, while women described how they played role-play games with dolls and horses. The results also show that male pre-school teachers expressed a willingness to play while the female pre-school teachers expressed that they tried to avoid participating in children's play. Male participation in play was described as being more physical, something that female pre-school teachers described as being a disturbing element since they preferred calm play. The study shows that male pre-school teachers' own experiences of different sports activities have a major impact on their work in pre-school. Cushman (2010) claims in research from New Zealand that male teachers who demonstrated dominant masculinities strongly associated with the national sport, rugby, were favoured by principals in the employment process.

Conclusions

From the discussion above, it can be concluded that efforts to counteract traditional gender roles and stereotypes are paved with difficulties and that an awareness and understanding of one's own behaviour and practice with regard to gender stereotyping is essential. On the question of whether we need more men in pre-school I believe the answer to be a clear 'yes' but, as indicated in the discussion above, there is still reason for us to be vigilant. More men do not automatically mean that pre-school opportunities to counteract gender stereotypes increase. Men, as well as women, need to challenge these gender stereotypes, which means that they need to be well-informed about gender-related issues. In order to understand teachers' thinking about gender and equality related to the pre-school environment the theory of social representation may offer a valuable theoretical support with the aim of identifying the directions of the teaching practice. This theory will accordingly allow for a deep examination of common-sense/'taken-for-granted' knowledge in a dialogical perspective of social representations. My hypothesis is that pre-school teachers' talk about gender and how to counteract gender stereotypes includes underlying social representations and common-sense knowledge which have an impact on how the work to achieve equality is done. Social representations are normative and they are bound to a nature of tradition. Ideas about gender and equality are definitely an issue which is deeply associated with tradition and common-sense knowledge.

In my study, it appears that gender equality is an up-to-date area of high priority in the Swedish pre-school. Pre-schools have different strategies to ensure that efforts to counteract traditional gender patterns are in progress. In the transcript extracts presented there is an effort to create an environment that compensates shortcomings for girls and boys on the basis of their gender. This results in an environment that actively divides children into groups based on gender in order to develop the qualities traditionally attributed to the opposite sex. Boys are expected to, for example, develop the ability to show and express their feelings.

The male pre-school teacher may then be in a position as a role model who exceeds stereo-typical gender boundaries by giving the boys, and of course in one sense also the girls, experiences of the sensitive male.

Another way to approach the question of how the pre-school should work to counteract traditional gender patterns is to create an environment which strives to give children opportunities to develop their full personality without limitations related to gender. Some pre-schools in Sweden consciously work with an education where gender-neutral toys are the norm. They claim that strict gender coding of the toys affects children's ability to choose freely because the expectations in the surroundings influence children. From this point of view the role of the male teacher, as well as the female teacher, seems to be able to challenge gender stereotypes by creating an environment based on gender-neutral toys and, of course, an awareness of how to introduce these toys to the children. Using the social representation theory as a point of departure, one has to ask what a gender-neutral toy is and the grounds upon which such a definition is given. It is obvious that objects can communicate different meanings depending on their use, and that activities can be identified as masculine or feminine in the context of the pre-school. I argue that this calls for caution and a substantial awareness of the dominating gender structures in pre-schools. More male teachers do not necessarily mean increased awareness about gender structures. Men and women are part of a society in which gender structures are taken for granted. Reflection is essential in efforts to counteract stereotypes. The theory of social representations could facilitate the process of understanding teachers' thoughts and ideas about equality and gender structures expressed in conversations about pre-school.

De Sousa (2011) argues that knowledge of teachers' social representations is crucial in efforts to develop and improve professional practice. Marková (2003: 119) highlights the importance of awareness by claiming that the representation process is the same as 'placing something in front of the eyes of another or into the front of the mind of another'. In pre-schools one way to achieve this awareness is to work with reflection and documentation in a critical way. A prerequisite for efforts to increase gender equality and combat gender stereotypes is the teacher's ability to see what is happening behind what appears to happen, to develop a capacity for critical reflection. Working with documentation using digital cameras also gives an opportunity to visualise underlying social representations in the reflections of everyday practice.

UNANSWERED QUESTIONS

- What does it mean to 'counteract traditional gender patterns and gender roles'? Is it the same as responding to all children equally or is it to respond to children differently?
- Is there a wish for a special type of masculinity in pre-schools in order to balance the female-dominance? What kind of masculinity is desired in such cases? Should men do the same things as women or is their role to support with special 'male' things?
- Are young children allowed to resist gender education and how are they challenged in their common assumptions about gender?

References

Baagøe-Nielsen, S. (2011) 'Hvordan har det blitt 8400 menn ansatt i norske barnehager?', *Nordiske mænd til omsorgsarbejde! En forskningsbaseret erfaringsopsamling på initiativer til at rekruttere, uddanne og fastholde mænd efter finanskrisen.* Roskilde:VELPRO – Center for Velfærd, Profession og Hverdagsliv.

Cameron, C. (2001) 'Promise or problem? A review of the literature on men working in early childhood services', *Gender, Work and Organization*, 8 (4): 430–53.

Cushman, P. (2010) 'Male primary school teachers: helping or hindering a move to gender equity?', *Teaching and Teacher Education*, 26 (5): 1211–18.

de Sousa, C. P. (2011) 'The teacher's work', in M. Chaib, B. Danermark and S. Selander (eds), *Education, Professionalization and Social Representations.* New York: Routledge, pp. 68–74.

Eidevald, C. (2009) *Det finns inga tjejbestämmare – Att förstå kön som position i förskolans vardagsrutiner och lek.* Jönköping: School of Education and Communication.

Granbom, I. (2011) *'Vi har nästan blivit för bra' Lärares sociala representationer av förskolan som pedagogisk praktik.* Jönköping: School of Education and Communication.

Granbom, I. and Wernersson, I. (2012) *Män i förskolan – kartläggning och analys av insatser.* Stockholm: Skolverket.

Havung, M. (2000) *Anpassning till rådande ordning. En studie av manliga förskollärare i förskoleverksamhet.* Malmö: Lärarhögskolan i Malmö.

Hellman, A. (2010) *Kan Batman vara rosa? Förhandlingar om pojkaktighet och normalitet på en förskola.* Göteborgs universitet, Acta Universitatis Gothoburgensis.

Hjalmarsson, M. (2009) *Lärarprofessionens genusordning. En studie av lärares uppfattningar om arbetsuppgifter, kompetens och förväntningar.* Göteborgs universitet, Acta Universitatis Gothoburgensis.

Howarth, C. (2006) 'A social representation is not a quiet thing: exploring the critical potential of social representations theory', *British Journal of Social Psychology*, 45 (1): 65–86.

Jovchelovitch, S. (2001) *Contextualising Focus Groups: Understanding Groups and Cultures.* Paper prepared for the Meeting of the Group 'Conversation et Langage', Laboratoire Européen de Psychologie Sociale, Paris.

Kampman, J. (1996) 'Gender and welfare work', in H. S. Olsen and P. Rasmussen (ed.), *Theoretical Issues in Adult Education.* Frederiksberg: Roskildes University Press.

Liu, L. (2004) 'Sensitizing concept, themata and shareness: a dialogical perspective of social representations', *Journal for the Theory of Social Behaviour*, 34 (3): 249–64.

Marková, I. (2000) 'Amédée or how to get rid of it: social representations from a dialogical perspective', *Culture and Psychology*, 6 (4): 419–60.

Marková, I. (2003) *Dialogicality and Social Representation.* Cambridge: Cambridge University Press.

Marková, I., Linell, P., Grossen, M. and Orvig, A. S. (2007) *Dialogue in Focus Groups. Exploring Socially Shared Knowledge.* London: Equinox.

Nordberg, M. (2003) 'Jämställdhetens spjutspets? – Rollmodeller, velournissar och andra män i kvinnoyrken', in T. Johansson and J. Kuosmanen (eds), *Manlighetens många ansikten – fäder, feminister, frisörer och andra män.* Malmö: Liber AB.

Nordberg, M. (2005) *Jämställdhetens spjutspets? Manliga arbetstagare i kvinnoyrken, jämställdhet, maskulinitet, femininitet och heteronormativitet.* Göteborg: Göteborgs universitet.

Sandberg, A. and Pramling-Samuelsson, I. (2005) 'An interview study of gender difference in preschool teachers' attitudes toward children's play', *Early Childhood Education Journal*, 32 (5): 297–305.

Skolverket (2010) *Curriculum for the Pre-school, Lpfö 98 Revised 2010.* Stockholm: Skolverket.

Tallberg-Broman, I. (1991) *När arbetet var lönen. En kvinnohistorisk studie av barnträdgårdsledarinnan som folkfostrare.* Stockholm: Almqvist & Wiksell.

Wibeck, V. (2002) *Genmat i fokus. Analyser av fokusgruppssamtal om genförändrade livsmedel.* Linköping: Linköpings universitet.

PART III

Gendered professional identities and practice

8

PIONEERS, PROFESSIONALS, PLAYMATES, PROTECTORS, 'POOFS' AND 'PAEDOS'

Swedish male pre-school teachers' construction of their identities

Jo Warin

Introduction

Men's engagement in the care and teaching of young children has increased within the sphere of home and family according to recent research on paternal involvement (see Lamb 2010; Pleck 2010). Yet this kind of caring is often hidden within the private domestic world. The professional roles of men working with young children in pre-school institutions have a symbolic significance with the potential to 'undo gender' because they are public and visible. Their engagement generates many questions for consideration:

- What sort of men choose to work in this world? Are they men who dare to be different?
- What actually happens to them when they start to work in the pre-school environment?
- Do they, as some have argued (Williams 1989, 1993; Skelton 2001), actually revert to being hyper-masculine within this 'feminised' work context or do they become more gender sensitive and able to help children counteract traditional gender patterns?
- How do they start to see themselves and how do they think others perceive them, be they fellow staff, parents/carers or pupils?

The research presented in this chapter goes some way to answer these related questions, drawing on formal interviews and informal conversations with men who work in pre-schools as carers and teachers of young children in both England and Sweden. This research has been rooted in a firm belief, informed by the developing relevant literature, that we are more likely to see a decrease in dysfunctional and damaging expressions of masculinity (e.g. violence, sexual abuse, misogyny) when we see an increase in more caring and nurturing masculinities.

These questions about men's self-images can be explored in the light of more general theories about the construction of personal identity (see Warin (2010) for an overview). While, at first glance, the construction of a personal sense of self appears to be an intensely personal and individualised business, it relies on our social existence and is essentially a *social* concept. There are three related ways in which this is the case. Firstly, a social group provides a 'reference group' for making social comparisons; we can only create identity through the comparisons we make with others in the various areas of our lives (Festinger 1954; Marsh *et al.* 2008). Secondly, a social group creates opportunities for the activation of self; we are only prompted to reflect on who we are when our social relationships trigger this kind of introspection and reflection (Stets and Burke 2000). Thirdly, and perhaps most significantly, interactions with others provide judgments and perspectives that are 'reflected' back, creating the reflexive 'me' that is identified in Mead's (1934) *Mind, Self and Society*, also known as the 'looking-glass' self, a phrase famously coined by Cooley (1902). Our insights into the perceptions that others hold about us lead to self-awareness and the possibility that we can control self-presentation and the performance of our identities (Goffman 1971). Gender is a key element of the construction of personal identity and related social awareness of others around us. Indeed, many sociologists and psychologists have argued that it holds a central position within the overall construction of self (Jackson and Warin 2000). Gender mediates the processes of identity construction outlined above, activated by and through our participation in a range of social groups and relationships.

Awareness of one's gender group membership is thrown into relief when our immediate social reference group is mainly, or entirely, made up by members of the opposite sex (Williams 1989). Being in a gender minority activates this element of self as King (1998) showed in his pioneering study of men who teach young children. In both England and Sweden men are in a clear minority status within the world of pre-school. For example, Baker (2012), drawing on data from the Department for Education (DfE) in England, claims that only 2 per cent of the early years workforce is male, while the official Swedish figure for men in pre-school is 3 per cent in municipal institutions and 5.5 per cent in 'free' (independent) institutions. These statistics are representative of wider European patterns, as discussed by Van Laere *et al.* (2014), and affirm the extreme minority status of men working in pre-school. We might therefore expect gender to be a very prominent aspect of identity in this work context. The purpose of this chapter is to examine how far this is apparent in pre-school male workers' reflections on their professional and pedagogic relationships, and to explore their gender awareness in relation to themselves and those around them.

Conversations with male pre-school staff

I start by providing some necessary background information about the context in which I carried out a series of interviews with male pre-school staff. A network of gender researchers from Sweden, England, Finland and Indonesia was formed in 2009 and funded by the Swedish Research Council (SRC) to research influences on gender imbalances in teaching and related roles. This forum produced the opportunity to contact pre-schools in one Swedish city, carrying out interviews with male teachers there in 2012. Four pre-school teachers agreed to be interviewed, together with a fifth man who had worked as a pre-school teacher for ten years and had then become a lecturer in teacher education. This sample, while small, is typical of research work in the area of pre-school and elementary school male teachers' constructions of their subjectivities because it is often hard to locate and engage large samples, in part due to their minority status. Consequently, a set of 'close-up' studies has emerged based on the interviewing undertaken, sometimes with repeat interviewing, with contributions by Murray (1996), Sumsion (1999), Smedley (2007), Martino (2008), Francis (2008), Mallozzi and Campbell Galman (2014) and Hjalmarrson and Löfdahl (2014). Taken together these small-scale studies have drawn out men's own constructions of identity conflicts and the intrapersonal issues confronting them in their professional roles. They have shown men at various levels of gender sensitivity and gender blindness as they perform on the public stage of teaching and caring for young children.

I now provide some brief contextual and biographical details about each participant (using fictional names for reasons of confidentiality) in order to ground an understanding of the identity work they undertake as male pre-school teachers, work that is rooted in their biographical employment trajectory and decisions about their professional career:

- *Per*, in his late forties, had worked in his current pre-school, situated in a leafy suburb, since the 1980s. A father with two grown-up daughters, he had no aspirations to move from the pre-school and expressed a strong enthusiasm for his work.
- *Linus* undertook pre-school work after leaving school at the time that it was still compulsory to do military service in Sweden. His decision to undertake 'unarmed service' led to the option to work in a pre-school. He then had a period of work in upholstery before deciding to return to pre-school teaching to train as a Montessori teacher. Following his training he worked as an au pair in London and then eventually came to his present role where he is now head of a small Montessori nursery/pre-school with five staff, including *Jonas* below. He was also studying, part-time, to gain his formal teacher training qualification in addition to his Montessori qualification.
- *Jonas* was the youngest man in the sample, in his early twenties. He came into pre-school work after being a forklift truck driver and was then unemployed, during which period of time his unemployment mentor got him a placement in a Montessori school. Jonas had been reluctant at first but the work had grown on him and given him the necessary experience to apply for his current post as a part time pre-school assistant. He had no formal teaching qualification at the time of our conversation.
- *Karl*, in his late thirties, was training as a kindergarten teacher. He had come into this work after a long search for the 'right' job which took him through employment as a construction worker, janitor, photographer, IT specialist and metalworker. He was also the father of a young child, which he claimed to be a significant influence on his work as a pre-school/kindergarten teacher.
- *Geir* had been a pre-school teacher for ten years in his home country of Norway. Like Linus, he did his 'unarmed military service' in Oslo in a pre-school for two years and then decided to move into factory work. However, he was persuaded back into pre-school teaching to join a very large pre-school that had a high proportion of male teachers (10 men and 30 women). He then undertook his formal teaching qualification, followed by postgraduate study, and then became a teacher educator.

In this chapter I also refer back to an earlier study undertaken as part of an evaluation of pre-schools within children's centres in the North of England focused on a male nursery worker – *Ian* – with whom I conducted a series of interviews over a three-year evaluation period (Warin 2006). Ian, an experienced pre-school teacher, became a local expert on the inclusion of male pre-school staff and fathers within the work of children's centres.

Performance and performativity: front-stage and back-stage selves in the pre-school

My analysis of my conversations with these five men relies on metaphors of performance, theatre and audience awareness. Indeed, the title for this chapter can be read as a cast list of the 'possible selves' (Markus and Nurius 1986) that men might adopt in the context of the pre-school. For Ian, gender was a very salient aspect of his identity in this work context due to his 'minority status' and he was very much aware of being in the public gaze:

> I'm definitely a minority. You know it's threatening, it's threatening ... you can feel you're like in a zoo if there isn't another male there.

While Ian used the metaphor of being in a zoo to draw attention to his feelings about being the object of public scrutiny rather than being on stage, he clearly recognised that his minority status placed him in the spotlight, centre-stage. Teaching, whether with four-year-olds or 14-year-olds, is a public practice which can be compared with the practice of acting since it necessarily involves a constant vigilance towards one's audience, efforts to imagine how one is coming across, and evaluation of whether one's attempts at communication are being understood as intended (Warin et al. 2006). Like an actor, it is part of a teacher's creative toolkit to develop the kind of self-awareness and awareness of others that inform their everyday practice. It is an essential ability within a pre-school teaching role.

Goffman (1971) suggests that human social interactions, like theatrical performances, include a front-stage region where actors are on show and a back-stage region that is private or hidden where individuals are able to be themselves. We may be especially aware of a back-stage and front-stage discrepancy which exaggerates our experience of *performing* when we move into very public front-stage positions such as the teacher within their classroom or the teacher confronting the interested and curious gaze of their parent audience when they arrive for picking up or dropping off their children. The five men in this study, together with Ian in the older English study, made many quite conscious decisions about the performance of certain identities. Our conversations in particular highlighted their performances of gender identities and the kinds of masculinities they were conscious of performing, for example the playmate role, a role that all of the men emphasised as a particularly positive aspect of their practice. For example, Linus stressed play as something distinctive that men bring to their pre-school work, claiming that 'we play in a different way with them' while Jonas explained his specific contribution to the staff team ('I like to play with them. I'm a fun guy') and Geir stated that men have a 'love of play'.

However, Goffman's ideas have been criticised because they overemphasise our agency in choosing identities to perform and imply that we are all equally free to choose who and what we want to be, a concept of individualistic identity choice that has been exposed by Rose (1997) and Skeggs (2004). The idea of self as something we can 'pick off the rail' and assume, much as we would do an item of costume, denies the influence of external and institutional pressures and influences. Identity is not freely chosen but is created through the cultural expectations and influences inherent in any social group, a view that is consistent with the social theorisation of identity as set out above. For example, in theorising about gendered institutions, schools have been described as 'masculinity-making devices' (see Connell 1995, 2000; Skelton 2001, 2002; Francis and Skelton 2001; Haywood and Mac an Ghaill 1996).

In these contexts, where ascendant definitions of masculinity prevail over others, men may, with the best intentions in the world, be tramlined into forms of gendered behaviour and conform to the gendered expectations of others. An example is Ian (in the English study) who spoke about a strong external pressure to become a regional figurehead and expert on paternal involvement strategies, running sessions for local nurseries, schools and youth services on 'Dads and Lads' work. Ian was drawn into performing the traditional gender script of the 'fast-track' male rising to a position of expertise and greater responsibility because of his rarity value as a male within early years educational settings, the phenomenon noted by Williams (1989, 1993) as the 'glass escalator effect'. He was aware of this dilemma and asserted his wish to maintain a 'hands-on' classroom role:

> *My primary role is with the children in the class. That's what I trained to do and that's what I enjoy … I want to stay in this work – as a class teacher.*

This example shows that we are often positioned by others in ways we may not always welcome or choose. A more extreme example is presented in Sumsion's (1999) account of a teacher named James whose fears about the way he was positioned by his parent audience came true when he arrived at his pre-school one day and was appalled to see the words 'James Straafe is a paedophile' spray-painted onto the walls. Johan, a very committed pre-school teacher in my Swedish study, was very much aware of managing his parent audience in relation to this highly sensitive aspect of gender performances, especially with regard to physical contact and touch with young children. He told me he was very deliberate in his provision of hugs in front of parents so that they could see this as an open part of his practice. So, as an actor in the spotlight, due to his minority status, the male pre-school teacher has to recognise and manage, as far as is possible, the gender perceptions of his audiences.

Like Goffman, Butler's (1990) approach to identity emphasises self as performance. Her work is also fundamentally about the gendered aspects of identity performances. However, Butler does not presuppose that the self is already 'there', back-stage, within the person, waiting to be brought out to show to audiences. She claims that it is the practices of self-presentation for others that bring about the creation of gender identities so her approach acknowledges the fluidity of gender identities which change in interactions with different audiences. The impression I have gained from talking with the men involved in my research is that they made conscious decisions about their performance of gender for a *range* of audiences, as I shall demonstrate below. The men talked about how they adapted their performances to the imagined perceptions of pre-school children, their parent audiences and their own fellow professional pre-school staff.

As a key element of empathic teaching relations with learners (Cooper 2004) a pre-school teacher has to enter into the minds of his three- and four-year-old audience and manage their view of him. Pre-school teacher trainees, both men and women, need to familiarise themselves with this audience, especially if they have had little experience of this age group. An arresting example of 'stage fright' was described to me by a young male volunteer in the English pre-school where Ian worked when he was confronted with this unfamiliar and unintelligible audience:

> *I've been over in the nursery where I would go and make time to go and sit in the classroom with the kids and that's the hardest thing I've ever done in my life … children … they're not an easy*

audience to please. They either like you or they don't and they're sat in front of you and you're singing 'Postman Pat' ... they're just sat there with a stern look on their face and you don't know whether they're liking you or what.

(Male volunteer in Warin 2006)

The Swedish men were very much aware of their pre-school audience in relation to gender and made many references to their imagined perceptions of the children about them. For example, Linus was aware that children witness him laying out the table for the midday meal, a practice that he undertakes quite consciously so as not to perpetuate the idea that it is women's work; for the same reason, Karl thought it important that the pre-school children saw him changing nappies.

A pre-school teacher does not only have to be sensitive to their child audience but needs awareness of two other audiences: their colleagues and the children's parents/carers. The Swedish male pre-school teachers touched on their thoughts and feelings about the perceptions of these intersecting pre-school audiences. Jonas, new to pre-school teaching, described himself as 'shy of adults' and told me that 'working with kids is not scary but working with adults is – the parents. I'm not so sure what to say when I talk with parents.' Managing the impressions of this group in particular can be experienced as a pressure for some pre-school teachers, especially for male teachers who are aware of equally strong public discourses of fear (male teachers as potential paedophiles) and adulation (male teachers as positive male role models).

Karl seemed very much aware of his identity as fluid and performed, claiming that he could adapt his performance to the different audiences and social groups that formed his private and professional life. At the time of the interview, Karl was undertaking postgraduate study alongside his classroom teaching role and was very aware of and interested in theories about gender, especially masculinities, and fluid identities drawing on the work of Connell (1995). He discussed this in relation to a 'line' or continuum of masculinity where he placed his engagement in his hobby of kick-boxing at the 'male end' and his role as kindergarten teacher as 'closer to the female'. He told me about his 'changing identities – being a child, an adult, a male, a female, a teacher, a student'.

Men in pink? Personal appearance matters

The dramaturgical theory of gender performance extends to choices about costume; indeed, my discussions with the Swedish pre-school teachers touched on several matters of personal appearance. For example, Geir emphasised his own very practical preference for clothes with big pockets when he was working as a pre-school teacher while Jonas explained his unusual decision to work barefoot as a deliberate strategy for emphasising his strong value for 'freedom', a personal choice that was very much in keeping with, and symbolic of, his role as a playmate and his enjoyment of outdoor physical play with children such as tree climbing.

Geir was able to offer an overview of men's choices about how to dress for a pre-school teacher role from his teacher trainer perspective, as well as his ten years of pre-school work. He told me he noticed two different sorts of men: those who are 'very sporty, or others who wear jeans and have piercings'. While Geir's categorisation of 'two types' was a necessarily superficial overview, my detailed discussions with the Swedish men revealed a very careful and conscious set of decisions about the presentation of the self and especially the presentation of the self as a male for the different pre-school audiences. These discussions about the physical aspects of self-presentation provided an inroad into the men's reflections on their performances of different types of masculinity. Choices about what to wear, colours, hairstyles and jewellery were significant surface clues to accessing deeper reflections on the construction and performance of gender identities in this context. For example, Karl was pleased to be able to challenge the children's stereotypical perceptions about gender through his own physical appearance. He reported a conversation he had recently engaged in with a pre-school boy who had told him that 'Boys don't have long hair' to which he had had been pleased to respond with 'Well I do!', indicating his own long hair which almost reached his shoulders. He explained that he believed his combination of long hair, ear rings and beard presented a gender-flexible appearance in keeping with his views above regarding gender-fluid performances and the disruption of traditional gender scripts.

The men also made choices about their personal appearance with a consciousness of challenging the children's gender perceptions so as to prevent the hardening of gender stereotypes. Like the other men in the Swedish study, Jonas was fully aware of the Swedish pre-school curriculum goal for challenging gender stereotyping: 'The pre-school should counteract traditional gender patterns and gender roles' (Skolverket 2010: 4). He discussed the ways he challenged gender stereotypes in the classroom, for example by putting on a princess tiara and pretending to be a princess, but he also told me he would not go as far as putting on a princess dress. Per told me that while he was careful to affirm children who arrived in clothing that is strongly associated with the opposite sex, he himself would never come to school in a dress, not even to challenge gender because it 'wouldn't fit my personality. I wouldn't be comfortable.' Linus adopted a similarly cautious approach in explaining his preference for pale purple shirts which he believed showed a degree of femininity but which do not make such a strong gender reversal statement such as dressing in pink. Both Jonas and Per seemed to suggest, in their thinking presented above, that they have a fixed idea of an authentic 'back-stage' self that they want to preserve and that might be threatened if they were to perform a very different kind of front-stage identity.

While the five Swedish men can all be positioned at various different stages along a continuum from gender blindness to gender sensitivity, my overall analysis showed a thoughtful positioning around how to present oneself physically within the pre-school as a male teacher: donning a princess tiara but stopping short of a princess dress; wearing a lilac shirt but not a pink one; having long hair but mixing this with a beard. Within the confines of the classroom, Jonas can wear a princess crown in front of his audience of pre-schoolers when at play, but when he dresses at the beginning of the day for his work he has to think of his adult audiences too. These choices demonstrate that a careful positioning is underway with an awareness of gender and sensitivity to the perceptions of audiences, balanced with a need to keep within a personal comfort zone.

Gender sensitivity and the management of identity performances within the pre-school

The research interview itself is also another stage and location for impression management and performance in which both parties – 'the researcher and the researched' (Brownhill 2014: 45) – undergo a mutual positioning of each other. My focus on gender was made quite explicit within the aims of the study, the men's engagement in the study, my briefing of them and the opening introduction which activated aspects of gender identity awareness, putting the men 'on their toes' with respect to statements about masculinity, femininity, and men and women. Perhaps because I had inevitably activated a degree of gender sensitivity I tried to counteract this effect by playing with different stances within the interview. For example, I sometimes adopted a 'Devil's advocate' position to prompt acquiescence or resistance to suggestions about gender differences in pre-school teaching. When Karl told me of his enjoyment of teaching about bugs and spiders I asked if this might be a contribution he makes as a *male* teacher and he was quick to say 'This is not because I am a male.' He went on to say that some of his female colleagues 'have *learned* to be afraid of bugs' (his emphasis). Later in his interview he reasserted this recognition of the socially constructed nature of gender by telling me 'I believe I have many classical male qualities but that is what I have *learned.*' Similarly, I used my own role as a female educator to challenge the men's emphasis on the value of their playmate role (in both fathering and teaching), an emphasis that implicitly theorised men's and women's different compensatory roles in the pre-school. For example, I suggested to Geir that men have appropriated this enjoyable aspect of childcare which consequently positions women with the more dull and routine aspects of childcare and teaching. Geir resisted this by asserting that 'Differences between male teachers may be bigger than differences between men and women.' I recognised that some of the men were highly aware of gender and were able to perform gender sensitivity in their presentation of self to me within this co-constructed conversation since gender was an explicit element of our interaction.

I also recognised a degree of gender sensitivity within the Swedish men's evident knowledge of their pre-school curriculum gender goals. The Swedish pre-school curriculum has a very specific statement about the need to address gender, putting this at the heart of its education on social and citizenship awareness development. This is quite a contrast with the English Early Years Foundation Stage (EYFS) curriculum (DfE 2014) which has no such explicit statement. I was struck by the men's familiarity with this pre-school curriculum goal. For example, Karl volunteered that the Swedish pre-school curriculum requires *active* work against gender (his emphasis). Per also mentioned that he was very much aware of this element of the curriculum, especially because parents frequently asked him about this aspect of his teaching and wanted to monitor it. Per pointed out that although the resources in his Montessori pre-school were gender neutral he was able to challenge gender roles through his influence on peer group formation and free play. Even Jonas, who had no formal training, mentioned his awareness of the pre-school curriculum aim to counteract traditional gender patterns. He added that 'nobody ever checks up that [you] are actually doing this [but] you have to check on yourself'. So my impression was that this particular group of men was very much aware of the Swedish curriculum statement on counteracting traditional gender behaviour and recognised that their familiarity with this principle was a strong indicator of their gender awareness and sensitivity.

It is of interest to note that two of the men in the study – Karl and Geir – were both engaged in the academic study of gender and teaching, Karl as a postgraduate student and Geir as a lecturer. So they might be expected to be highly gender-sensitive individuals and my analysis showed this was indeed the case. For example, in his teacher training role Geir was aware of the need to sensitise both male and female trainees to gender issues and found the use of single-sex teaching groups, as well as the presence of other male teacher trainees like himself, to be important influences on this element of their pre-school teaching preparation.

Conclusions

While my research methodology did not allow me to witness the impact of these men's beliefs through their practices with children, it was encouraging to encounter a degree of gender awareness in our interview interactions, especially from those men who have had opportunities to develop gender sensitivity within their professional training and further study. There were glimmers during these conversations of a way forward where reflexive and reflective pre-school staff are highly tuned, as many actors are, to managing skilful and self-aware gender performances with their professional pre-school audiences. I wonder how far the relative gender sensitivity of these pre-school staff mirrors the gender egalitarian context of Swedish social policies, which has a stronger record on policies for men as fathers for example, compared with the UK?

It is both possible and desirable to train children and young people to become much more alert to the ways in which they themselves and other people around them are performing and thereby creating gender identities. However, in order to be able to confront and disrupt gendered performances in children, we have to develop greater gender sensitivity ourselves as educators (Houston 1985). As Rogers (1967) points out, only self-aware teachers can bring about self-awareness in pupils. We cannot leave this kind of teacher self-awareness to chance. We need to take Butler's ideas (1990) on board within the training of those who teach and care for young children. We need to acknowledge that practices of self-presentation bring about the creation of gender identities and that gender identities are malleable when interacting with different audiences. The training of gender sensitivity has to become a key element of initial teacher training (ITT) and continuing professional development (CPD) if we want to disrupt the slow but steady progress of gender entrenchment.

UNANSWERED QUESTIONS

- Why is the gender pattern of work in ECE so resistant to change?
- How can we rescue the 'missing men' agenda from a preoccupation with men as 'male' role models who are likely to perpetuate gender differences through an assertion of traditional forms of masculinity?
- How can we reframe and promote this agenda as the all-important need to have adults, both men and women, who can perform in gender flexible and fluid ways to their young audiences?
- How can we train male and female pre-school staff to model gender flexible behaviours in front of their child and parent audiences?

References

Baker, R. (2012) '"Childcare is not just a woman's job" – why only two per cent of the day nurseries and childcare workforce is male', *daynurseries.co.uk*, 10 September. [Online.] Available at: http://www.daynurseries.co.uk/news/article.cfm/id/1557858/childcare-is-not-just-a-womans-job-why-only-two-per-cent-of-the-day-nurseries-and-childcare-workforce-is-male (accessed 19 August 2014).

Brownhill, S. (2014) 'The researcher and the researched': ethical research in children's and young people's services', in S. Brownhill (ed.), *Empowering the Children's and Young People's Services: Practice-based Knowledge, Skills and Understanding*. London: Routledge, pp. 45–61.

Butler, J. (1990) *Gender Trouble*. New York: Routledge.

Connell, R. W. (1995) *Masculinities*. Cambridge: Polity Press.

Connell, R. W. (2000) *The Men and the Boys*. Cambridge: Polity Press.

Cooley, C. H. (1902) *Human Nature and the Social Order*. New York: Charles Scribner's Sons.

Cooper, B. (2004) 'Empathy, interaction and caring: teachers' roles in a constrained environment', *Pastoral Care in Education*, 22 (3): 12–21.

Department for Education (DfE) (2014) *Statutory Framework for the Early Years Foundation Stage: Setting the Standards for Learning, Development and Care for Children from Birth to Five*. [Online.] Available at: https://www.gov.uk/government/uploads/system/uploads/attachment_data/file/335504/EYFS_framework_from_1_September_2014__with_clarification_note.pdf (accessed 4 September 2014).

Festinger, L. (1954) 'A theory of social comparison processes', *Human Relations*, 7: 117–40.

Francis, B. (2008) 'Teaching manfully? Exploring gendered subjectivities and power via analysis of men teachers' gender performance', *Gender and Education*, 20 (2): 109–22.

Francis, B. and Skelton, C. (2001) 'Men teachers and the construction of heterosexual masculinity in the classroom', *Sex Education*, 1 (1): 9–21.

Goffman, E. (1971) *The Presentation of Self in Everyday Life*. London: Penguin Books.

Haywood, C. and Mac an Ghaill, M. (1996) 'Schooling masculinities', in M. Mac an Ghaill (ed.), *Understanding Masculinities*. Buckingham: Open University Press.

Hjalmarrson, M. and Löfdahl, A. (2014) 'Being caring and disciplinary – male primary school teachers on expectations from others', *Gender and Education*, 26 (3): 280–93.

Houston, B. (1985) 'Gender freedom and the subtleties of sexist education', *Educational Theory*, 35 (4): 359–69.

Jackson, C. and Warin, J. (2000) 'The importance of gender as an aspect of identity at key transition points in compulsory education', *British Educational Research Journal*, 26 (3): 375–92.

King, J. R. (1998) *Uncommon Caring: Learning from Men Who Teach Young Children*. New York: Teachers College Press.

Lamb, M. E. (2010) *The Role of the Father in Child Development*, 5th edn. Hoboken, NJ: John Wiley & Sons.

Mallozzi, C. and Campbell Galman, S. (2014) 'Guys and "the rest of us": tales of gendered aptitude and experience in educational carework', *Gender and Education*, 26 (3): 262–80.

Markus, H. R. and Nurius, P. (1986) 'Possible selves', *American Psychologist*, 41 (9): 954–69.

Marsh, H. W., Trautwein, U., Lüdtke, O. and Köller, O. (2008) 'Social comparison and big-fish-little-pond effects on self-concept and other self-belief constructs: role of generalized and specific others', *Journal of Educational Psychology*, 100 (3): 510–24.

Martino, W. (2008) 'The lure of hegemonic masculinity: investigating the dynamics of gender relations in male elementary school teachers' lives', *International Journal of Qualitative Studies in Education*, 21 (6): 575–603.

Mead, G. H. (1934) *Mind, Self and Society*. Chicago: University of Chicago Press.

Murray, S. (1996) 'We all love Charles: men in childcare and the social construction of gender', *Gender and Society*, 10 (4): 368–85.

Pleck, J. H. (2010) 'Paternal involvement: revised conceptualization and theoretical linkages with child outcomes', in M. E. Lamb (ed.), *The Role of the Father in Child Development*, 5th edn. Hoboken, NJ: John Wiley & Sons, pp. 58–93.

Rogers, C. R. (1967) *A Therapist's View of Psychotherapy*. London: Constable.

Rose, N. (1997) 'Assembling the modern self', in R. Porter (ed.), *Rewriting the Self: Histories from the Renaissance to the Present*. London: Routledge.

Skeggs, B. (2004) *Class, Self, Culture*. London: Routledge.

Skelton, C. (2001) *Schooling the Boys: Masculinities and Primary Education*. Buckingham: Open University Press.

Skelton, C. (2002) 'The "feminisation of schooling" or "re-masculinising" primary education?', *International Studies in Sociology of Education*, 12 (1): 77–95.

Skolverket (2010) *Curriculum for the Pre-school Lpfö 98: Revised 2010*. Stockholm: Skolverket.

Smedley, S. (2007) 'Learning to be a primary school teacher: reading one man's story', *Gender and Education*, 19 (3): 369–85.

Stets, J. E. and Burke, P. (2000) 'Identity theory and social identity theory', *Social Psychology Quarterly*, 63 (3): 224–37.

Sumsion, J. (1999) 'Critical reflections on the experiences of a male early childhood worker', *Gender and Education*, 11 (4): 455–68.

Van Laere, K., Vandenbroeck, M., Roets, G. and Peeters, J. (2014) 'Challenging the feminisation of the workforce: rethinking the mind-body dualism in early childhood education and care', *Gender and Education*, 26 (3): 232–46.

Warin, J. (2006) 'Heavy-metal Humpty Dumpty: dissonant masculinities within the context of the nursery', *Gender and Education*, 18 (5): 523–39.

Warin, J. (2010) *Stories of Self: Tracking Children's Identity and Wellbeing Through the School Years*. Stoke-on-Trent: Trentham Books.

Warin, J., Maddock, M., Pell, A. and Hargreaves, L. (2006) 'Resolving identity dissonance through reflective and reflexive practice in teaching', *Reflective Practice*, 7 (2): 231–43.

Williams, C. (1989) *Gender Differences at Work: Women and Men in Nontraditional Occupations*. Berkeley, CA: University of California Press.

Williams, C. L. (ed.) (1993) *Doing 'Women's Work': Men in Nontraditional Occupations*. Newbury Park, CA: Sage.

9

BEING PROFESSIONAL

Norms relating to male pre-school teachers in Japanese kindergartens and nurseries

Anette Hellman, Chie Nakazawa and Kiyomi Kuramochi

Introduction

A gendered division of labour is still strong in Japan and care-related occupations are considered to be 'female work' in Japanese society. Accordingly, the number of men working as pre-school teachers in kindergartens and nurseries is low; in 2010 it was 4 per cent. At the same time, notions of gender and gender equality are changing in Japan. The prime minister's office founded an advisory council in 1994 that promoted the concept of liberation from culturally and socially shaped gender differences as one of its aims for participation in society (Mae 2007). Furthermore, these notions emerged in policy documents such as the Act on Securing of Equal Opportunity and Treatment between Men and Women in Employment (1972) and the Act on the Welfare of Workers Who Take Care of Children or Other Family Members Including Childcare and Family Care Leave (1991) and are thus gradually moving towards gender equality. These changes have made it possible for men to take up pre-school teaching, but teachers still have to negotiate conflicting norms about gender, care and professionalism in their everyday lives in pre-school.

This chapter focuses on norms concerning male pre-school teachers and the care of young children in kindergartens and nurseries in Japan. It does so by exploring ideas about being professional in relation to conventions about the male pre-school teacher. The chapter builds on a larger study (Hellman 2013) that shows that both male and female classroom teachers, as well as head teachers, consider the ideal pre-school teacher in terms of professionalism and they view the position to be 'gender neutral'. At the same time teachers also express how they are expected to perform 'traditional' gender activities in order to measure up to ideals of pre-school teacher professionalism. Professionalism is thus labelled 'gender neutral' while gender becomes clearly visible in relation to norms about gender, bodies and the division of labour.[1] Prompted by these results, we will explore female and male teachers' ideas about the gendered challenges they encounter in their daily work and their views about dealing with them. We ask: *Which of the tasks that professional teachers are expected to perform may differ in terms of gender? How do male and female teachers who work in mixed-gender teaching teams reflect upon these norms in relation to their daily work in caring for young children?*

This chapter illustrates how, in Japanese society, 'being professional' as a pre-school teacher means that both female and male teachers have to transgress their society's stereotypical norms of masculinity and femininity. This experience provokes reflection on an individual level but it also encourages the creation of a certain kind of 'safe' atmosphere. Research has described how common projects and the creation of solidarity may create spaces in which it is possible to transgress gender stereotypes (Thorne 1993; Butler 2004; MacNaughton 2006; Hellman 2011). Some of the teachers interviewed by Hellman felt that their colleagues could create an atmosphere in which they felt safe enough to transgress stereotyped gender borders in the pre-school environment. We will argue that solidarity, in terms of taking care of and standing up for each other, creates a safe space in which male and female teachers can negotiate gender in ways that make it possible to transgress gender stereotypes.

After a short section on our theoretical framework, methodology and research sites, we will present the ideas of some male and female classroom teachers and head teachers in relation to gender, professionalism and the teaching of pre-school children. We will show how gender differentiation becomes visible in relation to two strong discourses that manifest in kindergartens and nurseries: firstly, children's needs, and secondly, the gender division of labour in Japanese society. We will also discuss how teachers may negotiate and overcome the challenges these discourses pose. This discussion will be presented in the section entitled 'Gendered bodies: children's needs, strength and gentleness'. We will conclude by discussing our results in relation to previous research and we will indicate some implications for future understandings of professionalism, male teachers, masculinity and care.

Theoretical framework, methodology and research sites

This study explores how norms are negotiated in situations in which conceptions of professionalism are created and where gender norms are both entrenched and challenged. Our theoretical starting point is poststructural feminism and critical studies of men and masculinities (Connell 2000; Whitehead 2002; Butler 2004). In these studies, professional teachers (male and female) are treated as situated constructions for whom normative structures both constrain and influence their understandings of their work. Our analysis rests on the concepts of norms and normality, such as norms about masculinity and femininity (Butler 2004). We have also used the concepts of hegemonic masculinity and space (Connell 2000) as well as 'gender safe' and 'gender fair' contexts (MacNaughton 2006). The ways in which gender and normality are manifested in educational practice are culturally defined and some practices are more influenced by gender norms and hegemonic masculinity than others. Connell (2000) discusses three 'vortices' that tend to enforce hegemonic masculinity: *discipline, gender division of subjects/tasks* and *sport*. One of the reasons that stereotypical norms of masculinity emerge has to do with contextual norms about bodies and the way that bodies are made the focus of a normative gaze (Whitehead 2002). In order to transgress gender boundaries people need to feel 'safe' from the risk of exclusion and they need a sense of there being 'fair treatment' (MacNaughton 2006).

The fieldwork in Japan was conducted by Hellman as part of a post-doctoral study that was funded by the Japan Society for the Promotion of Science (JSPS).[2] The data concerned

TABLE 9.1 Interviewees in terms of gender, role and setting type

Gender	Role	Kindergarten		Nursery		Pre-school	
		Public	*Private*	*Public*	*Private*	*Public*	*Private*
Female	Teachers	12	4	8	5	0	1
	Head teachers	2	2	1	0	1	1
Male	Teachers	2	0	1	1	0	4
	Head teachers	0	0	0	1	0	0

the Japanese context in general and the nursery/kindergarten context in particular. The study was ethnographic in character and consisted of two months of observation and interviews in two pre-schools: a public kindergarten (Yochi-en) and a public nursery (Hoiku-en). Additionally, two days of observations and interviews were conducted at each of the following three setting types: one public pre-school (Kodomo-en), two private nurseries and one private kindergarten. The methods used were observations including participant observations, focus group interviews, photos and videos. After the observations, interviews with individual teachers were conducted and these were tape-recorded. The participants consisted of 26 female teachers, eight male teachers, seven female head teachers and one male head teacher. The names of participants used in this chapter are all fictional.

The public and private kindergartens were linked to faculties of education at universities and were often used as sites for researchers and students to conduct their studies. The way that education policy was interpreted at the university reached the teachers through these close relations between the institutions. This may have impacted upon the quality and profiles of these pre-school environments since it placed them at the 'forefront' of research policy in practice. These samples are therefore of particular interest for understanding discourses about 'ideal' nurseries and kindergartens in Japan.

Gender, professionalism and the teaching of pre-school children in Japan[3]

All of the teachers interviewed described the importance of behaving as a professional and defined this as a 'gender-neutral' position that focused on children's needs. The discourse about children's needs is powerful in many educational contexts, where children are seen as individuals who have universally 'childish' heredity and will develop in accordance with universal developmental scales (Dahlberg *et al.* 2002). Previous research from pre-schools outside Japan has shown how this discourse often intersects with norms about male and female role models (Nordberg *et al.* 2010). Researchers have also pointed out how common assumptions about 'boys' needs' for male role models and 'girls' needs' for female role models rest on ideas about biological differences between the sexes (Thorne 1993; Connell 2000). The way in which this discourse manifests in the context of a Japanese pre-school will be presented in the next section.

The discourse about children's needs and role models

Ideas about role models featured in discussions with the teachers interviewed in Japan but not primarily in relation to the child's gender. For instance, when giving her view of male role models in her nursery, Ms Takahashi explains:

> *Male teachers become role models, not for boys or girls but rather as good human beings and as good teachers, role models for the occupation of being a teacher. But age is important since younger children want to have female teachers, since they need to be handled more carefully and sensitively. Older children need to have male teachers since the older ones like to play more physically and powerfully. They like to run and get healthy bodies. This is true for both boys and girls.*

As this quotation shows, role models tend to be formulated as important for socialisation and for demonstrating the difference between childishness and adulthood, but they are not presented primarily in relation to gender. The *adult teacher* was posited as a role model for *children*, rather than the female teacher being presented as a role model for girls and the male teacher for boys. Nakata (2003) describes two types of expectation made of male pre-school teachers by their female colleagues. The first is that they should provide a 'gender-neutral' form of care, and this is understood to be part of a teacher's professional role (as discussed above). The second is that they should perform as 'the second father at home'. Takashima and Yasumura (2006) discuss the expectation that male pre-school teachers should play the role of an 'extra father' for the children, a finding from their research review in Japan. They claim that expectations of the teachers to teach the children a 'male way of life' since fathers are so absent from the home environment can be found in around half of all pre-schools. Research from outside Japan, such as in Sweden (Nordberg *et al*. 2010), has found similar patterns in terms of notions of the absent father. However, there is one important difference. In European pre-schools, male teachers are often considered to provide important role models for *boys*, whereas in Japan they are described as important for both *boys and girls*.

Age also seems to be a crucial issue in Japan. Older children of both sexes are said to 'need' male teachers since they are expected to enjoy physically expressive activities. Health ideals feature significantly in the activities at both nurseries and kindergartens (Ministry of Education, Culture, Sports, Science and Technology (MECSST) 2008; Ministry of Health, Labour and Welfare (MHLW) 2008), and physically demanding activities are considered important ingredients for good physical development. This kind of activity is therefore encouraged for all children, particularly older ones, and the children are expected to be taught by all teachers, both male and female. However, head teacher Ms Takahashi describes younger children as having different needs. Younger girls as well as boys are said to 'want' female teachers since women are expected to be more attuned to the needs of young children for extra care and sensitivity. These actions too are seen as offering a 'professional' kind of care for the youngest children and they are expected by both male and female teachers. Both men and women are therefore expected to teach all age groups according to prevalent norms about children's needs. However, both classroom teachers and head teachers in our study often pointed out that there are norms in Japanese society about women and physical expression as well as about men and care that can be challenging in their daily work. This will be discussed in the following section.

Gendered adult bodies: norms about strength and gentleness

The teachers and head teachers that we interviewed described the gender hierarchies and norms they experience in their daily activities with children, parents and other teachers. These norms may be understood as part of powerful discourses about the gendered division of labour in Japanese society. In this chapter we focus on two sets of norms that are associated with this discourse: masculinity and physical activity, and masculinity and the care of young children, particularly in relation to tenderness. We will also discuss how these norms may be challenged.

Norms about masculinity and physical activity

All the kindergartens and nurseries in this study, except for one kindergarten, had male teachers and all the staff seemed positive about this, a finding that echoes Honda *et al.*'s (2006) work. However, their reasons differed and there were also some differences between those from the nurseries and those from the kindergartens. For example, the head teachers from private and municipal nurseries tended to discuss male teachers as part of a welfare project whereby the nurseries provided a facility that enabled parents to work outside the home, a situation that they saw as altering roles in the family. The male teacher was thus presented as working at 'the forefront' of gender equality and modernity. All the male teachers in the study had made an active choice to become teachers of young children. Like their female counterparts, the reasons they gave were that they were interested in children, learning and care. Additionally, the male teachers talked of how they wanted to change norms of masculinity, femininity and care in society at large, and they often saw pre-school as an important platform for the negotiation of gender equality and modernity. Nurseries, in particular, were presented by the teachers and parents in the study as an institution that may help to enhance gender equality since the range of services it offers, such as the provision of cooked meals and full-time childcare, enable both men and women to work.

With regard to gender equality, head teacher Yamamoto is noteworthy for discussion. She heads two nurseries, each of which has highly qualified staff with academic training in gender studies and sociology as well as pedagogy; each nursery employs 50 per cent male teachers. Yamamoto's goal was to teach her employees an alternative masculinity that was less authoritarian and more in line with notions of the 'professional teacher' as discussed above. The head teachers from private and municipal kindergartens were also able to discuss the value of male teachers as a way to promote gender equality, but they tended to focus on how men bring something different into the pre-school environment rather than on changing stereotypical notions of masculinity. Their stance was associated with the idea of men's bodies as more suitable for physical activities (Connell 2000). They claimed that men should do all the things required of a professional kindergarten teacher but that they should also add extra physical activities – they might, for example, play with the children in a more active and dynamic way outdoors or encourage more indoor sports – and this was all clearly linked with the idea of masculinity. Men also teach physical training and health for older pre-school children since these subjects do not fit with traditional norms about the behaviour of adult women in public spaces. Head teacher Aikawa said:

> *In Japan people are often somewhat ambivalent about women being too sporty, physical or loud. Women are generally more tender and quiet and do not run around. So it is very much appreciated by many parents and also by some of the female teachers if men work here and take care of the physical training for the children, for both boys and girls. Physical training for children is less equivocal and is more about health than gender norms – it's about growing up and being healthy.*

Since both girls and boys are seen as individuals who need physical training for their development and health, this forms an important part of pre-school children's daily activities. However, as shown in the quotation above, it is considered strange for female teachers to be physically active or loud. Honda *et al.* (2006) suggest that kindergartens are more likely than nurseries to ascribe a stereotypical gender role to their male teachers. Male kindergarten teachers are expected to take the initiative and to perform an active teaching role that involves the body. For example, they participate in gymnastics, undertake physically demanding tasks at school events, assume responsibility for safety management and deal with 'suspicious' individuals. Several researchers within the field of critical studies of men and masculinity have shown that norms about male bodies reinforce norms about hegemonic masculinity (Connell 2000; Whitehead 2002). In the Japanese pre-school context, Takashima and Yasumura (2006) describe how male pre-school teachers are considered suitable for working with older children but not with young children.

There are evidently powerful norms about age and gender at work here and these place women's public physical activities outside normality (Butler 1990; Young 2000). It may therefore be 'safer' (MacNaughton 2006) to restrict gender transgressive teaching, which does not fit the traditional image of real women, to men. At the same time, men are supposed to perform physical activities publicly and perform them well. The same normative gaze that positions women as unsuitable and men as suitable also labels individuals performing the activities as more or less 'feminine' or 'masculine' (Whitehead 2002). In our study, there were several female teachers who performed physical activities together with the children, though they tended to draw attention to the fact that they did so. In one of the kindergartens in the study Ms Kawamura, discussed this:

> *I like to play physically or a little bit dramatically with the children in our group. The children really like it and I think it is important for their development. So the teachers here have decided that we all should participate in these activities, since it is good for the children. In Japanese society, it is more common for men to do these things but I am interested in gymnastics, so I like to do that kind of activity. I think it is very important that male and female teachers discuss how we can help each other and learn from each other. It feels better if we can trust each other and no one talks behind your back.*

This teacher alluded to the importance of the collegial ethos for facilitating a challenge of gender norms. MacNaughton (2006) also notes that teachers need a sense of gender safety – trust and gender – in order to dare to try other positions without risking marginalisation. Just as there are prescriptive norms for women, some practices may be considered strange or abnormal for 'real' men, and this forms the topic of the next section.

Norms about masculinity and the care of young children; tenderness in verbal and body language

Honda *et al.* (2006) report on the survey they conducted in nurseries and kindergartens which explained how the work and roles of teachers at nursery school are often considered to be gender equal. However, certain tasks are regarded as most suitable for male teachers (such as gymnastics, as discussed above) while others are thought more suitable for women, such as working with the youngest children in the so-called 'zero aged group' (0–1) in nurseries. Honda *et al.* describe how it is acceptable for male teachers to work in kindergartens with the 3–5 year age group. It is caring for the youngest children that seems to be most problematic in relation to masculinity. *What, then, is the problem?* The teachers in our study discussed two things: firstly, the Japanese language, and secondly, the use of body language. Both of these factors are concerned with norms relating to gender and gentleness.

In Japan, the appropriate manner of speech differs according to gender, both in terms of the gender of the speaker and the person being spoken to. This has changed over time and depends to some extent on location and occasions but it still exists (Nakamura 2007). Kreitz-Sandberg (2007: 154) refers to Taga, whose primary school study explored the impact of teachers' gendered expectations about the correct way to address children and how these influenced their use of voice and language in the classroom. Taga noted that if a male teacher used a loud voice – 'Nan ka, o-mae tachi wa!' – to reprimand his students for inappropriate behaviour, this rough way of speaking would be accepted by the students and their parents. However, female teachers were expected to address the students in a more polite tone. The male teacher in Taga's study reflected on these norms and described how he often wanted to use a more feminine, polite manner of speech – 'Anatatachi chanto shinasai' – but he said that he appreciated his freedom to use both ways of speaking.

The norms regarding the proper way for men and women to speak to children are also related to perceptions of children's needs at different ages. For pre-school children, particularly the youngest (0–1), normal masculine ways of speaking are considered too strict for the children's fruitful development. This was explained by pre-school teacher Mr Sato, a particularly reflective teacher from whom we quote at some length:

> *I grew up in quite a strict family, so when I started work I would speak sternly to the children and use harsh language without thinking about it. The head teacher then spoke to me about my use of language and encouraged me to engage in some self-reflection. The head teacher explained to me that even though he may not intend it, a male teacher may be understood by the children to be strict, harsh and frightening simply because of the way he speaks and uses his body language.*

Mr Sato alludes here to the expectations of 'real men' that are prevalent in Japan and that involve certain styles of communication that conflict with those expected of 'professional pre-school teachers'. Working as a male pre-school teacher in Japan therefore demands learning different ways of using both speech and body language. Upon reflection Mr. Sato understood that it was important to smile more and to use softer verbal and body language, and he tried to align his behaviour better with that expected of professional teachers. He also tried to follow advice he received to 'always have some space in his mind', an idiom that refers to maintaining self-control and pausing to reflect before saying what he was thinking to the children. He became aware of the importance of controlling his temper and reflecting on his behaviour so that he could come across as warmer with a more relaxed attitude and remain alert to the needs of others. Mr Sato continues by saying:

Men and women may differ before they start working together, but when they do it is really important to talk so that everybody understands one another and feels good. If someone is too direct, they may come across as performing the authoritarian, angry and disciplinarian paternal role. That is not good. But these are really difficult things to discuss and change. In Japan, the words used by men and women differ and consequently the mind becomes different – even if you don't want that. There is a lot to change when you start consciously working with it.

Mr Sato refers here to the way in which norms are manifested in language and how powerful this is since it shapes the way people think and conceptualise the world (Butler 2004). The Japanese language affects and also reflects gender power relations as well as age and status relations, and it is particularly important for demonstrating politeness and consideration. For example, female language forms seldom use imperative verbs towards children, women or men. This makes it difficult for a woman to tell a man or a child what to do in a 'strict' way, while this way of talking is normal for men (Nakamura 2007). However, in the pre-school context, the way adults are expected to talk to the children is the same for men and women. Our interviewees told us that male teachers are expected to learn to speak in the way considered appropriate for addressing children in the educational context. Speaking gently and unthreateningly is regarded as professional but is also associated with the norms of motherhood that involve caring, affection and sensitivity to the needs of others.

Norms about gentleness are also evident in relation to caregiving and body language. In an interview at a nursery, Hellman (herself a female teacher), a female teacher (Ms Eguchi) and a male teacher (Mr Inoue) discussed these issues. Ms Eguchi said that she did not think about gender and young children. Mr. Inoue nodded and said that he was not doing anything differently from his female colleagues. Hellman (AH) asked if this comment related to all his daily activities:

MR INOUE: Yes.

AH: Does this apply to all routines? Such as eating, toilet visits?

MS EGUCHI: I probably do more of the regular routines, like changing diapers ...

MR INOUE: That's true, especially with the girls' diapers. Maybe because you have to be gentle when you change diapers and even gentler with girls or at least that's the public expectation. So maybe a woman is seen to be better suited to this.

MS EGUCHI: Yeah, or maybe I am just gentler because I am more used to doing it ...

Recalling Connell's (2000) notion of the 'vortices of gender division of tasks/subjects', the pre-school may be seen to represent a space in which gender is highly relevant because of the association between the norm of gentleness that prevails in working with young children and norms about the different 'natures' of men and women (Mae 2007). Nakata (2003) notes that men's uneasiness about changing infant diapers may be due to the fact that Japanese society has not yet publicly accepted the idea of physical contact between men and infants since men are assumed to lack sufficient gentleness. This seems to be the main reason for men's reluctance to perform this work rather than any fear about men behaving in sexually inappropriate ways, a very strong discourse in other countries such as the UK. These normative frameworks construct gentleness as inherent in women but not in men. As Mr Suzuki told us:

> I believe that it is important that men and male pre-school teachers can be close to children too. This is good for children, both in order to show them that men and boys can be tender and close and also because it is good for boys as well as girls with physical contact. As a male pre-school teacher, I try to promote this, even though it is not in line with traditional values for men – but the traditional norms need to change.

Like Mr Suzuki, several of the teachers and head teachers we interviewed mentioned how they worked with their colleagues to change traditional ideals. Some of the teachers explained how their ideas about gender differences had changed over time. One male teacher, Mr Matsumoto, recalled when he had started to work as a teacher in a kindergarten with mostly female colleagues:

> Then I thought that men and women had quite different natures, but when I had worked together with my female colleagues for some time, I learned that the differences between teachers depend very much on the person. You have your gender, but you also have your personality.

However, this kind of realisation did not arise suddenly but required working with self-reflection, as noted by Mr Suzuki in earlier quotations. It also requires that a 'safe' and 'fair' atmosphere is created so that traditional norms may be challenged without people running the risk of being ridiculed. This kind of collegial atmosphere may be created by a group of male and female teachers as a common cross-gender project, as described by Mr Suzuki.

In their studies of male pre-school teachers, Nakata (2004) and Aono (2009) show that the men had initially believed that their teaching had nothing to do with gender but that after a while they realised that there were things that they could not do the way women did. The men described how change occurred as they worked alongside other male and female colleagues; they integrated images of women's and men's roles and developed their own unique practices according to their individual personalities. Mr Sato continues:

> We are many men here and we try to support each other in finding new ways of talking to the children. I think that it should be seen as natural for both men and women to raise children, both in the family and in nurseries. This should not be divided according to gender. I guess here in Japan it has been divided since the 'Samurai' time, and those old ideals continue to affect ordinary men and women in their relations to each other and to children, even though there is a great deal of discussion about the need to change them. It is really hard for both men and women with these traditional gender norms.

Both male and female teachers agree that traditional gender norms need to be changed. They propose that the way to do this is to create safe spaces for friendship, trust and shared collegial values about teaching, values that are inclusive in terms of gender. They imply that gender has to be discussed more openly and they raise questions about how to create a more inclusive way of understanding professionalism. *Is there a risk that discussion about 'gender neutral' environments in pre-school inevitably ends up creating one set of norms for men and another for women?*

Conclusions

In this chapter, we have explored female and male teacher's ideas about the gender challenges they encounter in their daily work and what they think about overcoming these. When Aono (2009) interviewed several male nursery school teachers she found that they experienced the role of the male teacher as distinct from that of the female teacher. They described how female teachers were regarded as children's 'natural' teachers despite the fact that their daily work and professional roles were ostensibly labelled 'gender neutral'. This paradox is also noted by the pre-school teachers in our study. Using this as our starting point, we have shown how teachers experience certain tasks as gendered. These tasks are linked to two discourses: firstly, that of children's needs, and secondly, the gendered division of labour.

The discourse about children's needs was found in all the kindergartens and nurseries in this study in the form of ideas about children's age and development. Young children were said to need extra tenderness whereas older children, both boys and girls, were said to need more healthy physical activity. However, the traditional gendered division of labour may make it difficult for female teachers to carry out this latter part of the 'professional role' since physical activity is traditionally associated with masculinity.[4] The discourse also makes it difficult for male teachers to care for young children and to demonstrate 'professional tenderness' through their body language and speech towards both boys and girls.

We have shown how the teachers used self-reflection and learned to cooperate with each other in order to develop their teaching practices for the children in their group. This meant creating or finding a shared set of professional values that all could subscribe to, regardless of gender. Some of the male teachers in the study said that from this 'safe platform' in the pre-school environment they wanted to show society new and different ways of fathering through their professional role as pre-school teachers. For instance, they often identified themselves as 'a father in the second home' in their process of developing a sense of professionalism and saw themselves as demonstrating a more attentive and tender way of relating to young children than the traditional authoritarian way.

Researchers have described how engaging in common projects and building solidarity may help people create spaces in which gender stereotypes become less relevant (Thorne 1993; Butler 2004; Hellman 2011). Some of the teachers interviewed in this study perceived that colleagues (in mixed- or single-gender groups) were able to co-create an atmosphere in which they felt safe enough to transgress stereotypical gender boundaries. We therefore wish to close by highlighting that solidarity – taking care of and standing up for one another – can create a safe space in which male and female teachers can negotiate gender in ways that make it possible to break with gender stereotypes.

UNANSWERED QUESTIONS

- Is there a risk that discussion about 'gender-neutral' environments in pre-school inevitably ends up creating one set of norms for men and another for women?
- How does language intersect with norms about gender in other contexts?
- How can we work in order to promote spaces for gender, safety and solidarity?

Notes

1. A sense of inherent aptitude based on socially constructed masculinity and femininity.
2. Hosted by Chie Nakazawa, Tokyo Gakugei University
3. Japan has two systems, with different curricula, for pre-school children: kindergarten for children aged three to six years and nurseries for children aged between zero months and six years. These institutions are linked to different government departments. The kindergartens are linked to the Department of Education and the nurseries are linked to the Department of Welfare; the departments are generally regarded as focusing on education and care respectively. Male teachers work in both systems.
4. Without male teachers female teachers lead the physical activity. But once male pre-school teachers enter pre-school, female teachers may put these expectations on men through a discourse about aptitude and the gender division of labour.

References

Act on Securing of Equal Opportunity and Treatment between Men and Women in Employment (1972) [Online.] Available at: http://www.ilo.org/dyn/travail/docs/2010/Act%20on%20Securing%20etc%20 of%20Equal%20Opportunity%20and%20Treatment%20between%20Men%20and%20Women%20 in%20Employment%201972.pdf (accessed 10 January 2015).

Act on the Welfare of Workers Who Take Care of Children or Other Family Members Including Childcare and Family Care Leave (1991) [Online.] Available at: http://www.ilo.org/dyn/travail/ docs/1971/Act%20on%20the%20Welfare%20of%20Workers%20Who%20Take%20Care%20 of%20Children%20or%20Other%20%20Family%20Members%20Including%20Child%20Care%20 and%20Family%20Care%20Leave%201991.pdf (accessed 10 January 2015).

青野篤子 (2009) 「男性保育者の保育職に対する意識: ジェンダー・フリー保育の観点か ら」『福山大学人間文化学部紀要』9号, pp. 1–29. (Aono, A. (2009) 'Male childcare workers' attitude toward child day care: from the view point of gender-free child day care', *Bulletin of Human Cultures and Sciences* (Fukuyama University), 9: 129.)

Butler, J. (1990) *Gender Trouble. Feminism and the Subversion of Identity*. New York: Routledge.

Butler, J. (2004) in S. Salih and J. Butler (eds), *The Judith Butler Reader*. Malden, MA: Blackwell.

Connell, R.W. (2000) *The Men and the Boys*. Cambridge: Polity.

Dahlberg, G., Moss, P. and Pence, A. (2002) *Från meningsskapande till kvalitet. Postmoderna perspektiv – exemplet förskolan. (From Creation of Meaning to Quality: Postmodern Perspectives – Examples from Pre-school)*. Stockholm: HLS Förlag.

Hellman, A. (2011) 'Gender learning in pre-school practices', in N. Pramling and I. Pramling-Samuelsson (eds), *Educational Encounters: Nordic Studies in Early Childhood Didactics*. New York: Springer.

Hellman, A. (2013) *Gender and Gender Equality in Pre-schools in Tokyo*. Tokyo: Japan Society for Promotion of Science.

本田潤子・小林育子・桜井登世子・安村清美・鈴木努・成田眞・高嶋景子・中原篤徳 (2006) 「保育現場において認識されている男性保育者の特徴」『田園調布学園大学紀 要』第1号, pp. 153–75. (Honda, J. *et al.* (2006) 'The characteristic of male childcare workers perceived in childcare centers', *Bulletin of Den-en Chofu University*, 1: 153–75.)

Kreiz-Sandberg, S. (2007) 'Gender and education: perspectives on schooling in Japan and comparisons from the Philippines', in C. Derichs and S. Kreiz-Sandberg (eds), *Gender Dynamics and Globalisation – Perspectives on Japan within Asia*. London: Transaction Publishers.

MacNaughton, G. (2006) 'Constructing gender in early years education', in C. Skelton and B. Francis (eds), *The Sage Handbook of Gender and Education*. London: Sage.

Mae, M. (2007) 'From culturality to transculturality. The paradigm shift in cultural and gender studies', in C. Derichs and S. Kreiz-Sandberg (eds), *Gender Dynamics and Globalisation – Perspectives on Japan within Asia*. London: Transaction Publishers.

文部科学省 (2008) 『幼稚園教育要領』 (Ministry of Education, Culture, Sports, Science and Technology, Japan (2008) *The Course of Study for Kindergarten*.)

厚生労働省 (2008) 『保育所保育指針』 (Ministry of Health, Labour and Welfare, Japan (2008) *The Guideline for Day Care Centers*.)

中村桃子 (2007) 『<性>と日本語: ことばがつくる女と男』日本放送出版協会. (Nakamura, M. (2007) *'Gender' and Japanese: Language Constructs Women and Men*. Japan Broadcasting Corporation.)

中田奈月 (2003) 「男性保育士による低年齢児保育の困難」『保育士養成研究』21号, pp. 19–27. (Nakata, N. (2003) 'Difficulty of male nursery teachers in baby-infant nursery', *Research on Nursery Education*, 21: 19–27.)

中田奈月(2004)「男性保育者による『保育者』定義のシークエンス」『家族社会学研究』16 (1): 41–51. (Nakata, N. (2004) 'Sequence analyses of a definition of "childcare workers" by male childcare workers', *Japanese Journal of Family Sociology*, 16 (1): 41–51.)

Nordberg, M., Saar, T. and Hellman, A. (2010) 'Deconstructing the normal boy: heterosexuality and gender constructions in school and pre-school', in L. Martinsson and E. Reimer (eds), *Norm Struggles: Sexualities in Contentions*. Newcastle: Cambridge Scholars Publishing.

Thorne, B. (1993) *Gender Play: Girls and Boys in School*. Buckingham: Open University Press.

高嶋景子・安村清美. (2006) 「『男性保育者』研究の動向: 男性保育者に求められる資質・役割に関する研究動向とその展望」『田園調布学園大学紀要』1号, pp. 153–76. (Takashima, K. and Yasumura, K. (2006) 'Recent trend of studies on "male childcare workers"', *Bulletin of Den-en Chofu University*, 1: 153–76.)

Whitehead, S. M. (2002) *Men and Masculinities: Key Themes and New Directions*. Malden, MA: Polity.

Young, I. M. (2000) 'Att kasta tjejkast. Den kvinnliga kroppens uttryck, rörelse och rumslighet', in *Att kasta tjejkast: Texter om feminism och rättvisa*. (*Texts About Feminism and Justice*). Stockholm: Atlas, pp. 255–80.

10

GENDERED IDEALS AND SPORTS COACHING

Reflections on the male as 'the centre' of sports in relation to child sports

Karin Grahn

Introduction

Sports coaching is regarded as an educational practice (Jones 2006); since sport is a popular leisure-time activity for children sports leaders/coaches play an important part in their social-isation. Sports also serves as an arena in which males engage with children. The majority of the sports leaders in Sweden are men (Riksidrottsförbundet (RF) 2013). Women tend to coach girls and young children more so than men, but according to Redelius' (2002) study a third of the sports leaders for children were men. Research suggests that fathers regard involvement in sports activities as a way of engaging in their children's lives (Gottzén and Kremer-Sadlik 2012). In Sweden a large number of coaches and leaders are parents carrying out voluntary non-paid work; in a study by Patriksson and Wagnsson (2004) fathers were more engaged as sports coaches than mothers. On the one hand, sports serve as an arena where men engage in educating and caring for children; on the other hand, sports are also criticised for being an arena that to a high degree celebrates male athletes and masculinity (Coakley and Pike 2009). Scholars are rather concerned with the masculinisation of sports in comparison to primary school settings in which the feminisation of practice has been the topic of much discussion (Skelton 2001).

Even though a number of elite sportswomen of today are highly valued, popular in the media and well paid, the male high-performing body is still central to the valuation of sports activities. Messner (2003) believes that traditional male sports and male athletes are positioned at the centre of sport. Sports activities also remain strongly segregated in terms of gender, which directly influences coaching practices. For this reason it is important to critically exam-ine and discuss the ideal of the male high-performing body and the central position of men in sports. This is important as values and ideals may influence sports coaching practices for people of all ages/gender identities/sexual orientations. Even young children who participate in sporting activities may be exposed to explicit or implicit ideals, both through practice and via the media (Fagrell 2000; Messner 2003; Bhana 2008; Bartholomaeus 2011). A study carried out by Fagrell (2000) showed that seven-year-old Swedish children already had a clear image of boys and men as being stronger and more suited for competitive sports than their female counterparts. When children grow up they may look to sports stars as role models and male-centred ideas of sports performance may influence their own relations to sports. This influence is, for example, reflected in interviews carried out with children in grades 3 to 6 (9–12 year olds) (Grahn and Berggren Torell 2014) which showed that sex-divided teams in organised sports were taken for granted by the children. Some of the children talked about boys and male football players as better and stronger.

The aim of this chapter is to reflect upon the male-centredness of sports and how gendered ideals may influence the coaching of athletes. Using examples from a previous study (Grahn 2008) the chapter examines how gender is constructed in textbooks used in Swedish coaching education. Interviews were also conducted with swimming coaches, taking note of how they talked about young athletes; these are also used as examples. By gaining more knowledge about gender discourses in sports and how coaching is gendered, it is possible to reflect upon how norms and ideals are reproduced or challenged. The focus of my research is on youth sports but the discussion raised is also of interest in relation to other age groups, not least impressionable young children. Many of these children will continue to experience sports in their future schooling and through their personal interests. Since sports are a common leisure activity among children it is important to reflect upon how gender discourses may affect children's participation. Sports are also consumed in different ways and young children may experience sports either as participants, spectators, through the media or through computer games. Raising awareness about gender issues is relevant for all coaches, leaders, parents/carers and teachers. There is also a wider relevance to this work as it is personally argued that gender ideals affect the life of the individual as well as society at large.

Background

To frame the context of this study a brief introduction to Swedish sports and coaching education is deemed necessary. The so-called Swedish Sports Movement includes all sports for people of any age – these are organised in sports clubs that are members of the Swedish Sports Confederation (Riksidrottsförbundet: RF). Usually sports clubs offer activities for children of a pre-school age. According to the RF the majority of Swedish children are engaged in a sport at one time or another from the age of seven (RF 2014). All sports clubs are governed by the policy document of the Swedish Sports Confederation (RF 2009) which contains guidelines that apply to child sports as well as elite sports and recreational sports. In Sweden, no official qualifications are needed to become a coach. A basic course usually provides specific sport knowledge and some instructions in coaching children. The courses are organised by specialised sports federations (floor ball, swimming, etc.) and they usually produce course textbooks.

This chapter draws on data from two research projects. In the first study a quantitative analysis of texts and pictures and discourse analysis (Bergström and Boréus 2000; Fairclough 2001) were used to analyse a total of 43 course textbooks for coaches in six different sports, these being football/soccer, floor ball, handball, athletics, swimming and gymnastics. The textbooks were intended for coaches of children and youth athletes from about 10 years of age and older, but the textbooks relating to floor ball, football, gymnastics and swimming also dealt with younger children. The chapter also draws on interviews with youth coaches (three men and one woman). They were included in a study of coaches and athletes in swimming.

A total of 20 interviews were conducted with four coaches and six athletes in three clubs. Discourses of gender, performance, training and the body were analysed, including the use of language and interpretative repertoires (Edley 2001). All of the coaches led co-trained groups of girls and boys.

Competitive sports

The notion of sports is one that is organised around the idea of ranking. The athlete or team that runs the fastest or scores the most goals is crowned the winner/s. To assure that sports offer equal opportunities for all participants it is divided into child, youth and adult sports, recreational, competitive and elite sports, disability sports, and women's and men's sports. The argument for these divisions is that it would be unfair, for instance, for women to compete against men based on physical strength and capacity. Even though physical capacity does not differ between non-adolescent girls and boys, most sports use the adult sex segregated organisation in training and competition from an early age (see Messner 2003). From this perspective sports activities are organised around the idea of the adult male high-performing body. Performing bodies in sports can be described in a continuum from fastest to slowest, strongest to weakest. In this continuum adult male high-performing bodies are positioned as the fastest, most agile and strongest, and all other bodies are positioned in relation to this ideal.

Even though the idea of the performing body as a continuum enables women athletes to be viewed as faster and stronger than male athletes, this is seldom the case. Since male bodies in general are positioned at the high end of the continuum, the male athlete symbolises high-performance athletes. According to Larsson (2001) this makes the male body the most desirable body in sport. The grown-up, strong (male) body may also be idealised in other educational settings, in which pre-school children are told to eat their food to become big and strong (see Chapter 5).

Social and performance orientation in sports

A social orientation emphasises personal relationships and having fun (Stuntz and Weiss 2003). This is viewed as especially important in sports for young children (Messner 2009). In a coaching context, this means that being caregiving, empathetic, working on relationships with the athletes and the social climate in the group are prioritised values. In other words these are traits and social skills that both women and men coaches in child sport are expected to have. For example, in a study by Gottzén and Kremer-Sadlik (2012) fathers involved in their children's organised sports activities emphasised a caring and supporting behaviour. The expectations of men coaching children to have certain social skills can be compared to desired qualities among men working in primary schools. On one hand they are expected to include traditional feminine aspects such as caring and sensitivity into their teaching; on the other hand they are expected to provide, for example, discipline (Skelton 2001).

Performance orientation is when achieving and winning are viewed as central in sports (Carless and Douglas 2012). This is considered to be less important in the early years (Messner 2009) but Gottzén and Kremer-Sadlik (2012) argue that over time there is an expectation that children will develop their competencies with an aim to succeed in sports. Competitive sports coaching has been shown to be developed on technical rationality, viewing bodies as biological objects that can be moulded into success. This has led to authoritarian coaching practices built on hierarchical coach–athlete relationships (Cassidy *et al.* 2009). Scholars have been critical of this way of conducting sports coaching; according to Ingham *et al.* (2002) even youth sports draw on a performance principle and thereby run the risk of bypassing the developmental perspective of participating in sports. Performance or social orientations are sometimes treated as opposites. Performance orientation is often connected to boys whereas social orientation is connected to girls (Larsson 2001). However, research shows that young athletes' descriptions of themselves contain both performance and social aspects as being important and integrated (Eliasson 2011; Larsson 2001).

Theoretical framework

The research draws on gender/intersectionality theory and discourse analysis, viewing language as a source for shaping knowledge. Discourses both enable us to talk and think about things such as sports or gender and to make sense of things. But discourses are also limiting in the way that they shape knowledge as truths or common sense. Our knowledge and the way we can talk about things are prescribed by discourses at the same time as discourses are shaped by language and social interaction (Fairclough 2001). Language use in coaching or coaching education influences ideas about coaching and those being coached (Cassidy *et al.* 2009).

Sports as gender regimes

Research on gender and sports has shown how femininity and masculinity are constructed as both separate and complementary, reproducing a gender order built on a binary classification model (Coakley and Pike 2009). To uphold this gender order organisers, coaches and sports participants actively keep the boundaries between women and men. This happens both in everyday sports practices and in Physical Education (Eliasson 2011; Oliynyk 2014). Children learn from an early age that sports are sex segregated and internalise this situation as the 'normal' way to do sports (Fagrell 2000; Messner 2003; Eliasson 2011; Grahn and Berggren Torell 2014). Gender divisions and stereotypical behaviour have been shown to be prevalent among four- and five-year-old girls and boys in soccer (Messner 2003); studies of primary school children (seven to eight year-olds) suggest that boys are already viewed as bigger, better and more suited for sports (Hasbrook and Harris 1999; Fagrell 2000; Bhana 2008; Bartholomaeus 2011). Different sports have, however, different gender associations and are arranged and practised differently. Children may learn different things about gender in rhythmic gymnastics than in handball. It has been previously suggested that diverse gender regimes apply to different sports (Grahn 2008). A gender regime (Connell 1987) can be understood as the ordering of gender, either at a local or institutional level. This means that the institution or practice frames the way gender is understood and thereby power relations between boys/girls, men/women and femininity/masculinity exist. By viewing different sports as gender regimes, different ways of reproducing or challenging the centre of sports can be explored.

Age and gender as intersecting

Krekula *et al.* (2005) emphasise the need to include age in intersectionality research and see both gender and age as axes of power that may intersect. Intersectionality can be analysed as processes which construct age, gender or other categories in everyday life, and which constitute power relations that mutually determine each other (Krekula *et al.* 2005). Gender and age is of interest in this chapter. Descriptions of athletes include both gender norms and age norms with the two needs being analysed as intersecting entities.

The adult male high-performance body as the centre of sport

The following section shows how the male body is produced as the centre of sport (Messner 2003) in textbooks used in sports coaching education programmes. I will exemplify how gender differences are constructed in relation to the norm.

The male body as the centre of textbooks

Results from the textbook analysis show how the male body is presented as the centre of the text. Five aspects were noted:

1. More men and boys than girls and women were portrayed in the pictures.
2. Elite athletes were most often presented as men or male teams.
3. Male athletes were presented as the norm, for example in sport instructions and in examples of exercises.
4. Male athletes were presented as the centre of knowledge on athletes.
5. Sports language often drew on male-associated words and idioms such as 'man-against-man play'.

In all of the included sports, with the exception of swimming, pictures of boys and men dominated, with more than twice as many pictures of male athletes than of female athletes being present in the football, athletics, handball and gymnastics textbooks. Textbooks about swimming contained an equal amount of pictures of girls, boys and girls and boys together. Although there was a disproportionate portrayal of male athletes, there were differences among the textbooks. Some textbooks had a more equal distribution of pictures of girls and boys while others had a high number of illustrations of males. In ten out of 43 textbooks studied there were pictures of boys/men but no pictures of girls/women at all. This domination of boys in pictures normalises the view of boys as natural athletes. From this perspective a mix of girls and boys in pictures is symbolically important to signal to the reader that sports activities are carried out by both girls and boys and, as in swimming, by girls and boys together.

In total, girls/women and boys/men were mentioned to the same extent in the textbooks, but there was a significant difference in how and when they were mentioned. For example, even if only a few elite athletes were mentioned, they were usually men. When books presented sports-specific knowledge, such as methodological instructions and examples of drills, athletes were most often presented as boys ('he'), as in the following example:

The first man in line starts with the ball, and dribbles around the cones. When he dribbles around the last cone he turns around and passes the ball along the center line to a player/coach and gets a pass in return. He receives [the ball], spins around the cone in the middle and shoots at the goal.
(Textbook about floor ball, Florin et al. 2001: 69)

This way of writing was most common in the textbooks about athletics, handball and floor ball. In those textbooks about swimming and football the expression 'he/she' was most common, but the second most common way of writing was 'he'. In the gymnastics textbook joint expressions like 'he/she' and personal pronouns (she or he) were used to an equal extent. While text about girls constructed gender-specific knowledge, for example menstruation or physical training for girls/women, text about male athletes was used to construct knowledge about athletes in general. For example:

In a state of rest you ventilate 5–10 litres of air/minute. At maximal work ventilation can increase to more than 100 and up to 200–220 litres/min for well-trained adult males.
(Textbook about hand ball, Månsson 2000: 23)

This example also emphasises the *adult* well-trained body as the centre of knowledge from which coaches for less well-trained men/women/boys/girls are supposed to gain knowledge.

The language used in textbooks to describe sports and teaching/coaching in sports was found also to be gendered. Exercises and games had male-associated names such as 'man-against-man games' or games named after male figures like 'The Gingerbread Man' and 'Following John' or exercises like 'Tarzan-swimming'. This masculinised language is most frequently used with reference to team sports. Since the Swedish Sports Confederation has emphasised that playfulness is important in sports for children (RF 2009) one can question the gender distribution of play role figures. *Is it the case that both girls and boys can pretend to be 'John' or 'The Gingerbread Man' but not feminine-associated figures?* With the current names of games, girls and *boys* are left out of the opportunity to pretend to be, for example, 'Pippi Longstocking' or 'Santa Lucia'.

To summarise, the male body symbolises the athletic body in the textbooks and in this way knowledge about male bodies comes to represent knowledge about athletic bodies. The priority given to boys and men in textbooks tends to be less explicit in books for younger children and in those textbooks aimed at coaching less advanced levels of sport. Even so, it is important for coaches/leaders/teachers of young children to reflect upon these findings since continued involvement in sports may include a more intense focus on boys/men as the centre of sports, including sports knowledge based on male bodies.

The idealised body in swimming

When describing the optimal body in swimming, coaches drew both on discourses of similarity and gender difference. The first is shown in coaches' descriptions of an optimal body for swimming. Coaches emphasised size: a tall body with large hands and feet. The 'right' genes would seemingly provide individuals with a performing body. Even though the optimal body for swimming was described by drawing on biology, there were few connections to gender in the descriptions offered. In this sense the swimmer's body was viewed as a one-dimensional, non-gendered body (it did not matter if you were a girl or a boy as long as you were tall). Both male and female swimmers were exemplified as possessing an optimal swimmers' body, such as in this example mentioning two of Sweden's best swimmers:

> *Therese Alshammar, she is like the archetype, and Sara Sjöstrand, she has gigantic feet.*
>
> *(Eva, coach)*

These women were not exemplified as 'archetypes' for female swimmers but for swimmers in general. In contrast to many of the textbooks analysed (besides those about swimming), the swimmer's body could be represented by either a female or a male body. Descriptions of the body draw on a discourse of gender differences when the interviewees talked about performance, physical development and muscles. For example, even though both female and male swimmers can represent the ideal body, achieving the optimal body was described in different terms:

> *[G]uys reach the swimming body much quicker than girls. […] for a guy it's enough to go into puberty and then you're done, you look like a swimmer, if you train correctly meanwhile.*
>
> *(Christopher, coach)*

Boys were described as developing a performing body: 'boys grow and become good at sports; girls grow and become less good at sports' (Eva, coach). This view of boys and girls seems to be connected to the onset of puberty. When younger swimmers were described girls were described as comparable to boys. This shows how intersections between age and gender are situated and changeable (see Krekula *et al.* 2005).

Both in the interviews and the textbooks analysed the positive effects of bodily changes for boys were emphasised (growth, muscles, etc.) and, as a result of these changes, an enhancement of performance would follow. In these descriptions of girls and boys during adolescence the adult male high-performance body is idealised and constructed as the end point of the boys' development. This can be compared to Krekula *et al.* (2005: 86) who argue that the 'working age' is the norm of a society which positions children as 'not yets'. In this manner boys can be described as 'soon to be' (high-performing) athletes. This is also in line with eight- and nine-year-old boys' imaginations of their future bodies as strong and successful in sport, as described by Bhana (2008).

Gendered coaching

In the textbooks analysed femininities and masculinities were constructed by drawing on both a performance and a social discourse. Both girls and boys were portrayed as performance and socially oriented, but the overall idea of girls was that they were in need of having specific social aspects taken into consideration while doing sports. Boys were less likely to be described in the same way. Boys were described more explicitly as performance oriented in textbooks: 'boys [are] more oriented towards performing' (Textbook about swimming, Ågren *et al.* n.d.: 13). Girls were generally constructed as being socially oriented: 'Girls are more social than guys and most often choose sport primarily for social interaction' (Textbook about floor ball, Florin *et al.* 2001: 63). Social orientation was constructed as essentially feminine, which is repeated in many texts, while only some texts tried to problematise this view.

The coach (as the intended reader) is important in how femininities and masculinities are constructed in the textbooks. Instructions to the coaches were given on how to coach boys and girls. These instructions construct an idea of how boys and girls are expected to act and what they needed in their training. Girls were constructed as in need of social support to do sports. Words like 'motivate', 'understand' and 'support' were reoccurring. *So what do swimming coaches have to say about girls and boys doing swimming?* The coaches interviewed sometimes portrayed boys as being more competitive and girls as being more socially oriented. For example, Hans (coach) told me that 'All of them want to win, girls and boys, but boys want to win more' and 'Girls love to talk, boys want to train'. Coaches' views of boys as more competitive can be interpreted as a result of boys learning to be competitive already at an early age. Studies of first-year grade boys [six-year-olds] (Hasbrook and Harris 1999; Oliynyk 2014) show that competitiveness is part of the construction of masculinity. While the coaches interviewed described boys as being more competitive, both girls and boys portrayed themselves as being competitive and performance-oriented athletes, particularly in the interviews with swimmers. More importantly, both girls and boys also emphasised the significance of having good social relations while engaging in sporting activity.

Even though the above quotes represent a stereotypical view of girls and boys, those coaches who were interviewed also talked about both girls and boys as being performance oriented *and* in need of social aspects like a friendly climate. In general, coaches portrayed the training as all swimmers doing the same things and training in the same ways. Gender differences were mostly described as being socially different, and these differences were said to sometimes influence interactions in the group or between coaches and swimmers, such as using a softer way to communicate with girls.

To summarise, coaching is portrayed as gendered, performance-oriented for boys and more caring and socially oriented for girls. This is particularly the case in the textbooks analysed. In swimming, the coaching of girls and boys draws on a discourse of sameness; all swimmers are trained in the same way and do the same things, but the coaching of swimmers also draws on a discourse of social differences since girls are portrayed as being different to boys and in need of a more attentive and caring style of coaching.

Reflections: male-centredness

This chapter has problematised the male norm in sports, especially by exemplifying how textbooks construct the adult male high-performing body as an ideal. It is not possible to say from this research *if* and *how* the content of textbooks influences coaching practices. However, according to Fairclough (2001), language is important in shaping discourses, which in turn shapes social practices. Drawing on discourse analysis, pictures, texts and talk are thus important in influencing social relations and subject positions.

When sports coaching practices draw on an idea of the adult male high-performance body there is a risk of subordinating female bodies, feminine bodies and other forms of masculinities. Textbooks may also leave coaches without practical tools to handle diverse problems that may be associated with socialisation into a narrow view of masculinity such as homophobia, aggression, injuries, body ideals and so forth. If only one (or select types of) masculinity is (are) idealised, sport educational practices will become tied to a gender regime leaving limited space for the development of diverse masculinities and femininities, leaving only a narrow space for boys to express femininity and/or to include homosexuality as part of a sporting masculinity. Sports activities could counter these ideas if sports leaders/teachers actively work for acceptance and diversity, starting when children begin engaging in sports. If coaches, leaders, parents and teachers gain knowledge of ideals promoted through sports they can actively work against them and towards a more acceptant and diverse coaching.

In the textbooks analysed there is a lack of discussion about the fact that not all boys are similar. It presupposes that boys are a homogenous group, a problem which has also been pointed out in educational research concerning boys' underachievement (see Skelton 2000). Boys who do not fit into the prescribed masculinity may be left out or dropped from sport settings. Other research that deals with Swedish child sports has shown results in line with the arguments of this chapter. Male athletes and the way men play sports have been shown to be promoted in sports settings. Eliasson (2011), for example, suggests that boys and a masculine way of playing is the norm in children's football. Oliynyk (2014) suggests that children's physical education in elementary school draws on a male norm. These results (among others) show that the adult male way of playing sports and being an athlete influences child sports. This influence becomes problematic if it excludes other values. For example, research has shown that idealised forms of masculinity in sports include heterosexuality, competitiveness, strength, aggression and power (Wellard 2007). These traits have also been shown to be highly valued among Afro-American first graders in US primary schools (Hasbrook and Harris 1999) and research involving Australian primary school children (Bartholomaeus 2011); findings highlight that sports were seen as the most common association to masculinity, and that taking part in sports was described as part of 'being' a boy. Similar results have been found by Skelton (2000) in English primary school football activities.

Reflections: gendered coaching

Results show that different types of coaching are prescribed for boys and for girls (see Larsson 2001; Eliasson 2011). Coaching of girls draws on a social discourse emphasising having fun, friendship and caring. Coaching of boys is framed by a performance discourse. This dichotomous way of viewing coaching strengthens discourses of gender difference and may lead to different sporting practices for boys and girls. These shape different experiences which do not depend on personal interests or aims for doing sports but on children's biological sex. In research interviews with swimming coaches they described their coaching practices as being built on an idea of sameness. Co-training of girls and boys enables athletes to gain similar experiences of doing sport. It can create a setting in which the individual is seen and where differences are not viewed as being based on the biological sex. The practices described by the coaches exhibit a potential to give swimmers an individual experience of doing sport that is less formed by gender, but there were also examples of gender stereotypical views of coaching athletes. The opportunity for co-training of girls and boys could be possible in a range of sports, especially in the early years, when differences in physical strength and bodily size are small between girls and boys. Sports for young children have a great potential to explore co-training of girls and boys.

When coaching is gendered there is a risk of strengthening gender stereotypes instead of being attentive to the necessity of different coaching styles depending on individual needs. If, for example, boys are viewed as performance oriented, there is a risk that they will be exposed to coaching practices imbued with a traditional coaching discourse, promoting authoritarian coaching which could lead to negative consequences for the athlete's health and well-being (Cassidy et al. 2009). This type of coaching could be contrasted to the ideals expressed in a study by Ingham et al. (2002) which argued for the value of youth coaching practices drawing on participatory and developmental discourses, and which emphasised equality, cooperation and caring as an alternative to solely drawing on the performance discourse in sports. As the interviews with swimmers have shown, both girls and boys point to the importance of a good social climate while engaging in sports. Based on their statements (also see Ingham et al. 2002) coaches for children should be urged to keep a social orientation in coaching for both boys and girls, even when athletes grow older.

Conclusions

In this chapter I have suggested that there are gendered views on coaching based on perceptions of girls and boys as different. I have also argued that men and male sports are constructed as 'the centre' of sports, but that this ideal may have more or less impact depending on the sport and the levels of sport. Even though sports for young children may not be as influenced by this ideal as competitive youth sports, I suggest that there is a continued need to reflect upon the ideal so that the male centeredness of sports does not negatively impact on sports practices for children.

UNANSWERED QUESTIONS

- How can coaches/leaders/teachers/parents working with young children challenge the male as being the centre of sports?
- What actions need to be taken to develop a more inclusive and diverse sports practice?
- How can sports coaching practices become more focused on every child's personal interests and aims for doing sports instead of being organised around believed gender differences?
- What can sports learn from other forms of educational or leisure time activities for children?

References

Ågren, B., Ståhl, G., Mellhammar, G., Jonsson, G., Lindgren, R. and Ahrreman, S. (n.d.) *Baskurs, barn och ungdom. Deltagarmaterial*. Stockholm: Gymnastikförbundet.

Bartholomaeus, C. (2011) 'What it means to be "manly": Gender, sport, and primary school students', *Outskirts*, 24. [Online.] Available at: http://www.outskirts.arts.uwa.edu.au/volumes/volume-24/bartholomaeus (accessed 4 September 2014).

Bergström, G. and Boréus, K. (2000) *Textens mening och makt: Metodbok i samhällsvetenskaplig textanalys*. Lund: Studentlitteratur.

Bhana, D. (2008) '"Six packs and big muscles, and stuff like that". Primary school-aged South African boys, black and white, on sport', *British Journal of Sociology of Education*, 29 (1): 3–14.

Carless, D. and Douglas, K. (2012) 'Stories of success: Cultural narratives and personal stories of elite and professional athletes', *Reflective Practice: International and Multidisciplinary Perspectives*, 13 (3): 387–98.

Cassidy, T., Jones, R. L. and Potrac, P. (2009) *Understanding Sports Coaching: The Social, Cultural and Pedagogical Foundations of Coaching Practice*, 2nd edn. London: Routledge.

Coakley, J. J. and Pike, E. (2009) *Sports in Society: Issues and Controversies*. London: McGraw-Hill Education.

Connell, R. W. (1987) *Gender and Power: Society, the Person and Sexual Politics*. Cambridge: Polity & Blackwell.

Edley, N. (2001) 'Analysing masculinity: interpretative repertoires, ideological dilemmas and subject positions', in M. Wetherell, S. Taylor and S. Yates (eds), *Discourse as Data: A Guide for Analysis*. London: Sage, pp. 189–228.

Eliasson, I. (2011) 'Gendered socialization among girls and boys in children's football teams in Sweden', *Soccer and Society*, 12 (6): 820–33.

Fagrell, B. (2000) *De små konstruktörerna: flickor och pojkar om kvinnligt och manligt i relation till kropp, idrott, familj och arbete* (*The Small Constructors: Girls and Boys About Womanliness and Manliness in Relation to Body, Sport, Family and Work*). Dissertation. Stockholm: HLS.

Fairclough, N. (2001) *Language and Power*, 2nd edn. Harlow: Longman.

Florin, P., Hällgren, T., Pettersson, S., Wallin, P. and Larsson, N. (2001) *Innebandyledare för barn och ungdomar*. Malmö: UPAB & SISU Idrottsböcker.

Gottzén, L. and Kremer-Sadlik, T. (2012) 'Fatherhood and youth sports: A balancing act between care and expectations', *Gender and Society*, 26 (4): 639–64.

Grahn, K. (2008) *Flickor och pojkar i idrottens läromedel. Konstruktioner av genus i ungdomstränarutbildningen* (*Girls and Boys in Sports Textbooks. Constructions of gender in Youth Coaching Education Programmes*). Dissertation. Göteborg, Acta Universitatis Gothoburgensis.

Grahn, K. and Berggren Torell, V. (2014) *Barndom och genus i Idrottslyftsprojekt på skoltid*. Stockholm: Riksidrottsförbundet. [Online.] Available at: http://tinyurl.com/pr6ffb3 (accessed 4 November 2014).

Hasbrook, C. A. and Harris, O. (1999) 'Wrestling with gender: Physicality and masculinities among inner-city first and second graders', *Men and Masculinities*, 1 (3): 302–18.

Ingham, A. G., Chure, M. A. and Butt, J. (2002) 'From the performance principle to the development principle: Every kid a winner?', *Quest*, 54 (4): 308–31.

Jones, R. L. (2006) 'Introduction: coaching as an educational enterprise', in I. R. L. Jones (ed.), *The Sport Coach as Educator. Re-conceptualising Sports Coaching*. Abingdon: Routledge, pp. 3–13.

Krekula, C., Närvänen, A.-L. and Näsman, E. (2005) 'Ålder i intersektionell analys', *Kvinnovetenskaplig tidskrift*, 2–3: 81–94.

Larsson, H. (2001) *Iscensättningen av kön i idrott. En nutidshistoria om idrottsmannen och idrottskvinnan* (*The Staging of Gender in Sport. A Contemporary History About the Sportsman and the Sportswoman*). Dissertation. Stockholm: HLS.

Månsson, B. (2000) *Fysisk träning och träningslära för handbollspelare och tränare*. Stockholm: Svenska handbollförbundet.

Messner, M. A. (2003) *Taking the Field: Women, Men, and Sports*. Minneapolis, MN: University of Minnesota Press.

Messner, M. A. (2009) *It's All for the Kids: Gender, Families, and Youth Sports*. Berkeley, CA: University of California Press.

Oliynyk, I. (2014) *Att göra tudelning. Om att synliggöra och diskutera ämnet idrott och hälsa för de yngre åldrarna ur ett genusperspektiv* (*Making Dichotomy. About Making Visibly and Discussing Physical Education for the Younger Ages from a Gender Perspective*). Malmö Studies in Sport Sciences, Licentiate Theses. Malmö: Malmö högskola.

Patriksson, G. and Wagnsson, S. (2004) *Föräldraengagemang i barns idrottsföreningar*, FoU-rapport 2004:8. Stockholm: Riksidrottsförbundet.

Redelius, K. (2002) *Ledarna och barnidrotten: idrottsledarnas syn på idrott, barn och fostran* (*The Leaders and Child Sports: Sports Leaders Views on Sports, Children and Nurturing*). Dissertation. Stockholm: University of Stockholm.

Riksidrottsförbundet (RF) (2009) *Idrotten vill*. Stockholm: Riksidrottsförbundet. [Online.] Available at: http://tinyurl.com/pd7vv9m (accessed 24 November 2013).

Riksidrottsförbundet (RF) (2013) *2013 Verksamhetsberättelse med årsredovisningar.* Stockholm: Riksidrottsförbundet. [Online.] Available at: http://tinyurl.com/kv6arok (accessed 19 August 2014).

Riksidrottsförbundet (RF) (2014) *Barn och ungdomsidrott.* [Online.] Available at: http://www.svenskidrott. se/Barnochungdomsidrott/ (accessed 30 May 2014).

Skelton, C. (2000) '"A passion for football": Dominant masculinities and primary schooling', *Sport, Education and Society,* 5 (1): 5–18.

Skelton, C. (2001) *Schooling the Boys: Masculinities and Primary Education.* Buckingham: Open University Press.

Stuntz, C. P. and Weiss, M. R. (2003) 'Influence of social goal orientations and peers on unsportsmanlike play', *Research Quarterly for Exercise and Sport,* 74 (4): 421–35.

Wellard, I. (2007) 'Inflexible bodies and minds: exploring the gendered limits in contemporary sport, physical education and dance', in I. Wellard (ed.), *Rethinking Gender and Youth Sport.* London: Routledge.

CONCLUSIONS

Inga Wernersson and Jo Warin with Simon Brownhill

To raise male participation in educating and caring for young children seems to be an objective in many countries in Europe and elsewhere. Norway currently 'leads the way' with around 10 per cent of staff in kindergartens being male. This, however, falls short of the 20 per cent set as a goal (Norway: Handlingsplan, 2004), even though an elaborated and long-ranging campaign has been at work in that country. Interestingly, Sweden seems unable to meet the 20 per cent 'quota', despite it being a country that had a clear policy and has used affirmative action as early as the 1970s.

Two questions were posed in the Introduction to this book. One question asks what is it with masculinity that keeps men away from teaching and caring for young children; the other is about what difference more men would make. To put it bluntly: *Are men so badly needed that it is worth all this fuss?* The lack of males in professional teaching and care for young children can be posed as a simple or as a complex question, the simple one being: *How do we go about recruiting more men to the job?* There need not be any worries about competence; that many men are suitable for the job has been proven (as well as there are, of course, women who are not very suitable). The answer may then be a concern for marketing experts. *How do we present the connection between men and children in a 'selling' manner?* Not even the most effective countries are, however, very successful as the goal of 20 per cent has not been met despite massive media visibility, economic incentives and affirmative actions of different kinds. The experience to date indicates that we have to deal with a more complex interpretation of the problem. Viewed as a complex question, the issue of male absence in professional teaching and care for young children contains ingredients from most of the 'all-too-well-known' aspects of a hierarchical gender order: power and status differences, division of labour, ideas about inevitable gender-related personality differences and the image of males as violent and dangerous, to mention a few.

The chapters in this book use several different angles to highlight the issue: as part of a structure/gender order, from a pedagogical/teaching perspective, from the perspective of children and from within different cultural contexts. Let us start with the children, or rather the perception of how children are, and what consequences this may have for men as professionals and gender equality in childcare.

The image of the child

Adriany (Chapter 6) takes a critical stand towards the 'child-centred approach' in Indonesian kindergartens. Her main point is that the idea of a natural sequence of development restrains ECE teachers since they believe that they are not supposed to influence children and try to change stereotypical gender patterns. The assumed naturalness of young children implies that gendered inclinations are innate rather than constructed in social interaction. Under some circumstances there might also be a potential conflict between ideas of children's competence and agency, and pedagogical efforts to counteract unwanted social patterns. Löfdahl and Hjalmarsson (Chapter 3) describe similar tendencies from the Swedish horizon where tacit assumptions of inevitable sex differences form the base for methods of gender pedagogics. They refer to the slogan 'Add but not deprive', stressing that gender pedagogy is *to add to* rather than to *change* children's repertoire of behaviour patterns, activities and competencies. This serves as an example of how boys and girls are viewed as '… representing distinct characters, with different needs, personality and skills, [which] thus fail[s] to see the differences within the groups "boys" and "girls"' (p. 38). When considering children's sport activities, as discussed by Grahn (Chapter 10), it seems hard to separate the biological fact that adult females and males have different average physical capacity in some aspects from how individual children are experienced. The gendered organisation of sport activities and the image of the adult male body is a lingering problem in children's sports. Systematic research on sex and gender, as well as everyday experiences and political debate related to social changes during recent decades, has formed understandings of gender as social constructions in numerous shapes. Several studies presented in this book show that the child, regardless of these findings, is believed to have a biologically given, gendered personality. Such beliefs are also clearly present in the very efforts to promote gender equality. This makes the importance attached to men as role models even more puzzling. *Why are role models needed if girlishness and boyishness are seemingly innate?*

The image of men and masculinity

Men and the mystery of masculinity serve as the core of this book – *why are there so few men in ECE?* Warin (Chapter 8) stresses the general importance of gender in the creation of a personal identity, and that belonging to a minority group (e.g. being a male teacher in preschool) underscores this even more. Individual/psychological mechanisms might magnify gender identity in a situation where gender is supposed to be played down by intentional or even programmatic crossing of traditional gender lines. All primary actors involved – be they children, parents or female colleagues – form expectations and demands that may become extremely gendered because of the minority status of men. The male carer may become very self-conscious in the 'performance of self' and it may become complicated to simultaneously have a 'male approach' and be a sensible adult demonstrating equality and similarity between men and women. The minority status as such, rather than inherently male needs that are not fulfilled in the 'feminised' world of childcare, would then be an active force in keeping men away from this kind of employment. It may then, in a sense, be the absence of real and profound differences that keep men out of ECE. The lived experience that there is nothing very special that discerns them as men from all those women may be a confusing, or even scary, experience for some male adults who are keen to perform the longed-for 'male role model'.

If there is such confusion it could be interpreted as a loss of identity and/or a kind of shame related to the loss of legitimacy for general male hegemony.

The emphasis on masculinity in ECE seems to be stronger in the USA than in other countries represented in this book. Mallozzi and Campbell Galman (Chapter 4) describe how a female teacher marvels at a demonstration of militaristic manliness by a male teacher and the question is asked *whether this emphasis on the soldier as an example of unique and spectacular maleness in some way serves the interests of other ways of being male?* Maybe the image of masculinity is fragile and elusive and needs extreme attributes and femininity as a contrast to make it visible and 'true'?

Political action, as well as a substantial body of research, has focused on the seemingly parallel problem for women to enter male occupations. Women appear to have integrated comparatively well in some traditionally male strongholds like engineering and politics. Two aspects may be important for understanding the difference between male and female crossings of gender lines. Firstly, women move upwards status-wise when they enter traditional male areas and, secondly, femininity needs not be as safeguarded as masculinity. That the individual personality, e.g. as 'role model', is used as an important tool in carework may serve as a third form of difference between traditionally female and male occupations that makes it harder for men to integrate. Difficulties for women entering male occupations have been related to the questioning of competence and different kinds of harassment, while the difficulties for men seem to be more of a loss of identity and downgrading of social position.

Brownhill (Chapter 2) asks the question: *If being a role model is indeed 'part of the job' of an educator, does that mean that females are strong role models for children?* If the answer is yes, meaning that all adults are role models, males might find themselves in a kind of cross-pressure, feeling at risk of losing their male identity and at the same time not really knowing how to be a male role model. There are stories presented in this book of male ECE teachers who exaggerate the male role; Löfdahl and Hjalmarsson (Chapter 3) give mention to practice which sees aggressive behaviour among boys being more or less supported and documented for parents to view by professionals. A woman who becomes an engineer or a carpenter or some other 'male job' may have similar problems with dual pressures and images of self. One important difference may be, however, that gender identity is much less, if at all, important in the actual performance of job tasks. If being a 'role model' is part of professional teaching and caring for young children then the male professional may end up in the contradictions of trying to perform a distinctly male role and, at the same time, be a gender neutral individual.

It is often more or less taken for granted that caring is 'feminised' because it is performed mostly by women. It may, however, be more relevant to 'turn it on its head', i.e. that the idea of a 'female individual' has been formed by the traditional gendered division of labour by the needs of children, and thus that it is more about a 'careification' of women than a feminisation of caring. Should this be the case, it may be very hard for a man to remain within the male gender frame and still do the work properly. There is a logical difference between seeing tasks and behaviour as present in a female and a male type and to see men and women as shaped by the things they do and have done for generations.

The role model argument can be understood at the psychological/individual level. If identity is created/constructed in interaction, then basically all individuals, regardless of age and sex, are potential role models, good or bad. What is expected from male pedagogues are performances of 'manliness' that are supposed to have the potential to guide children (boys) when learning how to be or respond to a proper (adult) man. Very early in the Nordic context (Tiller 1962) the specific importance of male role models was connected to (1) 'compensatory masculinity', meaning the risk of boys picking up violent or otherwise unwanted aspects of masculinity from fictional heroes/villains, and (2) the risk of boys being effeminate if they were raised by women only. A similar kind of reasoning is found in the Indonesian context (Adriany, Chapter 6) where a boy's 'girlish' (and in other situations aggressive) behaviour is explained by his living with female relatives. In the example taken from the North American context (as previously discussed), we find a related idea in the marvel over a male teacher who expresses extreme masculinity. Also, in the Swedish studies, there is a similar boosting of maleness present when in one case boys are motivated to eat food they do not like by referring to strength and big muscles. The chapter by Hellman *et al.* (Chapter 9) is especially interesting because there are clear gender differences in manners and language. The male role model function is not emphasised in the Japanese context and it is expected to be difficult for men to express the tenderness needed for handling young children.

The image of male superiority is also present in the context of children's sport where the adult male body is presented as 'the ideal' and not attainable for girls/women, nor yet present for young boys, as discussed by Grahn (Chapter 10). In most examples in the book it is the male body that is used to make masculinity visible and spectacular. When the idea of masculinity is made concrete it seems to be a matter of body and muscular strength. Interestingly, there is no sex difference in young children in this aspect, but there is an undeniable average difference among adults.

The body is also in focus when it comes to the view of the male professional as a potential threat to the children. Statistically there are very few cases of paedophilia, but the impact of their presence on men's willingness to work with children is enormous. Warin (Chapter 8) shows in her chapter that the men she interviewed were very aware of the risk they put themselves in simply by being male carers. It is easy to understand why men are reluctant to put themselves in a situation where they may be suspected of molesting young children, but a question proposed by Wernersson (Chapter 1) hints to the possibility of other interpretations of the situation: *How far does it function as a symbol of dangerous masculinity, connected to power and supremacy, and how far does it present a rationale for men not to work with children?*

The image of the profession

The male as role model could also be placed in the frame of professionalism. The 'role model' argument has been presented but also contested when female pre-school teachers in the Swedish context discuss how to neutralise stereotypical gender patterns among the children: they talk about pedagogics and the organisation of the physical context, i.e. they 'professionalise' rather than 'personalise' their influence on the children (see Granbom, Chapter 7).

The emphasis of profession over gender (and, one might guess, education over personality/ the individual) is especially strong among Japanese kindergarten and nursery teachers, as highlighted by Hellman *et al.* (Chapter 9). The Japanese context seems to be more visibly gendered than some of the other countries represented in this book, and it is described how the ECE teachers in discussions and self-reflection try to find a gender-neutral professional conduct that is comfortable for both men and women teachers. Hellman *et al.* discuss how some of the male teachers in their study said that they wanted to show society new and different ways of fathering through their professional role as pre-school teachers from this 'safe platform' in the pre-school environment. These men use their professional knowledge and experience as a tool to transform Japanese masculinity, while the role model idea, as discussed above, is at least, in some interpretations, thought to strengthen masculinity.

Maybe one way to get around the problems with the quest for 'male role models' as essential parts of a teacher's function is to put the actual professional competence and the performance of job tasks in focus? Human development takes place through interaction and it is likely that all adults, including teachers, as well as other children or fictional characters, will in fact function as (potential) models in a wide and general sense (see Brownhill forthcoming: 159). The ongoing professionalisation of childcare ought to have the consequence that a teacher/carer is able to function as a model beyond their individual, immediate personality. This implies that one of the core competencies in this kind of profession is to teach/care for children that are not of their own sex, ethnicity, class, cultural background, etc. One of the pre-school teachers quoted in Brownhill's chapter (Chapter 2) makes the distinction between a 'male role model' and a 'role model who happens to be a man'. Among the professional competencies hopefully expected from a teacher, regardless of gender, is the knowledge and ability to identify needs for all kinds of children.

Upon reflection, a further unanswered question could be added to those presented by Brownhill: *Is the whole idea of 'role models' – not only those related to gender – a reminiscence from another kind of society where a child's life course was expected to be more or less identical to that of their parent/elders of the same sex?* We argue that the 'roles' of modern-day 'role models' are expected to be more abstract, being related to personality and attitudes rather than skills and actions. This fits well with the lack of solid examples in empirical research of what a male role model is expected to do or be. Vague references to physical play or team sports like football or the ability to handle the tools supposed to be used by males are not very convincing. We must then take a step further and ask: *Why does this obsolete idea of the importance of role models survive when most children do not learn skills nor lifestyle from same-sex elders anymore?*

There are several possible answers to the question posed above. A simple one is, of course, that it can take a long time before individual minds and social discourses are changed in accordance with contextual/structural/material changes. Another answer is that the 'division of labour' in reality has a diminishing part in the construction of gender orders, and that other dimensions, such as power in social relations and power in relation to sexuality, are much more important. The function of the 'male role model' is then not to teach young boys the things you should be able to do as a man, but rather to demonstrate men's power over women. That could be one part of an explanation as to why men, who seem to let women take the responsibility of children and household work without any problem, are troubled by the lack of men in teaching. If teachers are pictured as authority figures and teachers are mostly women right through the school system this means that women have power over male individuals for a very long period of their lives. The cries for male professionals as role models could be interpreted as a somewhat disguised protest against female power. It is not about women being inappropriate teachers or inadequate carers for boys but more about an anomaly in the gender order hierarchy. To talk openly about restoring male power would be politically incorrect in most contexts. Many men today, even in countries where a hierarchical gender order is openly accepted, have female colleagues that they trust and respect as competent workmates. It is important to add that ideas of male supremacy are not maintained by men alone; women also do their share. No real consensus exists on what is desirable or acceptable in individual expressions of sex/gender or in the common gender order. Depending on the context and the angle, very different ideas can be brought about even by the same person. *If the children in kindergarten are brought into the centre how does the picture then look?*

Adriany (Chapter 6) criticises, from a gender-equality perspective, the child-centred approach in Indonesian kindergartens for making the children's developmentally piloted needs the sole judge of what is good care and teaching. The problem with this, says Adriany, is that gendered patterns in the children cannot be questioned or counteracted. She writes: 'If schools promote the child as an active individual who can construct their own meanings, I recommend that teachers, too, need to be constructed as active individuals' (pp. 78–9). Here again, the competence and professional practice of teachers as the tool for changed gender patterns is pictured in opposition to a passive female carer without individual agency.

This could be compared to the Swedish situation, as described by Granbom (Chapter 7) and Löfdahl and Hjalmarsson (Chapter 3), where the curriculum for pre-schools since 1998 states that teachers should actively promote gender equality and find ways to present alternatives to traditional stereotypes to the children. Granbom shows how pre-school teachers, when discussing how to work with gender, take the inevitable differences between boys and girls as a given. The teachers try to enrich the environment for all children, but when they do they are guided by clear pictures of what boys and girls really like and how they are. Löfdahl and Hjalmarsson also show in their study, however, that it is not a simple task to construct neutral patterns. They argue that the 'gender-conscious pedagogy' developed in the Swedish context sees boys and girls as different and in need of different kinds of compensatory experiences. The girls are expected to develop and value bodily strength, while boys need to develop social and emotional sensitivity. 'Add but not deprive' asserts that there should be no criticism of traditional gendered activities, but activities connected with the other sex should also be provided for. In a way this pedagogy also takes a gender split in early interests and abilities for granted. Stereotypical gender patterns and the sex of the child are self-evident points of departure in efforts to create gender equality.

Care and teaching can be described as different aspects of a professional carer's knowledge base. How care activities in pre-school might be more difficult to control compared to learning activities in terms of gendered communication is shown by Hellman (Chapter 5) in her description of how messages based on ideas of proper masculinity are produced in meal situations. Boys are encouraged to eat their food by references to strong fictional figures like Popeye and Pippi Longstocking. Such references or explicit comparing of biceps are not found in talk to girls. In conditions when the intentions are teaching and learning it is possible to keep gender equality objectives in mind, but when activities are framed as care (and maybe play) it is easy to fall back on internalised gendered manners. We argue that this is probably unavoidable if we want to avoid life in childcare institutions turned into 'total institutions' with absolute control. We recognise that many of us carry a lot of 'dead weight' in the form of dated ideas and manners better suited for the days of our childhood.

A comparative perspective

A comment on the comparative perspective of this book is also needed. The interiors of childcare institutions from five different countries – two in Asia, one in North America and two in Europe – are used as examples or study objects in different chapters. This does not even come near to a proper comparative study and all discussions of cultural differences and similarities must thus be speculative. It is obvious, however, that there are some common features. One is that in all of the five countries the proportion of male teachers is similar, i.e. in every 100 pre-school teachers two or three of them might be men, and in all of the countries this is put forward as more or less of a problem. A need to recruit more male teachers/carers for young children is thus identified in many countries.

Löfdahl and Hjalmarsson (Chapter 3) pose important questions about how to work actively with what in Sweden/the Nordic countries is called gender sensitive pedagogy. A vital aspect of this kind of working/thinking is that gender is perceived as a system/structure/ abstract order present in society but not as a trait in individuals (cf. Sinnes 2006). In many situations a teacher needs to know something about a child's context to decide how to act on and react to different types of behaviour and actions. The story told by Adriany (Chapter 6) involving the violent boys and the destruction of the dolls corner is enlightening. The idea was that by breaking up the structuring of the room/space related to a gendered division of labour the children would be unrestricted in creating their own spaces for play that was not guided by gender stereotypes. In theory this sounds like a great idea, but it may be based on romantic/obscure suppositions of a natural and free creativity in the child, related to the child-centred perspective, as criticised by Adriany. Children use the experiences and tools they are afforded, and even if play allows them to mix them in partly new ways the very serious endeavour to learn how to function in the real world is always present.

We recognise that there are many unanswered questions, many of which are offered at the end of each chapter. One of these asks: *Why are the strategies used to get more men into care/ teaching of young children ineffective?* We know that men are able to do the job, but they chose not to do it. A loss of social status, the need to safeguard masculinity, the avoidance of wishing to take on a minority position and the paedophilia threat are some of the reasons for men to keep out of professional childcare. The need of the 'male role model' is an argument that does not hold. Traditional 'strong' division of labour is long gone in many countries and there are not many 'roles' left to model if men and women are working in all areas and are able to choose from the same variety of lifestyles. The arguments for more men in childcare should maybe relate to the idea that men should not be deprived of a possible career, that professional childcare is a growing field of work, that there is a need for competent adults regardless of gender, and that it is easier to advance gender equality if both men and women are present in kindergarten and pre-school. A final argument may be the most important: caring for children as a natural occupational choice for men could be an important part of the necessary development of much needed new kinds of masculinity.

It is hoped that reading this book allows readers to recognise the importance of professional competences, including knowledge about the consequences of gender structures, and that this is trusted as the base for high-quality caring and teaching *regardless* of the sex of the teacher.

References

Brownhill, S. (forthcoming) *The 'Brave' Man in the Early Years (0–8): The Ambiguities of the Role Model.* Saarbrücken: LAP LAMBERT Academic Publishing.

Dahlström, E. (ed.) (1962) *Kvinnors liv och arbete: Svenska och norska studier av ett aktuellt samhällsproblem.* (*Women's Life and Work: Swedish and Norwegian Studies of a Current Social Issue*). Stockholm: Studieförbundet Näringsliv och Samhälle.

Norway: Handlingsplan (2004) *Den gode barnehagen er en likestilt barnehage. Handlingsplan for likestilling 2004–2007.* (*The Good Kindergarten Is a Kindergarten with Gender Equality. Action Plan for Gender Equality 2004–2007*). Barne- och familiedepartementet (Department for Children and Families). [Online].

Available at: http://www.regjeringen.no/upload/kilde/bfd/pla/2004/0001/ddd/pdfv/205598-q-1071-likestilling.pdf (accessed 11 December 2014).

Sinnes, A. T. (2006) 'Three approaches to gender equity in science education', *NorDiNa*, 1/06: 72–83. [Online.] Available at: http://www.genderinscience.org/index.php/downloads/doc_download/120-sinnes-2006-three-approaches-to-gender-equity-in-science-education (accessed 7 January 2015).

Tiller, P. O. (1962) 'Rollefordelningen mellom foreldrerne og barns personlighetsutvikling' ('Division of roles between parents and children's personality development'), in E. Dahlström (ed.), *Kvinnors liv och arbete: Kvinners liv og arbeid: svenska och norska studier av ett aktuellt samhällsproblem*. Stockholm: Studieförbundet Näringsliv och samhälle.

AUTHOR INDEX

SUBJECT INDEX

#0199 - 081217 - C0 - 246/174/9 - PB - 9781138797727